GENO

GENO

IN PURSUIT OF PERFECTION

GENO AURIEMMA

WITH JACKIE MacMULLAN

FOREWORD BY DIANA TAURASI

w

WARNER BOOKS

NEW YORK   BOSTON

Warner Books

Time Warner Book Group
1271 Avenue of the Americas, New York, NY 10020
Visit our Web site at www.twbookmark.com.

Printed in the United States of America

First Edition: January 2006
10 9 8 7 6 5 4 3 2 1

Library of Congress Cataloging-in-Publication Data
Auriemma, Geno.
    Geno : in pursuit of perfection / Geno Auriemma with Jackie MacMullan.— 1st ed.
        p. cm.
    Includes index.
    ISBN 0-446-57764-2
    1. Auriemma, Geno. 2. Basketball coaches—United States—Biography. 3. University of
Connecticut—Basketball. 4. Connecticut Huskies (Basketball team). 5. Basketball for
women—Connecticut. I. MacMullan, Jackie. II. Title.
    GV884.A85A3 2006
    796.323'092—dc22
                                                                              2005022208

Book design by Giorgetta Bell McRee

To the two best coaches—my parents,
Donato and Marsiella.
To Kathy, Jenna, Alysa, and Michael,
you comprise the best team I could ever be on.

—Geno Auriemma

To Alyson and Douglas, with all my love

—Jackie MacMullan

Acknowledgments

To all the people who have stayed by my side, supporting me through the best and worst times in my life. I appreciate all of you and the experiences we've shared. A special thanks to my parents, for all the sacrifices they made so my life could be better. To my wife, Kathy, and my children, Jenna, Alysa, and Michael, for all the concessions they have made. They are the only ones who know just how much they have done for me. Thanks to Jackie MacMullan for having the tenacity to get my thoughts on paper. Thank you to Time Warner and Esther Newberg for taking a chance on me. A special thanks to my coaches, starting with Chris Dailey, who has been there from the beginning and has been instrumental in our success; to Jamelle Elliott, who played for me and coached with me, and has been such a valuable sounding board; to Tonya Cardoza, who has provided quiet wisdom; to Jack Eisenmann, who grew up with me and stood by me. To Sarah Darras, I offer my gratitude. This book never would have happened without you. To my family, staff, administrators, past assistant coaches, old friends, new friends, colleagues, and players—*cent anni*!

—GENO AURIEMMA
May 2005

Acknowledgments

I am grateful to Sarah Darras—you are truly amazing. Thanks to Chris Dailey, Jamelle Elliott, Tonya Cardoza, and Jack Eisenmann for letting me intrude. Kathy Auriemma, Peg Myers, Robyn Danahy, and the Connecticut players, past and present, were not only helpful, they were good company. Rick Wolff, Ed Kleven, Esther Newberg, Randy Press, Joe Sullivan, Don Skwar, Ian Thomsen, Todd Balf, and Michael Holley were great sounding boards. Michael, Aly, and Douglas Boyle mean the world to me. Fred and Margarethe MacMullan, Sue and Vinny Titone, and the entire Boyle clan have provided a lifetime of support. Janice McKeown and Jane (Cavanaugh) Smith are two of the best friends anyone could ever have. Thanks to the Ya Ya's, the Westford moms, and the Fourth of July gang. To my boondoggle buddies, Liz Douglas and Stephanie Baird, thanks for keeping me sane during this project. Lastly, thanks to Geno. You sure know how to spin a yarn.

—JACKIE MACMULLAN

Foreword

I was in the WNBA for about two minutes before everybody started asking me the same question: "What's Coach Auriemma like?" It was amazing. It was the first thing everybody wanted to know. People are very curious about what kind of personality he has, and how he approaches the game. They all want a little insight into how he's been able to win five championships and produce all these great players.

How do you explain Geno Auriemma to someone that has never met him? They probably already have the wrong impression about Coach. He isn't very well liked in the women's game, mostly, I think, because of jealousy. They want what he has, and they don't know how to get it. He's also very confident and outspoken, and they don't always like what he has to say.

The biggest mistake people make is thinking that we must hate Coach because he was so hard on us. They figure we couldn't possibly like someone who yells at us and screams at us as much as he did. But, very early on at Connecticut, you realize he's on you because he wants to get the most out of you.

Nobody likes to hear the stuff he says. I didn't. Before we started my freshman season, I would see Coach on campus and he'd be smiling and having fun. We'd be joking all the time. I was thinking, "This guy is incredible."

But then practice started, and it was over. He was on my case constantly. He was busting me, big-time. As soon as we stepped in that gym, boom! He flipped a switch. He was this completely driven, competitive guy who was never satisfied. Whatever I did, I couldn't please him. It took a toll on me at first. Sometimes you need a compliment.

But he wasn't giving you one until March.

In my freshman year, we made it to the NCAA semifinal game against Notre Dame. I played horribly. I shot 1 for 15 from the floor. I was upset, and when I fouled out with about a minute to go, I came out of the game with my head down. I couldn't even look at the scoreboard. I knew if I had just made two or three more shots, we would have won. I felt so badly about letting my team down, especially the seniors.

Coach came over and talked to me. He rubbed my head. He wasn't going to let me feel that way. He wasn't going to let me blame myself.

Right after that, we had our individual end-of-the-year meetings. I figured he was going to say to me, "Hey, you did a really good job this year." Instead, he sat me down and said, "Next year we're going to suck with you on the team."

I couldn't believe it. What happened to the "it's not your fault" stuff he'd said the week before? But that's what makes Coach Auriemma different. You go in there thinking one thing, and he hits you with something totally different. I'm expecting all these compliments, and he's telling me, "We can't win with you next year. You took no responsibility for that championship game."

At the time, I was really angry with him. But you know what? He was right. If he had said to me, "Diana, I know you did your best in that game, it's okay," I don't know if I would have been as determined or as hungry the next season. He knew exactly what he was doing. I came out in my sophomore season and had, I think, the best year of my career. Oh, and by the way, we won the national championship.

While you are playing, you are not going to see the comforting side of Coach that often. You'll see it off the court when he's busting your chops, or goofing with us on the bus, or checking in to make sure everything is okay at home, but on the court those times are rare.

The most emotional moment I had with him was when we beat Penn State in my senior year in the regional final. We had played like crap the whole year. It was our last game at the Hartford Civic Center, and he took me out with one minute left, and there were a lot of emotions running through me. I came out, and he just gave me a huge hug. I'll always remember that one. It solidified everything for me. I remember thinking, "You know what? Coach has been on my side for four years. I might not have always known it, but he was."

The women I played with at Connecticut like to tease me. They call me Little Geno. They tell me, "He's your long-lost father." I say, "Hey, shut up," but I know they're right. I'm competitive, just like him. We're both hardheaded. I made him step his game up, and he put me on a different level. He focuses on the little stuff that at the time you don't think is that important. But later on, you understand.

I get it now.

One of his biggest things is communication. He expected us to be talking to one another all the time on the floor. If you didn't talk, you didn't play. Now I'm in the WNBA and you go to practice and you don't hear a word, for the most part. It's a different atmosphere. People have their agendas. They punch in, and they punch out when they're done. I'm out there clapping my hands, trying to get people going, because that's how we were successful at Connecticut. We were twelve people who were all on the same page. I miss that.

I know I can go to Coach Auriemma for anything. I have enough confidence in him that I've told him things I haven't even told people I've known my whole life. People think I'm this outgoing person, but actually I'm very reserved. I'm not one to put my problems out there. I'm not going to sit down and tell you my life story. Coach really worked on getting to know me. He figured me out like no one else ever has.

So that's why I'd trust him with anything. I don't know a whole lot of people who go to college and play for the same coach for four years and leave with that kind of relationship. It happens because he invests in you—so you end up investing in him.

The thing about Coach is he invests in all of us. Not just the stars. Everyone. We're all part of the family. There's nothing like the UConn connection in the WNBA. Whatever city I'm in, if someone played for Connecticut, we're hooking up for dinner. I never played with Rita Williams or Nykesha Sales, but it doesn't matter. We're getting together. It's the same with Swin Cash, and it was the same with Rebecca Lobo and Kara Wolters when they were in the league.

If you're on the outside looking at Connecticut basketball, all you see is this machine on the court, and this intense coach pushing the buttons. You don't see how much Coach Auriemma cares. You don't see him welcoming us into his family. You don't see his mother, Marsiella, making us pepperoni bread, or the times we go to his house and play stupid kid games like Pictionary and Mix and Match. You don't see us piling into a gym to watch his son, Michael, play basketball. You don't see us confiding in his wife, Kathy, and complaining to her about him.

Coach Auriemma isn't for everyone. If you can't take criticism or motivate yourself, go somewhere else. But if you love basketball, there is no other place for you, especially if you are competitive and you want to be really good. Here's the thing: everyone else is going to kiss your ass. They're going to spend four years telling you how great you are, and you will never find out how great you could have been, because nobody is pushing you.

Coach pushed the pedal for four years. And when I look back on it, I'm not just talking about basketball. He made me become a better person.

If I had never played for Geno Auriemma, I would be just like everyone else. I really believe that. He forced me to become somebody special, and I'll always be grateful.

People always wonder why all the UConn players always come back. It's because we have something—somebody—worth coming back for.

Thanks, Coach.

—DIANA TAURASI
Spring 2005

GENO

ONE

All of my scars are hidden.

My physical scars are on my stomach, covered by my clothing. They are my reminders of the hot coals that seared my flesh.

The emotional scars aren't as easy to see. I've got plenty of them, but there isn't one person that knows all of my scars. I've acquired them from a life of questioning myself, of constantly striving to prove myself.

The scars come from being seven years old, coming to America from Italy and not being able to speak English.

I arrive in Norristown, Pennsylvania, and I don't know the language. I don't know the customs. I don't dress the right way. I feel out of place, so I'm constantly self-conscious and unsure of myself.

Scars are part of you, whether you like it or not. Once you've been scarred, the marks remain forever. The key is, what effect does it have on you going forward?

I'm always amused when I hear people who don't know me describe me as arrogant, insensitive, and overconfident.

They have no idea how wrong they are.

They don't understand that even after winning five national championships at Connecticut, I still doubt myself all the time. They don't understand that the image of me on the sidelines, the person they see on television prowling back and forth, is not who I am. You need a certain level of confidence to be successful at anything. I certainly have confidence. People think I have too much of it, and say it comes across as cocky, but the truth is, no matter what I accomplish, I'm never sure it's good enough.

It's never as good as it could have been, because I've never coached the perfect game, and my players have never played the perfect game. And when that flawed game is over, I'm convinced it's my fault, even if we win big. It's like the pitcher who throws a perfect game in nine innings. If he doesn't strike out every guy, then he's going to talk about the line drive that was hit and caught by the third baseman. If he's a perfectionist, even after his amazing accomplishment, he's probably going to be ticked off about a slider that just missed the strike zone.

Even after our perfect 35–0 season in 1995, the year we won our first national championship, I found myself going back and saying, "Why didn't we execute that backdoor cut better? Why did their pressure bother us? Why didn't I do a better job?" Those questions dog me. They stay with me, those scars, even though no one else can see them.

I'm not sure what the scars on my stomach signify. Maybe it is a reminder that I came from nothing. Even though I never had anything growing up, my expectation level was still pretty high. Some people who have nothing growing up have very low expectations. If my parents' expectations were higher, they would have accomplished more. Their goals were modest: to get out of Italy. I'm not sure my father even did that of his own volition.

I think he came because his older brothers were already in America and said, "Hey, Donato. Get over here."

I grew up in a little village in the mountains east of Naples called Montella. Most of the homes in the village were made of stone. My name in Italy was Luigi. It was always very cold in the winter, and very warm in the summer. There were no screens in the house, but no flies either.

We used to sleep in front of the fireplace because we had no heat. We didn't have any electricity. We heated up our water over an open flame.

My mother worked, just like all the other mothers in the village. The girls who were too young to work would stay behind and take care of all the brothers and sisters and cousins.

One morning, when I was two years old, it was really cold out. The only way to keep the little ones warm was to place the hot coals on the floor and place the babies in a circle around that pile of heat. On this particular day, I guess I fell asleep. My mom was out working, and no one was paying attention, and I toppled over into the coals. You can imagine what it must have been like to have eight or nine coals stuck to your burning skin, and no one there to help you.

By the time they pulled me out, my stomach was burned pretty badly. I don't remember the pain. I don't remember any of it. My mother said one of the reasons it took so long for someone to notice me was that I hardly made a sound.

In the context of today's world, that's a pretty horrible story. God forbid some little kid trips and scrapes his knee and there's no parental supervision around. That kid would probably be taken into custody by the state. But back then, what happened to me, in the big scheme of things, was not so tragic. Think of all the other children of that era who were born in the mountains of Italy. Many of them never survived their own birth, and others died of various diseases at a very young age. So I got a few scars. I was one of the lucky ones.

Montella was a remote region with no doctors or hospitals. Our family didn't have a car, a television, or a radio. If you wanted to go somewhere, you walked. When you are young, and you don't have anything, you don't even realize you are poor, because you are just like all the people around you. I always felt like a normal part of the universe. I had no idea what the world was like beyond my little village. And on some level, I guess, I wasn't really aware of the struggles the elders in my town had gone through when they were my age.

I just never had a sense of how incredibly difficult it must have been to be my parents, to be ten years old during World War II, to live in fear every single day. I look at my own children now. They have such a comfortable life. My daughters are at the University of Connecticut. My son goes to a private Catholic high school. I can't even imagine what it would be like if all of a sudden an army marched through the center of Manchester, Connecticut, and occupied our town. It's impossible to fathom.

My mother, Marsiella, remembers all of the difficulties of her childhood, but I think it's very painful for her to talk about it. She and her five other siblings lived a life I can't possibly understand.

My mother has never set foot in a school. She can't read. She can't write. She can sign her name, barely. But here's the funny part. In "real world" terms, my mother can do almost anything. The only things she can't do are the things we assume every intelligent, functioning person can do. She can take care of almost every single thing that requires you to get through life. She can manage almost anything that comes her way—as long as she doesn't have to read it.

Even though she was sent to work at the age of ten, that didn't necessarily mean she was going to get paid. She worked in exchange for goods and services. Someone might give you seeds in exchange for your labor, so you can grow vegetables in your backyard. Or they give you livestock. They give you a piglet to raise, and you keep that pig, and feed him, and make him as big as a house, because you know you are going to eat every single piece of that pig before the year is over.

My mother loves to tell the story of my grandmother's pig. At the time, World War II is on and the Germans march into their village. My grandfather has already gone off to war. Typically, when the Germans come to town, the mothers and the children flee to the mountains and hide there.

My grandmother sends her children out the back door of the house and tells them to hide in the hills. But she refuses to leave. She doesn't want the Germans to get her pig. The pig is downstairs in the basement of the house, so she hides there with it, doing her best to keep it quiet so they won't find her.

The Germans stay a few days. My mom and her brothers and sisters forage for whatever they can find in the mountains. My grandmother manages to keep that pig alive. The soldiers leave without discovering her.

The problem during that time was there were no men left behind to protect their families. If they stayed behind, it was either because they were too young, or had been injured in some way, or were unfit for battle. The women that were left behind to fend for themselves became pretty strong and pretty determined and pretty tough. My mother is all of those things.

You learned to protect your family, to stay one step ahead of the Germans. If they came knocking on your door, you better have already left for the mountains. Otherwise, if you were still there, and you had a young daughter, they might take her. People hid their daughters for that reason. There were plenty of unspeakable things that went on in my mother's childhood.

My mother remembers a family that was forced to evacuate their home so the Germans could take it over. A little boy was looking for his dog. He's calling for the dog, and the dog starts barking, and the soldiers tell the mother the dog is making too much noise. But the little boy won't leave without his dog. He calls and calls for him, and finally the dog runs over and starts barking at the soldiers, so they shoot the dog—and the boy.

That is the kind of environment my parents were raised in. My grandmother worked in the fields all day, in the heat, harvesting hay with a sickle. My mother was born on June 11, 1931, and four days later, my grandmother was back in the fields with her sickle. She would come home at lunch and breast-feed my mother, and tell her, "You're the only baby in Italy who is having warm milk for lunch." Then she would go back to work.

Before she came to America, my mother never ventured outside of Montella—except to hide in the mountains.

My father, Donato, was born in 1927. He and his brothers were fortunate enough to have a horse and a wagon, so they were able to get hired by other people to transport things from one village to the next. That's how he made his living.

He was a very proud man, a very hardworking man. He brought us to this country to give us a better life than the one he had, and he succeeded. His life was very simple, and that's how he liked it.

My life, I know, was a mystery to him. He was proud of me, I'm sure of that, but I don't think he ever really got it. A women's basketball coach? That's a job?

Donato died of cancer in 1997. He had been sick for a while, and I remember arriving at my parents' house in Norristown, the same one that I grew up in, and my mother telling me he was gone. She was sitting there, so sad, and I really broke down, but it was as much for her as it was for my own grief. I felt for her, because I was never really able to develop a close relationship with my father.

He was very distant. He just didn't share a lot. And he definitely did not understand what I was doing. He just couldn't grasp why basketball was so important to so many people. He had a hard time understanding why everyone made such a big deal of what I did. In his mind, you measured success and hard work by how much physical labor you put into it.

I've been very fortunate to be successful as the women's basketball coach at Connecticut. It has provided my family and me with just about everything we could ever need. Yet there's a tremendous amount of guilt that comes along with knowing how much easier your life has been because your parents brought you here. Those scars are the ones that never heal.

I remember my mother visiting us once in Connecticut. She was staying with us in my comfortable home, and I was bitching about something stupid, about something that happened in the office, or something that happened with recruiting. She listened, like she always does, but didn't say much.

Later that night, the topic of my grandmother came up. My mother starts talking about her, and before you know it, she's getting very emotional. She starts telling me that when her mother got sick, they couldn't figure out what was wrong with her, so they took her to a hospital about fifteen miles away from Montella. Well, back then, fifteen miles away might as well be the end of the earth.

For seven days, my mother and her family don't hear anything. Finally they get word their mother has died. My mother has tears in her eyes as she tells the story, and she never cries, unless it's for a happy reason.

She tells me, "I never got to see my mother before she died. Even worse, they buried her and nobody had any idea where, because we had no way to go and look for her."

You sit there and you listen to that, and suddenly all that stuff you were bitching about earlier seems so small and so meaningless.

It wasn't until more than thirty years later, on a trip back to Italy, that my mother was able to visit her mother's grave. Her brother located it and took her there to pay her respects. It's an old story, really. If you talk to anybody who is seventy or older, who has come to this country from somewhere else, particularly an Eastern or Western European country, I bet they've had similar experiences.

It's the old-fashioned tale of searching for the American dream. Move to America, get a job, make nothing, scrape up enough to buy a tiny little place, and become one of those families that George Bailey talks about in *It's a Wonderful Life*. There's a part in the movie where George is accused by his boss, Mr. Potter, of sucking up to those "garlic eaters."

My parents and I were those garlic eaters.

I remember my younger days in Italy, but not as well as I would like. I wish I could close my eyes and retrace the steps I took every day. I wish I could see the guy who made the bread, the guy who delivered the groceries, and the woman who would lower her basket from the second floor and pull up her parcels. I wish I could remember my parents as young people raising a family.

When I was younger, I took great pride in my history. Then I got a little older and I lost sight of it a little bit, because I got so wrapped up in my own life and what I'm doing. But now I'm past fifty, and my mother is in her mid-seventies, and my father is passed away, and I find myself reaching back and trying to recapture my roots, because once it's gone, it's gone.

All my father's brothers who were over there have died. My mother has no other family left except my brother, my sister, and me. The information stream is starting to dry up.

I've asked my mother what the kids in our village did for fun. There were no organized sports leagues. Montella certainly didn't have any kind of teams with fancy uniforms. There was a residual military presence from the war in our village, and as a result, there were some kids who knew how to play a little baseball. There was a field not far from our house in Montella, and there were kids who gathered there informally. I was too young to take part in any of that, but my mom said I would get up and walk there every day, just to watch. I remember going there, but not the specifics. I don't believe there was a backstop on the baseball field, or any nets in the hoops for basketball. Sports were certainly not a priority in the countryside of Italy at that time.

I tell my kids these stories about my birthplace, about the

history of their grandparents, and they really aren't that interested. They'd be much more excited and much more impressed if I told them, "Your grandfather played in the NBA," or "Your grandfather played major league baseball." Instead, I'm telling them, "This is what they went through," and I don't think they get it, nor should you expect them to, I guess.

I remember vividly the day our family moved to America. My two uncles had already come over and settled in Norristown. My dad went over next, and left us behind in Italy with our mother. He got a job in a candy factory making hard candy, the kind you eat at the front desk when you check into a nice hotel. I think he made something like seventeen dollars a week.

He sent for us around November. I was so excited about going. I was excited because I had never been in a car, and we were taking a car from Montella to Naples, which was about an hour's ride. I just sat looking out the window, watching everything speed by. To this day, there's nothing I like better in the world than getting into a car and driving real fast.

When we get to Naples, we board a boat to America, and my life as I know it begins. We are on that boat for thirteen days. My mom, I remember, isn't feeling so hot. She suffers from seasickness. My sister, Anna, is only one year old, and my brother, Ferruccio, is four years old. I am in charge of them, especially when my mother isn't feeling good. My brother is a bit of a wise guy. He spends the entire thirteen days learning every swear word the sailors know. All the sailors are Italian, and they get a kick out of my brother.

We are on our own a lot. My brother spends most of the time running around the boat. I spend most of the time chasing after him, making sure he doesn't get himself into any trouble. I am one of those kids who likes to do everything right, and I know if my brother gets into trouble, that means I am going to get in trouble, too.

I swear, I spend most of my time saying, "Have you seen Ferruccio?" It's amazing that we all make it to America in one piece. We land in New York City, sailing past Ellis Island and the Statue of Liberty like every other European following a dream.

My uncle picks us up at the dock. I'm wearing all my little dark clothes and my little cap. Classic immigrant picture. We get into the car, and I'll never forget it. He's driving an Impala, with big fins. It is a bronze-gold color. I'm sure it's the most beautiful thing I've ever seen.

My uncle has a job at the steel mill, and he's in the union, and he can speak a little English, because he has been over here a couple of years. As we're zooming down the New Jersey Turnpike, I'm thinking to myself, "Man, this is unbelievable. This is some kind of dream."

We move in with my uncle Stefano, his wife, and their four children. You throw in my dad, my mom, me, my brother, and my sister and you've got four adults and seven kids living in a three-bedroom house.

I'm sleeping with a pack of kids in one room but I don't care. My uncle's house is right across the street from a school and a playground. He lives two blocks from a Catholic school, St. Francis. That's where my cousins went, and that's where I'll be going.

They take me for my first day of school. I don't speak any English. I walk in, and I'm supposed to be in second grade. I don't speak the language, and I've already missed the first two months of school, but I've already done first grade in

Italy, so this is how it goes. Nobody is feeling sorry for me. Nobody is giving me extra help. Nobody is going to make it easy for me.

They talk to my aunt, and she interprets for me. They tell me, through her, "This June is graduation. If you pass the test, you graduate. If you don't, you stay behind. Do you understand?" I nod my head, but I have no idea what they are saying.

Pretty soon, I figure it out. I don't want to stay back. I'm going to figure this out. I show up for class the first day, and I sit in the front so I can pick up as much as I can. I'm living with cousins who speak English, and that really helps. Every time they open their mouths, it's an education for me. I ask them so many questions they get sick of me in a hurry.

I'm only seven, and I'm a sponge. I'm at the playground across the street with all the kids, and I want to fit in, so I *have* to understand. When you think about it, what is second grade, really? It's numbers and letters. It's not physics. So little by little, I start to pick it up. Once I learn to read, I read everything I can get my hands on. I read all the cereal boxes, cover to cover. I think Battle Creek, Michigan, is the center of the universe, because that's where all our cereal is from.

At the end of the school year, I pass that test.

I tell my players all the time when they have a problem: "Figure it out." When they say, "I can't," I stop them and tell them, "Don't tell me that. You can if it really matters to you."

That first day when I walk into that strange school, I'm wearing the clothes my mother made for me. I only have two pairs of pants. The kids make fun of me. I say I don't care, but of course I do. Maybe that's where, without knowing it, I got this sensitivity to what people say about me. When people criticize me, it bothers me. My friends will say, "Why do you give a damn about what that person thinks?" but I do.

I've always been overly concerned with what people think, right from the beginning.

The last thing I ever wanted to be was different—but I was.

My first year at school in America, we eat lunch at our desk, which is a good thing, because I don't have to sit in a cafeteria alone. Everybody is grossed out by my lunch. My mom packs me eggplant Parmesan, our dinner from the night before. Sometimes she gives me sausage and eggs. No matter what she makes me, it's dripping in oil, and it's wrapped up in foil. The other kids are eating peanut butter and jelly and ham and cheese and they are looking at me and saying, "Who wants to eat that?" It's just one more way I stand out, one more way that makes me different or strange, or whatever it is those kids think about me.

We have recess after lunch, and after a few days of running around, a couple of kids take me under their wing. My first friend is Steven Watson. He is a little guy, but he is really tough, and they don't make fun of me when I am around Steve. The guy next door, Tyrone, he is older, probably about twelve. He sits on the porch and talks to me about the neighborhood.

We play baseball across the street. Tyrone teaches me how to hit. He's so nice to me, but all these years later, I can't even remember his last name. He lets me use his glove, because I don't have one of my own.

When I am in the fourth grade, my parents buy their own house in Norristown. It costs $13,000 and it is about a mile and a half away from my uncle's house, in what you'd call a lower-middle-class neighborhood. They are brand-new homes, row houses, all lined up, all the way down the block. My mother takes a job working at a rug factory making braided rugs. My father gets a job working across the street from the steel plant. They make construction blocks. I'm playing sports and going to school.

At this point, I'm talking to my parents strictly in English. It is hard for them, but necessary for me. I know they need to understand English. They also need to speak Italian to me, to make sure I never forget.

When school gets out, it's summer vacation, but both of my parents are working, and we're not living with my older cousins anymore, so I've got to watch my brother and sister. I'm twelve, my brother is nine, and my sister is seven. From seven in the morning to five at night, I'm in charge of the kids.

I was probably too young to take on that much responsibility, but what could my parents do? They need to work. We need the money. We don't have a car, so my mom and dad take the bus to work every day. We stay in our neighborhood and try to stay out of trouble.

I play baseball every chance I can. I really think I'm going to be a major league baseball star. I become a Philadelphia fan, and we are living through tough times in 1964. That is the year of the great Phillies collapse. Richie Allen is a rookie that year. Jim Bunning pitches a perfect game. I'm thinking to myself, "This is what I'm going to do with my life."

I'm a pitcher. I'm pretty good. From the time I am in the seventh or eighth grade, I have the same catcher. His name is Donnie Sobek. Donnie is a year older. We are a great team.

Little League tryouts were unbelievable back then. It wasn't all this nonsense like now, when everyone makes it and every kid is guaranteed playing time. Back then, five hundred kids would show up, and these guys would be walking around with clipboards, and you'd hit some grounders and throw a few balls, and after about two or three days of tryouts they'd cut something like three hundred kids, and you are devastated if you don't make it.

I don't even try out until I am eleven years old. I don't even know where the field is. There is only one in my town, but when I lived with my aunt and uncle, it was too far away. I couldn't walk to it, and I didn't have a bike.

Once we move, I meet this kid who tells me all I have to do is go out the back, hop over the stones on the creek, go down the other side, and the field is down the hill from there.

You never forget your first glove. I didn't get a decent one until I was much, much older. The first glove I own is made by some obscure company that doesn't even exist now. That's all we can afford. My mom gets it for me. That is the one great thing about her. She knows it is important to me.

I never ask my father for that stuff, because he won't understand. My mom always manages to find an extra ten dollars here or there to help me.

If they let me, I would have played baseball morning and night. I still have a scar from the time I slid into second, and there was a piece of glass on the bag, and it stripped my skin right off. There is glass and nails and all sorts of stuff everywhere. We don't care. Also, there are no adults. We pick our teams and fight our own battles. I hurt my arm really bad throwing breaking balls. If someone were around to supervise us, they probably would have told me I was too young to throw that kind of pitch.

When I get to be thirteen, I end up playing for a Salvation

Army team. Our coach is Vern Schlotzhauer. He is a really big old guy who is always smoking a cigar. Donnie Sobek is on the team, too. No matter what I do for old Vern, it is never good enough. One year I go 8–0 on the mound, and bat something like .350. I lead the team in hits and runs scored and I'm second in RBIs, but it doesn't matter. He gives the MVP award to Donnie. I guess Vern felt I had a lot of talent and a lot of potential, and I was a guy he could keep pushing. He is right. I can take it.

Now that I'm a coach, I never bother with kids who can't take it. If they can't handle the challenge, I find that out early, and we don't recruit them. I kill guys like Diana Taurasi and Sue Bird when I first get them. They might not understand at first, but eventually they realize what it is all about. They know I'm pushing them to get the absolute best out of them. Svetlana Abrosimova got it right away. Swin Cash, she didn't like it all the time, but she knew the drill.

As much as I love baseball, the sport I really want to be good at is basketball. I am okay, but not the best. I'm not quite big enough. I'm not quite good enough. Baseball isn't as rewarding or as sexy as basketball. Being on the basketball team is what matters. I play baseball all summer long. I never even play for the school. It isn't that kind of sport.

I can still remember the first time I try out for the high school basketball team. I'm in the ninth grade. I never practice. I play baseball all the time and I don't do much of anything to work on my basketball skills.

So I go out for the team. After a couple of days, they post the list of the kids that make it on the wall. I check the thing, and I'm history, man. I'm cut. It's like a big sign telling you, "You ain't good enough." I kind of blow it off. I don't want to admit I'm hurt about it, so I say, "Ah, that's not what I really do anyway. I play baseball. I just tried out for this because all my friends were playing." That is true, but it is also true that when they make it and I don't, I'm pissed. I'm also crushed.

I end up playing a lot of basketball. They have an open gym in the afternoons, and I'm there every day. But I have no intention of going out for the team again. My feeling is, "Screw it. If they don't want me, I have other things to do." I don't need to experience failure like that again.

There's this kid, Jack Eisenmann, who plays there every day, too. He's a year older. He's playing with me one day, and he says, "Hey, you ought to try out for the team." I say, "Nah, I've already done that." He says, "No, really. Coach Gardler was asking me about you the other day. He was watching you play. He thinks you should try out."

Jack Eisenmann convinces me to try out, and I make the team. I've known Jack thirty-five years. We grew up together, and now he's my director of basketball operations at Connecticut. It's kind of a frustrating job, I think. He's a person who wants to coach, but the NCAA won't let him. So Jack ends up doing film exchanges for us, puts together our playbook stuff, and organizes about a hundred other things.

I'm sure he'd rather be coaching and working with players on a daily basis. He spent thirteen years coaching a men's college team in Ottawa. Of course, basketball is as popular in Canada as hockey is in Barbados.

Anyhow, because of Jack, I end up playing two years for Coach Buddy Gardler. I'm a backup point guard, and I love the game, but I've started so much later than everyone else, and for whatever reason, I don't commit myself to improving the way I should.

One of the things that bothers me to this day is that I

didn't pay enough attention in high school to what was going on. As a result, when it comes time to graduate and go on to college, I'm not prepared. I use as an excuse, "Well, my parents didn't help me. They didn't know any better," but the real reason is I didn't pay enough attention to my future.

When I get to college, I develop this personality where if something isn't important to me, I just don't do it. If it doesn't excite me or make me feel better, I ignore it. If a class is interesting and the teacher is charismatic and the subject matter is thought-provoking, I can't wait to go to class. But if the subject is mundane and I'm not that interested, I say to myself, "Why do I have to be there?"

Well, you have to be there because it's part of the curriculum. You have to be there because it's part of your responsibility. How come I didn't understand that?

Maybe that's why I'm so hard on my players. I make them go to class and pay attention to their studies and get on them far more than normal because I know firsthand how easily it can get away from you.

My players pay for the scars of my past.

Because of my background, because of where I come from, I have this feeling that I have to constantly prove myself—over and over again, just like when I was seven years old, trying to fit in, trying to show everyone I was just as good as they were.

Every game, every practice, every possession, I need to get it right. I need to make it perfect.

And, of course, I never do.

⊕

I've created this world where everything I do is subject to inspection and scrutiny. My wife, Kathy, will tell you that there have been times I haven't felt as connected to my family as I should because I'm always distracted by my job. Some coaches are really good at being totally committed to their job and still able to remain connected to their family at the same time. I had to learn how to do that. I didn't grow up in a family that was very connected, because of our circumstances and the disparity of our experiences.

My father is getting up early in the morning and going to work. My mother is doing the same thing. We go to school. When we get home, my parents are dead tired. What, did you think we were going to sit around the dinner table and have them ask me, "So, how was school today?"

I lived a different life than most fourteen- and fifteen-year-old kids my age. I am on my own with a lot of responsibility. Don't get me wrong. I never feel unsafe or unloved, just not that connected.

I have created an environment for my own family that includes a great deal of material things. I just hope I've also created a sense of belonging to something. I hope Kathy and I have created an awareness of how important relationships are as opposed to what kind of house you have, or what kind of car you drive.

We've done a pretty good job of keeping the kids out of the limelight. You're not going to ever see my son, Michael, cutting down the nets when we win a championship. You've never seen my children sitting on the bench, poking their heads in our huddle during timeouts. My daughters Jenna and Alysa don't run around trying to get certain things by saying they are Geno Auriemma's daughters.

You'd think I'd be a lot more content considering all we've accomplished at Connecticut. We've gone from a program that was invisible, with a 36–74 record in the four years before we got there, to one of the premier basketball programs in the country. I wish I could enjoy it more.

There's an old Irish saying that Guinness is what sustains you during the brief moments of happiness while you wait for the next disaster to hit. I really believe that's part of my makeup. I have these brief moments of happiness in life, whether it's drinking a pint of Guinness, or a great bottle of wine, or playing a great round of golf, or seeing my team play 40 minutes of great basketball. I enjoy those things for the shortest amount of time, as I wait, down the road, to fall into the hot coals.

I know it's just a matter of time.

There have been plenty of times I've landed face first in the fire. In 1998, I allowed Nykesha Sales, who was two points shy of breaking our school's scoring record, to score a layup against Villanova after she injured her Achilles tendon (more on that later). I've made some offhand comments about Tennessee coach Pat Summitt that caused all sorts of controversy (more on her later, too). I've gotten into a shouting match in a restaurant on campus with a mother of a recruit. I've dressed down a student reporter for asking a stupid question and wound up on *SportsCenter* for it.

My assistants tell me I talk too much. I tell my players all the time, "Your biggest strength is your biggest weakness." The media loves to ask me questions. Why? Because they know I'm going to give them a straight answer. What's my biggest weakness? I give them a straight answer.

Who wants people to be honest anymore? People want you to be politically correct. That's not my personality.

And so I accumulate these scars, these lessons in life.

I take what I've learned, and I try to save my players from making the same mistakes I've made. I push them, prod them, challenge them, and take them to the brink.

I don't want them ever to land face first in a hot bed of coals.

Believe me. It hurts.

TWO

I must be crazy to take the Connecticut job.

It is 1985, and I am an assistant coach at Virginia, which is a Top 20 women's program in the ACC. I leave for a program that has no history, no office, no fans, no real gym, and metal bleachers they only roll out for the really big games. The problem with that is, back then, there are no big games.

I really need and want to be a head coach. Debbie Ryan, who was and still is the head coach at Virginia, will tell you that. I drive her crazy my final year there, because I want our team to be *my* team. I have big dreams. To tell you the truth, my plan is to stay at Connecticut two or three seasons, win some games, them move on to an elite program.

The people at Connecticut will tell you I was hardly their first choice. Pat Mizer, who is spearheading the search for a new coach at the time, doesn't want me. She wants a woman. She tells the players, "We're going to get the best female candidate we can get." Peggy Walsh, one of the returning players, is pissed. She's saying, "Why not just get the best coach?" Pat and I laugh about it all the time now. She turns out to be one of my good friends.

The person they think they want is Nancy Darsch, who is Pat Summitt's assistant at Tennessee. When she doesn't get this job, she goes on to take the head job at Ohio State. When I find that out, I'm saying, "Damn, you take this job and I'll take the Ohio State job."

Who knows why they give it to me? I think I come across well in the interview. I bullshit them about how I think Connecticut can be in the Top 20, even though I don't believe that. No way. Not with what we have. What I am really thinking is, "You're not going to beat Tennessee. You're not going to beat Virginia, or UCLA, but you certainly can try to catch Villanova and Providence." It's not like the job offers nothing. It is in the Big East with an opportunity to create something. Also, I don't have a lot of confidence in the rest of the women's basketball community at that time. Very few schools are fully committed to their programs and offering the proper support. So it's not like I have to climb Mount Everest.

Or so I think.

John Toner, the athletic director, offers me the job over a cup of coffee at Dunkin' Donuts. It isn't a moment that is exactly dripping with pomp and circumstance.

Right away, I find myself talking all the time to Dee Rowe. He's a former coach at the school and the resident UConn legend. He becomes extremely important to me almost immediately. He is so helpful. Does he come down and give me tips on how to coach? Does he tell me what to run? No. What he does on a regular basis is find a way to connect with me and tell me, "Hey, you're all right. I like the way you do things." This is from a guy I admire as much as anybody. I always say I hope I die before Dee Rowe does so he can say my eulogy. Not one person on this earth dislikes Dee Rowe. If you do, you should reevaluate who you are. Dee Rowe is there for me at the beginning, and he's still there for me now.

When I get to UConn, it is hard to believe it is a Division I program. We hold practice in the field house. It isn't a gym; it is a basketball court in the middle of a track. And it isn't like we have the place to ourselves. We have track athletes working out in there. We have the baseball team doing indoor drills. We have weightlifters all along the perimeter. We also have students, faculty, and workers getting into shape.

Before we can accomplish anything, we have to work really hard to get people off the track. The faculty members are jogging around and we're saying, "Could you please get off the track?" They say, "Why?" and we say, "Well, we have a game tonight, and we've got to pull out the bleachers," but they don't care. They just want to get their laps in.

When we practice, we pull the curtains around our little area, like that would make any difference. We're still competing with the weightlifters, who occupy a little corner of the field house. They blast their music so loud we're shouting out instructions to the players.

Then you have the track team running around the oval. The hurdlers are the ones that get to my assistant, Chris Dailey, who everyone calls CD. We're trying to show the kids a play, and you hear this *Boom! Boom! Boom!* It is the runners knocking over those hurdles. One day CD can't take it anymore. She opens up the curtain and shouts, "I'm sorry, but isn't the object to jump *over* those things?"

In the other corner, the baseball team is working out. It isn't unusual for errant baseballs to go whizzing past our heads. The basketball court itself is in bad shape. When it rains, the roof leaks, and we have to strategically place buckets all around the court.

We don't have chairs on the sidelines. We have one big long bench. We share a tiny locker room with the softball team. In the winter, we are in. During the fall and spring, we are out.

Our uniforms are hideous. We have no equipment. Meanwhile, during the game, you've got my daughter Jenna running around and jumping into the high jump pit, with my wife chasing after her. It is insane.

But it is also a lesson. It makes us focus on what we have, not what we don't have. Years later, when we get good, schools that are our size are going to their athletic directors and saying, "We need what Connecticut has." CD and I laugh about that. We want to tell them, "Be careful what you wish for. You have more facilities than we do right now."

One of the things that I am pleasantly surprised about during our first season, in 1985–86, is the competitiveness of some of the kids. Kids like Peggy Walsh, a tough, hard-nosed player who just wasn't used to winning. That is true of all of them. Things just haven't gone their way. When you finish with a 9–18 record, then 9–18 again, then 9–20 and 9–18, it's almost like you get to 9 wins and say, "Okay, that's enough." So the first thing I do is try to set some team goals.

Now, I'm telling you, I don't think we have more than one legitimate Division I player on our team. We have Peggy, who is fantastic. She is very aggressive. She grabs 25 rebounds in a game against Pittsburgh. That's about it in terms of true talent. But we do have Audrey Epstein, a 5-foot-8 lefty from Long Island, whom I love. Audrey's most important traits are that she is very bright and a very good team player, which offsets the fact that she is slow, can't run, and can't jump. She is so conscientious, though. You know she is going to succeed in life. She's a lawyer now, as a matter of a fact.

Besides Audrey and Peggy, who is our team captain, we have another girl, Tammi Sweet, who seems really excited about what we are doing. She is our second leading scorer behind Peggy, and she is a big help to us. We have a real nice kid named Anne Fiolkowski. She is a smart player, too. We have a girl named Jill Brumbaugh, who is a mess when we get there, but seems to have a bit of an idea of what we are about by the time she leaves.

Actually, when you look back on it, the team is full of exactly the kind of kids you would recruit at a school that has a lousy record with no facilities and what appears to be no commitment from the university. What kind of kid would be attracted to that kind of program? A kid who always gets a high grade point average and who loves basketball. I think our team GPA that season is 3.5. They may not be the most talented group in the world, but they are intelligent.

On the first day, I gather them all together and ask them what our team goals should be. I say, "Where do you think we're going to finish?" They say, "Fourth." I'm looking at them in disbelief. I say to them, "Fourth? You guys should have your heads examined. What makes you think you can finish fourth?" They answer, "Because we have a new coach." Apparently, they are under the impression that as long as we just change the coach, everything will be fine.

I'm thinking to myself, "I'm glad we changed coaches, but what I'd really like to do is change some of the players." But I don't tell them that. Instead, I coach the hell out of those kids. I am so tough on them. I do not let up. I make them do drills over and over and over again until they get it right. I run them, and run them some more. They do more defensive slides than any team I've had. I'll never ever forget that group.

You coach kids that don't have the ability much differently than a group of elite players. You work them just as hard, but the approach is not the same. It's almost like coaching a high school team. There is so much drilling of fundamentals. We almost never scrimmage in practice, because we only have one or two players that would make it worthwhile. How are you going to play five-on-five when half your team doesn't really get it? The only time we really play is in the actual games. The rest of the time we do breakdown drills. Breakdown how to shoot off the dribble. Breakdown how to box out. Breakdown how to defend on the weak side. Breakdown this, breakdown that. It is two solid hours of drills. Because of it, we are in great condition.

Peggy is a terrific game player, but she will be the first to tell you she isn't crazy about practice. I tell her early on, "You have to put into practice what you put into games."

The first three weeks of preseason, Peggy is so sore she takes the elevator in her dorm to the first floor, because she can't climb the one flight of stairs. She has a loft in her bedroom where she usually sleeps, but her legs are so achy she can't climb the ladder, so she pulls the mattress down and sleeps on the floor instead.

As we get closer to the first game, I pull her aside one day and tell her, "If the season started today, I'd start Jennifer Weideman at center over you." Now, Jennifer is a thin 6-foot-3 kid who isn't nearly as talented as Peggy. But she is a hard worker, and she is giving me everything she has in practice.

Peggy gets the message. She busts her rear end after that, and when the 1985–86 season starts, she is our starting center for that game, and the other 26 we play the rest of the way.

Back then the Big East is made up of only nine schools. The conference tournament features only eight teams. So if you finish in the bottom two, you have to play in the dreaded eighth-versus-ninth game for the right to go to the league tournament. Connecticut has been in the eighth-versus-ninth game every year, and the kids are sick of it. It is humiliating. They nickname the game the "toilet bowl."

So I say, "Here's the goal. No matter what, we're not playing in the eighth-versus-ninth game. I don't care where we finish, but we're not playing in that game."

So what happens? We go out and finish seventh. You'd think we've won the national title. When those women walk into the tournament, they walk in there with their heads high. They strut in like, "Hey, look at us. We're not playing in that dumb toilet bowl game."

Our record that first season is 12–15. We start out 7–0, including a huge win over UMass. In all my years at Connecticut, that is the closest I ever get to being really satisfied as a coach. That's because we win some games we have no business winning. That never happens anymore.

UMass is that kind of game. They are a good team, well coached by Barbara Stevens. She's great. She's now the coach at Bentley College, and she's made them a national power in Division II. Anyhow, UMass beats UConn by nine the previous season, and they are leading by a whole bunch of points early in this game, too. But then, all of sudden, something clicks. All of a sudden, our players start taking what they've learned in practice, and actually start applying it on the court. We come back to win the game by three points, 62–59, and it will always rank as one of my favorite memories.

At that point, after losing 18 or 19 games for four years in a row, the kids are ecstatic. After that UMass win, they think we are on our way to the NCAA tournament. Instead, we lose 6 in a row to finish that season, including 11 of the last 14 games. Their effort is there. Their effort is fantastic. We just aren't good enough.

We do have another big win that season. We beat Syracuse 78–72 in our home gym. Connecticut has never beaten them before, so that means a lot to our players. We change around our approach for that game, and put Peggy at the top of our 3–2 defense. Syracuse has never seen that, and it seems to throw them off.

Although there are some high moments that season, there are a lot of tears, too. Many of the kids we have simply don't belong in a Division I program. Many of them won't—or can't—make the commitment I am asking them to make.

It is obvious to CD and me that we need to get our own kids. We need legitimate talented players with a winning attitude, and we need them quickly.

Kris Lamb is our first big recruit. She actually recruits *me* when I'm at Virginia and she is a high school player. She used to call me and ask me for tickets to the games. She is a huge North Carolina fan, so I get her tickets when the Tar Heels are in town.

We meet at a Five-Star Basketball Camp in Roanoke, Virginia. Dave Odom, who was a men's assistant at Virginia at the time, and I run the camp. I'm doing a lecture on boxing out, and I ask for some volunteers from the audience. Kris jumps up, and as I'm demonstrating how to create your space when you go up for a rebound, I accidentally elbow her in the nose. She barely flinches. I like her right away.

Kris really loves basketball, but she doesn't have a whole lot of people in her life at that time that know the game well, so I begin talking with her a lot. I help her get into the Blue Star camp the following summer, which features a lot of the top players in the country, and it gives her some exposure.

When I take the Connecticut job, Virginia isn't really recruiting her. She is one of those players who could probably make it at a place like Arizona, but not one of the elite programs. There are the elite teams, the mid-majors, and then there is us. She is probably a mid-major player, but because of our relationship, we get her.

Kris ends up being the heart and soul of the team while she is here. Coaches always ask the question, "How well do you know your players?" and in the case of Kris Lamb, I know her very, very well. I know what drives her—and believe me, I drive her hard. I am a real hard-ass. My players today don't know how easy they have it. They should ask Kris Lamb.

It's like when you raise a bunch of kids. Do you really think you're harder on your last kid than you are on your first or second kid? Of course not, not in a million years.

We bring Kris in, and she's part of my family right away. She's babysitting my kids, coming to the house for dinner, the whole thing. We just love the kid. This is mostly in the summer. Now school starts, and we're two weeks into it and she calls me up one night. She says, "Coach, I've got a problem." I say, "What's wrong, Kris?" She says, "I have this English paper due and I'm stuck." I say, "Well, today is Friday. When did you get this assignment?" She says, "Yesterday." I say, "Well, when is it due?" She says, "Tuesday." I ask her, "Have you been to the library and researched it?" She answers me, "Well, I tried, but I'm stuck."

I say, "Well, get unstuck."

And then I hang up.

I guess Kris wanted me to do the paper for her. She is an okay student, nothing special, and she is thinking, "Coach really likes me, so anytime I get in a jam, he'll help me." I think she got the message that my feeling is, "Screw that." But that's what is great about Kris. She never asks me anything like that again. She ends up having to work really hard at her studies, because nothing comes easy for her, but she is taking master's courses before she is done.

In her first couple of years here, she is a scorer all the way. All she wants to do is shoot. If she doesn't score, she thinks something is wrong with her. One day, we're beating Pittsburgh by 15 or 20 points, and she's 1 for 12 from the floor. She's out of the game toward the end, and she's weeping a little bit. I go storming up to her and say, "You've got to be kidding me. We're up 15, and you're an idiot. You're sitting here crying because you're not shooting well. This is so much about you it's unbelievable. You are never going to make it." And I march off. She is speechless.

I call her into my office at the end of the season, and I tell her, "Kris, the only way we're going to be any good is if you stop scoring. You need to be our defensive stopper, and become everything else other than a scorer. If you do that, we have a chance to really be something." Well, she turns about seventeen different shades of purple, and she looks like she's going to have a stroke, but you know what? She does it. She sucks it up, and she comes back to be our best defender, and don't you know, she scores more points than ever. All that stuff is really, really hard for her to hear, but she responds.

That has always been the way I've handled my players. I say things to kids they really don't want to hear. In the end, if they look at it, the only reason I'm saying it is because I can see past what they can see. That's what experience is. I tell them, "If you trust me, I can get you where you want to be." It's a tough way to go about it, but it's a lot better than blowing smoke up their ass and telling them what they want to hear—even if it's not true.

Here's what makes it work. On the other side, my players know they can come in here and say, "Coach, you screwed up the other night. You shouldn't have been so tough on Barbara Turner," or "You handled that situation with Kara Wolters wrong," or whatever. And I have to be big enough to tell them, "You're right."

That happened a lot more frequently in those early years than now. I'm probably more defensive now than I was back then. I've been inflicted with the same disease most coaches get when they've been coaching a long time and had some success. It's that disease where you always say, "I'm right and you're wrong." It takes me a lot longer now to admit, "I made a mistake."

The other problem is the players are too intimidated now. When I was coaching Kris Lamb, Kerry Bascom, Meghan Pattyson, Jamelle Elliott, and Rebecca Lobo, we were never on TV. When they came here, I was simply Coach Auriemma, who seems like a good guy, who is young, energetic, and has some ideas. Now every kid who comes here has seen us play for four years on television. They know everything about me, because they've read it or heard it or seen me in action.

So now they walk in here and they have this certain vision of me. They are afraid to talk to me, because in their eyes, I'm this bigger-than-life figure. Even though they might have some ideas of their own and they want to share them, oftentimes they can't. So I have to force the issue. I have to drag them into my office and say, "Tell me what's on your mind." Or I have to rely on my assistants to find out what they are thinking about. It's too bad, really. The kids who played for me early in this process certainly got a chance to know me a lot better.

Kris's freshman year, we go 14–13 and everyone is all excited. Everyone thinks we're on our way and everything is hunky-dory, but the truth is we end up losing some kids along the way. I inherit all these kids I didn't recruit, and as we start playing and drilling, my way of doing things doesn't fit in with what they want to do.

As we start moving forward and bringing in the kids we think are really going to help us, there's some natural resentment from the holdovers. Some of my early recruits bear the brunt of that resentment.

After Kris's freshman year, we take the biggest step in the program's history when we sign Kerry Bascom. Kerry is from Epping, New Hampshire. She is big and strong and fearless, and she can score. I have often told my players, past and present, that if we're down one with ten seconds left in the game, I want the ball in Kerry Bascom's hands. That's how good she is and how much confidence she has.

We also bring Laura Lishness, an immensely skilled player who, I'm sure, was put here on this earth to torture me. She is magnificent one day, and you think, "All right, here we go," and then she's in the tank the next. She drives me crazy. Thank God she is really talented and really nice. She could have been better than Kerry. She has the potential to get a triple double every night. She is six feet tall, with great hands and great feet, a three-sport star from Bristol, Connecticut.

I know things aren't perfect for Kerry and Laura with the

older players on the team, but I don't find out how bad it is until it is over. The upperclassmen refuse to call Kerry or Laura by name. They always call them "freshmen." If they were doing it as a term of endearment, that would be one thing. But they are doing it to be demeaning, to set the pecking order. I can tell you one thing: they never say it in front of me. If they did, I would have taken care of it.

Jill Brumbaugh is a senior on that team and so is Renee Najarian, a transfer from South Carolina who averages 18 points a game that season and feels like this is her team. So apparently one day, the girls are getting ready for a shootaround, and Laura Lishness is putting her uniform on. They are in the so-called locker room, which is the size of a shoebox. Laura is just about dressed, when one of our upperclassmen, Krista Blomquist, says, "Hey, freshman, give me your shorts. I want to wear those." Laura doesn't even look up. She just says, "Get your own damn shorts." The next thing you know, the two of them are rolling around on the ground fighting. I don't hear about this until years later. Nobody says anything. But we know there are problems with this group.

Kerry is rooming with Jill Brumbaugh, and it's not going well. She goes to the library to study, and occasionally she comes back to find her dorm room locked. Here's this kid from Epping, New Hampshire, a small-town girl who just wants to play ball, and too many nights she comes home and can't even get inside her room. Most of the time, she ends up staying in Kris Lamb's room. I'm sure it is terrible for her. I can tell you this, though: Kerry keeps her mouth shut. She never once comes and complains to me about anything. I think she and Laura and Kris and Heidi Robbins, who is a sophomore that year, feel they can handle it themselves, as long as they stick together.

Meanwhile, I'm being really, really hard on Kerry in practice, because I can see how great she's going to be. She is a gifted scorer, but she needs to be a better defender, so I ride her all day. I tell her, "You are the saddest excuse for a defensive player I've ever recruited." Things like that. But she can take it. I think she may have actually *liked* it. Kerry Bascom doesn't back down from anybody—not even me.

Kerry Bascom is one of those people who craves the give-and-take. She likes the interaction. Whether it's positive attention or negative attention, it doesn't matter. She just likes the challenge of it all. When you look back on what she did, it's incredible. If we needed a clutch shot, we looked to her to take it, at a time when there were not a whole lot of other stars on the team. If we were down one, everyone in the gym knew she was going to get the ball, and she still was able to make the big shot. That's pretty good.

I don't see Kerry as much as I'd like anymore, but every time she comes down for a visit, I'm all over her. I tell my current players, "Do you know how many losses I have in my career? Do you realize this kid gave me half of them?" Truth is, we wouldn't have won *any* games without Kerry and Laura during that 1987–88 season.

So it's right around Christmastime of their freshman year, and we've won four in a row, and we go to play the University of Hartford. Now, obviously this is not a game we want to lose. Connecticut is the state university, and we're supposed to be the best team. I don't remember what the score is at halftime, but I do know I am really, really upset. We are playing like crap, and the attitude of these players is really getting to me. I've never been around a team that fostered so much animosity and tension among themselves.

I walk into the locker room and I throw the clipboard to the ground so hard that it breaks into a hundred pieces. Then I let them have it. I tell them they are sloppy and look like they don't give a damn. I tell them they are not playing like a team. I am really, really hot.

I look over at Kris Lamb and she is sitting with her elbows on her knees, and she has her head down. She's playing awful, just like everyone else, but it just totally ticks me off that her head is down like that. I go over to her, and I whack her arm off her knees and I tell her, "You look me in the eye when I'm talking to you. Do you understand?" She's a little startled, but mostly she's ticked off, so she stares at me with complete disdain, and I rant a little more, and then we go out and win the game by 23 points.

That's in December. By February, our team is really splintered. We manage to win games, but there are two distinct groups: the kids CD and I have brought in, which includes Kris, Kerry, Laura, and Heidi Robbins, and the other nine kids we inherit. Those nine kids, for the most part, aren't playing as much as they think they should, feel like they are second-class citizens, and want things, I guess, to go back to the way they used to be.

It is a very difficult year for everyone. We go 17–11 that season, but I cancel the banquet that spring. The point of a banquet is to celebrate your seniors. We have nothing to celebrate.

The first player to leave is Lynne Reif. She is dealing with some personal tragedy in her family, and she's gone before the season ends. She turns out to be the first of many to jump ship.

CD, who makes a living out of being able to communicate with players, is so bothered by this group. She just can't reach them. She sits in the bleachers with tears in her eyes. She says more than once that season, "If this is how it's going to be, I'm getting out of coaching."

What she doesn't realize is that's what these kids want. They want to get us fired. At the end of the season, a group of them go to our athletic director, Todd Turner, and complain about how we run the program. They tell Turner we are physically abusive with our players, and bring up the incident with Kris Lamb back in December in Hartford.

I am stunned. All I did that day was go up to Kris and whack her arm as if to say, "What the hell are you doing?" I wouldn't have done that with just any player. I knew Kris Lamb so well it was like she was my own daughter. I had a familiarity with her that didn't make me hesitate to do that.

Now, if you are sitting there watching that, I can see where you could say, "Hey, that's kind of abusive." The other players didn't have the level of comfort with me that Kris had.

I learn from that. I can understand where those kids are coming from. I don't think I've ever done anything like that again, because I understand now how it can be misconstrued. And yet, I still come up to Barbara Turner from time to time and give her a little bump and say, "Hey, how are you doing?" The day I can't do that is the day I'm getting out of this business.

When Kris Lamb finds out some of her teammates have gone behind her back to the athletic director, she is horrified. She wasn't happy with me the day our disagreement happened, but we talked the next day about it, and that was it. It was over. In fact, when she told her father what happened, he said, "Sounds to me like you deserved it."

Now, three months later, she's in Turner's office trying to reenact what happened. She is so loyal to us anyway, but the truth is there's nothing to tell. These kids have taken one incident and blown it up. Kris Lamb sets the record straight. In the meantime, the parent of another player is calling up Kris's parents and trying to pressure them into getting involved. The Lambs want no part of it. The only way they will be involved, they say, is to support our coaching staff.

Once Turner listens to Kris and her version of what happened, it quickly becomes apparent to him that there is no real issue here. I am not reprimanded, nor do I receive any kind of punishment, but by the time it is over, the damage is done. There are rumors all over the state that I had punched Kris Lamb.

I was disappointed that the kids went behind my back like that. If they had a problem with me, I wish they came to me during the season. But they didn't. It shows you the character—or lack of character—we were dealing with that year.

The truth is, we were trying to do some things to turn around the program. They didn't like it because it was too hard, or because they weren't playing enough, or because they weren't "our players." But that's the part they got wrong. They could have been. We wanted them to be. They made a conscious choice not to be.

At the end of the season, Jill and Renee graduate. The rest of the upperclassmen quit. We come back with four returning players, and we bring six new kids in. It is a blessing in disguise. That's when it all starts to turn around. We bring in Meghan Pattyson, Debbie Baer, Wendy Davis, Kathy Bantley, Stacey Wetzel, and Pam Rothfuss. They are great kids who support each other and their teammates, and overnight, everything changes.

The chemistry these kids have is obvious from the very first day. Kris and Kerry take the recruits around, and the bond between them is established very early on. Finally, it feels like we are on our way. It's amazing how you can go from hell to heaven in such a short time.

Some of those kids from that 1987–88 season figure it out after a while. They start to feel badly about how they behaved. I get a letter from Krista Blomquist a few years later telling me, "Coach, sorry I was such a jerk when I was there." I understand. When you think about it, they're just kids. They're just kids trying to figure everything out.

We go 24–6 during that 1988–89 season and we win the Big East tournament for the first time in school history. We also go to the NCAA tournament. The next season, we are 25–6, and advance to the second round of the tournament. And by the 1990–91 season, which is Kerry and Laura's senior year, we have something special going on.

Kerry has been through a lot by then. Her mother suffered from multiple sclerosis, and she starts to deteriorate rapidly. We talk about it a lot. Kerry's dad and I agree the best thing Kerry can do for her mom is to stay at Connecticut and be successful and be a good student and make the most out of her experience, because that will make her mom happy. It's hard. Sometimes Kerry needs to go home. Of course we understand that.

I have never been through anything like this. Kerry is so fun to pick on and spar with, but obviously during this time we all see another side of her. She knows I love her, because I only pick on the people I care about, but once in a while you need to make sure you say it.

Kerry's mom dies during her junior season. We play a game without her down at Fairfield and we almost lose. We pull it out in overtime, and obviously, it's closer than it should be. Our minds are somewhere else. We make the trip to the funeral, and it is an emotional time for all of us. You feel helpless. You want to make everything better, and you can't. Kerry's not one to wear her heart on her sleeve. She's very guarded. But we can all see how tough it is. I treat Kerry with kid gloves the rest of that season. We end up losing the Big East tournament to Providence and lose to Clemson in the second round of the NCAA tournament. Kerry hits a shot that goes halfway down, then out.

By the time we come back for the 1990–91 season, Kerry is coming out of it. I'm back to my old Mr. Grinch self with her. I know she's as good a player as there is in the country, and I want her senior year to go well.

The game that really stands out from that season is when we play Auburn in our own tournament, the Connecticut Classic. Auburn is ranked second or third in the country at the time, and they are heavily favored, but we beat them, 67–63. That feels really good.

They have this vaunted zone defense that has gotten them to the Final Four a couple of times. Joe Ciampi, the coach down there, is famous for this matchup zone. He flies all over the country lecturing about it. Auburn plays it really well, and no one can attack it, and they are flying high, one of the top teams in the top conference, which at the time is the SEC.

Meanwhile, we've got a whole bunch of kids no one has ever heard of. We start the game, and right off the opening tap they score two points. So now we come down the floor, and Auburn is in its famous zone, and we knock down something like six straight three-pointers. It is just unbelievable. We go up something like 19–5, just like that. Everyone on the floor is hitting threes for us—everyone except Meghan Pattyson, who isn't a perimeter shooter. We put Meghan in the middle of the zone, and we're moving the ball so fast they can't catch up with it.

Auburn calls a timeout. I think they are shell-shocked. Nobody has done that to them before. You have to realize we're hitting some pretty deep shots, too. They are coming from all over the floor: the top of the key, way in the corner, you name it. Kerry and Wendy are just nailing everything.

So now we're in a timeout, and the kids come running over to the bench. We have, for us, a big crowd there—about eight hundred people. How about that? Just eight hundred people, but in our minds, every seat is full. Our kids are feeding off all the excitement, and they start saying, "We've got 'em now. We've forced them out of their zone."

Sure enough, Auburn goes into a man-to-man defense. I see our girls walk out there, and I know what they are thinking: "They're playing right into our hands."

Wrong. We don't score for the next five minutes. They just come out and stuff us. Their athletic ability is impressive. We can't run anything against them. Even so, somehow we hang on and win that game. Kerry and Laura won't let us lose. That is the first one that gets us noticed, a little bit. We may have even sneaked into the Top 25.

We build on that win all the way to the Final Four. We beat North Carolina State and Clemson to get there. Those are huge, huge wins for our program. Back then, those wins used to wash over me. I would revel in them for days and days. I went around thinking, "Man, we're hot stuff. We're really good. We've taken nothing and made it into something." Our coaches and our players share that same feeling. We let those big wins linger.

Now, all these years later, the enjoyment of a big win lasts until I wake up the next morning. If we practice the next day, it's over right there. If we don't practice, it's awesome, because we can sit back and enjoy the game for another twenty-four hours.

I miss pulling off the upset. It used to be, "We are going to take on Mike Tyson and knock him out." Well, now Connecticut is Mike Tyson. Everyone wants to knock us out. That's a much harder challenge than trying to upset someone yourself. When you are on top, everyone is gunning for you, and if you're not on your game, you're dead.

When I look back to those early years, I realize how much I challenged those players. I did not give them an inch. Kerry Bascom comes down once a year or so to take in a game, and she'll tell me, "Man, Coach, you've gone soft." That's probably true. Everyone has their own way of motivating their players. People have this idea that coaches manipulate their kids so they'll band together against the coach and hate him. But here's my question: if they all hate you, how are they going to play their hearts out for you? I don't want my players to hate me. I want them to hate what I'm asking them to do.

If they enjoy everything I'm asking them to do, then it's probably too easy. I'm sure there have been times my players have hated my guts, but I don't think, for most of them, that it was long-lasting. I don't think it's ever gotten to the point where I'm calling a timeout with three minutes left, and I've got a player on the bench thinking, "I hate this son of a bitch so much I'm not going to listen to a word he says."

I'm not saying all my players leave here loving me. Not every kid feels the same about me. I've had kids that played for me who graduate and I never hear from them again. I wonder what went wrong with those kids, and how I could have treated them differently.

When Rebecca Lobo graduates from Connecticut, she writes me a long letter. It is a very nice letter detailing her thoughts on our relationship, and how she feels I helped her become a great player. After I get it, I call her up and say, "I really appreciate you writing this letter, because I got a pretty bad letter about two days before your letter came."

The bad letter is from another former player of mine, Heidi Law. She is a nice kid who had a world of potential. She is a Connecticut native, a really nice young woman with long arms and some very fine basketball ability. In fact, she helps us get to the Final Four in 1991.

Heidi had a variety of injuries, some worse than others. When she was healthy, she was unbelievably good. But it seemed like every time she played great, I'd go up to her and say, "Heidi, I think you've finally turned the corner, man. If you could do this every night, I'll tell you what—there is no way anyone is going to beat us."

Right after that, almost immediately, Heidi would go under again. I don't know why. I think it's because she wasn't really sure she could deliver when it mattered. So when you put the onus on her and said, "Hey, Heidi, we're really counting on you today," that was too much for her.

By the time she is in her final season with the team, in 1992, she isn't playing much, and we part on bad terms.

It's funny. All the things that I believe kept Heidi from becoming a great player come alive again in that letter she writes to me. Believe me, it is a tough letter to read. In essence, Heidi is telling me I am the reason she quit the team, and I am the reason things didn't work out for her, and I'm the reason she has struggled so much and left school.

Heidi wrote that she could have been really good, but that I didn't understand her. Obviously, a letter like that bothers you. I am in the office when I get the mail, and I see the return address and I have no idea what I am about to get, because it's from someone I haven't talked to in a long time. So when I open it and I read all those things, I feel really bad.

I think about it for quite a while, but I can't seem to put my arms around it. I know Heidi is struggling, and she's lashing out, and I have to let her do that. I probably could have done some things differently with her. Maybe I could have made it easier for her. I understand that, but I guess I wasn't ready to accept all the blame for the things that had gone wrong in her life.

I used to kid Rebecca Lobo in public all the time. I'd say, "Rebecca is on the dean's list, a Rhodes Scholar candidate, first team All-America, and poster child for women's basketball. But you know what? That's a bunch of crap. Without me, she'd still be picking tobacco up there in western Massachusetts," which, believe it or not, was a job Rebecca used to have in the summertime.

Obviously I was joking. With or without me, Rebecca Lobo was going to be tremendously successful at something. The fact that I had a small hand in it is fate. I take one-hundredth of the credit for what happened to Rebecca Lobo, and I'll take one-hundredth of the blame for what happened to Heidi Law.

In the summer of 2003, nearly eight years after the first letter, I hear from Heidi Law again. She is living in New Jersey. She wants to come up to talk to me because, she says, she finally sees the side of things I want her to see. She says she regrets how everything ended, and she wants to make things right.

You know what? Me being an idiot, I've kind of put it aside. I keep telling myself, "I'll get to that later." But I know I need to get to it now. I need to give Heidi a chance to get beyond it. Sometimes coaches underestimate the impact our relationships with our players have on them as they go forward.

I've thought about the players that haven't stayed in our program for one reason or another. There's this old saying, "Players are only as good as the coach thinks they are," and there is a lot of truth to that. Think about it. If I think you suck, it doesn't matter how good you are, because you ain't playing, and everything you do bothers me. It's like being in a relationship. The first couple of years everything is great. I say, "Do this," and you say, "No problem. Kiss, kiss, kiss." But after a while, you wake up in the morning and you say, "Stop bugging me. Leave me the hell alone."

When a kid comes to your program, and you say, "This kid is really good," you are going to do everything you can for that player to make it true. You are going to work with her, give her playing time, and give her the confidence she needs to succeed. But once you turn, because a kid starts to screw up, or fights you in a lot of different ways, then you say, "You know what? This kid can't help us." And from that point on, no matter what that kid does, it's not going to matter. There's no turning back.

Everybody who coaches young kids needs to remember that they need a lot of confidence from you. They pine for it. They have to have constant reassurance and reinforcement that, "Hey, I believe in you. I'm with you." Even someone like Rebecca Lobo or Kerry Bascom needs that.

I have immortalized Kerry Bascom to the point where my current players are tired of hearing about her. In the spring of 2004, just before we win our third consecutive national championship, I bring up Kerry again, how she's my all-time money player. Diana Taurasi, who is probably the best women's basketball player who ever lived, can't take it anymore. She says, "Kerry, this, Kerry that. Why are you always talking about her?"

So Kathy and I have this great idea. We decide to hold a Kerry Bascom night at our house. Diana comes over, and one of our other seniors, Morgan Valley, comes with her, and I show them films of us playing in 1990 and 1991. They are stunned. Kerry is our tallest player on the floor at 6-foot-1, but she kicks everybody's ass up and down the floor. Diana doesn't say much, but she's impressed. I can tell.

A few months later, just moments after we've won another championship, Diana is being interviewed on national television. She looks right into the camera and says, "This is for all the past players, for players like Kerry Bascom and Rebecca Lobo." I can't believe it. But that's Dee. She gets it. Whether it's real or whether it's fake, Dee has always given respect to great players, even though she shows them no respect on the court.

Everyone knows they better respect Kerry Bascom. She was there at the beginning. She never got to play Tennessee, or win a national championship, but without her we never would have been able to do those things. She scored 2,177 points during an era where we were just getting started.

I don't cry very much—hardly ever. But I can honestly tell you I cried the night Kerry Bascom graduated. I couldn't help it.

A couple of years ago, Kerry came down to Storrs for a visit. At this point we sell out every home game, and the university has gone to a point system to dole out the choice seats. The way it works is the more money you donate to the school, the more points you accrue, and the better seats you get.

So the game is about to start, and Kerry walks down the aisle to some pretty choice seats right in the front row. Someone is kidding around, and they yell to her, "Hey, Kerry, are you sure you've earned enough points for those seats?"

She turns around and says, "I've got 2,177 points, baby. That should be enough for any seat in this place."

THREE

After our first visit to the Final Four in 1991, I know I'm not going to be happy until we win a national championship. And after meeting this kid from Southwick, Massachusetts, I know how we're going to do it.

Rebecca Lobo is going to take us there.

Sometimes, I have these feelings. My wife, Kathy, calls them premonitions. I don't know if it's quite that, but I do know sometimes I have a certain sense about a situation or a person, and when I say it out loud, it comes true.

All I know is after I meet Rebecca and begin recruiting her, I have one of those feelings. I come home after spending time with her and I say to Kathy, "We've got to get her. She's supposed to be here."

I can't believe how entertaining and engaging this kid is. I've had more interesting conversations with Rebecca Lobo during the recruiting process than anybody. She is just so insightful and provocative, and, actually, quite funny. She's also smarter than me, but then, most of the kids I recruit turn out to be that way.

We are pretty far into the recruiting process when I say to Rebecca one day, "You were meant to play at Connecticut." She is the first player I ever tell that.

The problem is Rebecca has Vanderbilt, Stanford, Notre Dame, and Duke recruiting her as well. They all are pushing hard for her and they all have great academic reputations.

Rebecca's parents understand how good she is, but they are very focused on the academics. Rebecca, meanwhile, seems to really like what we have to say. When she comes down for her visit, she stays with Meghan Pattyson. Now, if you can't have fun with Meghan Pattyson, there's really something wrong with you. She's just so outgoing and so much fun, and has a way of making you feel like you've known her your whole life.

After Rebecca's visit, Meghan comes into my office and says, "She's coming here. There's no doubt about it. She's a perfect fit for our team."

Rebecca gets to the point where she says, "I want to go to Connecticut." But her mother, Ruth Ann, says, "I'm a guidance counselor, and my best students don't go to Connecticut, and Rebecca is number one in her class, so why should she go there?"

Ruth Ann asks me that question on our home visit with Rebecca. How are you supposed to answer that? I say, "You can't make that decision until you come down, visit the school, talk to the professors, then decide whether Connecticut isn't the place for you or your daughter."

So her mother comes down and starts talking to professors on campus. After every visit, she comes away saying, "Really, I didn't know that. Really, I didn't know that." She is learning things like how many Merit Scholars we have, and what a solid honors program we have, and how competitive it is academically.

Now, Rebecca isn't telling her mother this, but she's saying to me, "Coach, I'm not going to pick Connecticut based on whether they have a strong honors program or not. That's important to my mom and dad, but that's not the reason I'm coming to Connecticut. I know I can get a good education here because I'm a smart kid."

That smart kid signs with Connecticut, and she becomes a legend.

But first she goes through hell.

And first we almost lose her at the eleventh hour.

Rebecca verbally commits and we're ecstatic, and everything is perfect, until I get a call one night from Ruth Ann. She leaves me a message. She says it's important.

I call her back, and she stops me in my tracks. She says she's heard some things about me. She wants to know if I've ever struck a player.

It's the whole Kris Lamb thing again. I do my best to explain to Rebecca's mother what happened, and how one small incident was misconstrued. I hang up the phone, and I'm sick. I can't believe this is happening. Kathy takes one look at me and says, "What's wrong? You look like the life has been drained out of your body." I tell her what's just happened. Neither one of us sleep very well that night.

Thankfully, Ruth Ann Lobo takes me at my word. Rebecca is still coming.

Rebecca Lobo is almost 6-foot-5, can handle the ball pretty well, especially compared to other people her size at the time, and she can shoot the jump shot, pass like nobody's business, and see the floor as well as any point guard out there.

So she's supposedly the best player in the country, and

everyone is telling her she's the best player in the country, but the one thing she is missing is she doesn't quite have the mental makeup at that time to be the best. So, especially in the early going, everything is a struggle.

There are a lot of expectations when Rebecca Lobo steps on campus, and I'm not sure she is ready for all of them. People forget that her sophomore year we only win 18 games. We should have won 22 or 23. We have some bad losses that season. Kentucky smokes us. Vanderbilt beats us by 20. We lose to Miami at home by three, then lose by 18 down at their place. We finish the season losing five of our final seven games, and we are going nowhere in a hurry.

I'm on Rebecca Lobo's case all the time. As far as she's concerned, she can't do anything right. Rebecca calls home after her sophomore year and says, "I can't stay here. I've got to get out of here." Ruth Ann isn't hearing any of it. She says to her daughter, "Listen, Rebecca, this is where you wanted to go. That's where you thought you were going to reach your goals. So either buck up or quit."

Anyone who knows Rebecca knows there is no chance that she is quitting. It's obvious to me we need Rebecca to take us to the next level, but it's also obvious to me she isn't quite ready to assume that responsibility. She is like this big jigsaw puzzle, only a few of the pieces are missing. It's my job to make sure we get all the pieces to fit.

Just before her junior season begins, I sit her down and I ask her some questions. I say, "What is it that you want, Rebecca? I'm guessing you want to win a national championship, be an All-America, and maybe be an Olympian." She agrees. Then I ask her, "How do you expect to accomplish all those things? What do you think has to happen?"

She's thinking about it, but before she even answers, I get

right to the point. I say to her, "Did your team ever win a championship in high school?" She answers, "No, we didn't." I ask her, "When you played AAU basketball, did you ever win a championship? When you played for the United States in the Olympic Sports Festival for the 18-and-under team, did your team win a gold medal?" I know the answer to both of those questions. It's no. I say, "When you went with (current Ohio State coach) Jim Foster to Korea with USA Basketball, didn't your team finish fifth? Now you've been here for two years at Connecticut, and we haven't even won a Big East title, never mind a national championship. Are you starting to see a pattern developing here?"

I tell her, "Whatever you are doing needs to change. You are obsessed with winning a national championship and becoming an All-America, and you know why? Because you are afraid you won't. And because you are afraid you won't, it's paralyzing you when it comes time to make plays.

"So here's what we are going to do. It's a process that is going to involve the next two years. Understand that whatever happens, you are in the process of becoming all the things you want. Let's stop focusing on the end result and start focusing on what happens every day in practice."

She's sitting there and obviously she's upset, but she is listening to me. So I keep going.

I tell her, "If I start busting your chops about something, stop looking at me like the world is about to end and understand I'm trying to do something. Understand I'm giving you responsibilities others won't have. But don't dwell on that. Live for the moment and stop worrying about what will happen in the future."

The next season, in 1993–94, we go 30–3. She's a first team All-America. Her mother, Ruth Ann, is diagnosed with breast cancer, and just like that, Rebecca's whole outlook on life changes. She starts to see everything in a different light. The year after that, we go 35–0, and in the second half of the national championship game she makes every single big shot she needs to make, and she becomes Rebecca Lobo, the symbol for everything that is right and good about women's basketball.

It was—and still is—one of the happiest moments of my coaching career. She is the first kid I ever recruit who has the expectation level that she should be an All-America, should take us to a title, and then goes out and actually does it. I feel so content about that. I am so happy for her.

I have so much respect for how she handled herself here. People don't understand the tremendous pressure that was put on her. She had the personality and the maturity to deal with it. She was just so bright, but not in a nerdy 4.0 way. She was smart, for sure, but also a fun-loving kid. She single-handedly allowed us to take a huge step forward in our program by being willing to take a chance on us. Everyone told me, "You're not going to get her." But they didn't know her.

I'm sure if you ask Rebecca, she'll tell you her time at Connecticut is the highlight of her basketball life. When she starts playing pro basketball, she has to contend with a fair amount of jealousy and pettiness. There are some people who want to tear her down, for whatever reason, to call her overrated, to try and somehow diminish what she has accomplished.

But what people forget is that in Rebecca's first season in the WNBA, she averages double figures in points and rebounds, and her team loses in the Finals. Her second year, she averages a double double again, then gets hurt. It is a downhill path from there, because physically she can't do certain things anymore.

Was she what everybody projected her to be as a pro

player? Maybe, maybe not. But Rebecca's strength is how she handles herself no matter what the expectations or demands are. She has this ability to carry things to the next level with just the right amount of diplomacy and grace. She is the perfect person at the perfect time for our program.

Obviously she isn't alone out on that court. Rebecca wouldn't have won a championship without Jen Rizzotti and Jamelle Elliott there by her side. Their team chemistry is unbelievable, and part of that is because Rebecca never acts like, "I'm the face of women's basketball, I'm the reason we're so good." She is one of the guys, no different from her teammates, and because of that, she is eagerly accepted by everyone.

One thing I've always noticed about our program is that during our greatest moments our players have come in pairs. Our first great pair is Laura Lishness and Kerry Bascom.

Our next great pair is Jen Rizzotti and Jamelle Elliott. I'm not taking away anything from Rebecca. Without her, none of it happens. But Rebecca would have never been able to lead us to a national championship by herself. As talented as she is, she is destined to be a David Robinson—a really good player, really smart, a great human being, the kind of person you want to know the rest of your life. But if it comes down just to her, it isn't going to get done, because she doesn't have that cut-your-heart-out instinct.

Jen and Jamelle have it. And the interesting thing is, they get it growing up in completely different environments. Jen is from a very stable and accomplished family. She grows up in New Fairfield, Connecticut, and her father works for IBM, and they live in Japan for a time, and they have a very comfortable upbringing. Jamelle has a great family, too, but she comes from one of the toughest places in Washington, D.C. I don't think you would ever call her childhood comfortable. So if you look at their two backgrounds, these two kids have nothing in common.

But they are so alike in so many ways. Both come to Connecticut flying way under the radar. They play on AAU teams, but they never go to any of the big-time camps where you get noticed by the big-time programs.

I remember watching Jen in one of her high school games. She has all the intangibles. She is a leader, the best player, and she makes all the big shots. But she is also so tough. I use the analogy of the great Philadelphia Flyers hockey player, Bobby Clarke, to describe her. Bobby Clarke was this blue-collar, rough-and-tough guy who was missing all his front teeth, and because he had that persona, you forgot sometimes how incredibly talented he was. It's the same thing with Jen. She's out there diving all over the floor wearing those two knee pads, playing with so much fire and intensity that sometimes it actually overshadows how talented she really is.

Jen Rizzotti can pass, dribble, shoot, and play defense. Nobody plays harder. And nobody loves to play more. I'm at an AAU game watching her once, and there is a holdup because there is water on the court. Nobody seems to know what to do. They're waiting and waiting and waiting, and finally Jen says, "Screw this." She grabs a towel and wipes up the wet spot and says, "Okay, let's play."

When we go on her home visit, she cooks us dinner. That is a first for me. I want this kid in my program.

I have the same feeling about Jamelle after the first time I see her. She is out there doing all the little things, the dirty work, like setting a hard screen, taking a charge, grabbing rebounds in traffic. And when the game is on the line, she always makes the play—whether it is scoring herself, or setting someone else up to do it. She is truly a *team* player in every sense of the word.

I'm with Georgetown coach Pat Knapp in the D.C. area, and we are going to see a summer tournament. There's a stronger, much more high-powered tournament going on at the time, but I want to see these other kids. I watch Jamelle Elliott for five minutes, and I am in love with her game. I ask the people in the stands, "Who is that kid?" At the time, Jamelle has generated some interest, but not among the elite teams. Her final choices have been narrowed to Temple, Syracuse, South Florida, and Providence. Pretty soon, Connecticut is added to the list. We sweep in and convince her to come with us.

Jen and Jamelle come in together, and right away there is a connection. When they aren't trying to beat each other over the head, they are instilling an incredible toughness in our team. They fight all the time because they are so competitive. I remember Rebecca coming into my office one day in preseason and telling me, "I can't wait for the season to start. I hate this time of year." I say, "Why is that?" She says, "Because we have to play pickup all the time, and every game ends in a fight between Jen and Jamelle. They fight over calls. They fight over the score. They fight over everything." I say to her, "Well, why don't you put them on the same team?" Rebecca looks at me like I'm crazy and says, "Because then they'll win every game."

By the time Jen and Jamelle are seniors, I really don't know what I'm going to do without them. One of my favorite moments of my coaching career is watching the two of them on Senior Night. We call them out individually, and Jen is called first, then Jamelle, and the two of them get locked into this incredible hug, and I just remember watching the two of them, thinking, "Jen and Jamelle. Together forever."

They have to move on, of course, but they are still as close as ever. When Jen gets married, Jamelle is a bridesmaid in the wedding. I don't want to speak for Jen, but I'm guessing Jamelle is the player she respected the most in her career.

When Rebecca is a senior, she wins every award there is to get: the Naismith Award, the Wade Trophy, first team All-America, the Broderick Cup. Then she graduates, and the following year, Jen wins everything.

Jamelle gets nothing. It's not right, but that's just how it works. So we're at the Big East banquet, and Jen is named Big East Player of the Year, and she stands up and thanks the coaches, then says, "If I could split this award right down the middle, I would. Then I'd give half of it to Jamelle Elliott."

Naturally, the two of them go into coaching. Jamelle is one of my assistants at Connecticut, and one of the most valuable people you can have. Her toughness as a player has translated into her coaching. At the same time, she has become the confidante for all our players. Jamelle cares deeply about our program, and it shows—every single day.

Jen, meanwhile, becomes the head basketball coach at the University of Hartford and puts that program on the map. We make sure we play Hartford, and I can tell you, it's pretty strange coaching against one of my all-time favorite players.

You can understand why we go into the 1994–95 season with a great feeling. We have Rebecca, who is a senior and ready to get it done. We have Jamelle and Jen, who are juniors. We have Pam Webber, a senior who is really liked and respected by our players. We have Kara Wolters, who is a bit flaky, but everyone loves her, and at 6-foot-8 she is very, very difficult to guard. We have Nykesha Sales, who is a freshman, and you just know she is going to be special. We have Carla Berube, one of those solid, quiet kids who doesn't say much, but will go on to make one of the biggest plays of the season. We have Missy Rose, who is tremendously fit, and a little nutty, but an integral part of our team personality. We have Kim Better, who fits the mold of the kind of player who is attractive to us. She is more of an athlete than a basketball player. She is a 'tweener, and she needs to grow in terms of skills, but she is very bright and very well-spoken. She is a really solid role player who epitomizes what our team is all about.

I admire how Kim juggles everything. She is a computer engineering major, a very difficult choice, and she spends a lot of time balancing her academics and her basketball and her responsibilities at home. But she does it.

That is our team. Can I tell you we started the year thinking about winning a national championship? I don't know. I know we are good. We've been 30–3 the previous year, and we've added Nykesha, a big, athletic guard, which is exactly what we are missing.

We go to Europe the summer before the 1994–95 season and we can tell right away that something is going on. You aren't allowed to take incoming freshmen, so Kesha has to stay behind. We play a couple of really top European teams, including one with Margo Dydek, who is now a star in the WNBA for the Connecticut Sun. We come home feeling pretty good about ourselves.

CD and I decide to put in a whole new offensive style of play. We start to experiment with the triangle offense, which Tex Winter made famous by convincing the Chicago Bulls and Michael Jordan to use it.

Jack Leaman, the former UMass men's coach, used to run something like it when he had Julius Erving. The summer we are practicing for our Europe trip, Leaman comes down to watch, and we start talking. He thinks the triangle offense will be a good match for our talent. We figure we'll go over to Europe and try it, and if it works, we'll have something. If it doesn't work, we'll scrap it and go back to what we did before when we were 30–3.

It is just amazing how quickly our kids pick it up. I am blown away by some of the stuff they do out there. Our offense becomes so unscripted. The whole key to the triangle offense is movement and cutting without the ball. It is a very unselfish offense, and our kids get it right away.

In mid-December, we go down to North Carolina to play NC State, and it is a very big game for us. We're down there, and I have a date to play golf the next morning at Pinehurst with Todd Turner, the former athletic director from UConn who is now working at NC State. I tell my players, "I don't want to be ticked off all day playing at this great course. So c'mon, let's play well."

We go into that environment, in the ACC, which takes its basketball very, very seriously, and we play unbelievably well. We make these cuts that looked like a choreographed dance. Everything is one movement to another movement to another movement, and it is just beautiful to watch. It is magical.

We beat NC State 98–75, and I am excited. I'm starting to think this is the year. It gets to the point where I'm itching to go to the games. I tell Kathy, "I can't wait to see what happens. I can't wait to see what they come up with today."

We get into our Big East schedule and we are just rolling over everybody. We are beating teams by an average of 30 points. We're feeling pretty good about ourselves, but people are questioning our schedule. They say it's not tough enough. Hey. We play who we play. We have a league schedule that is nonnegotiable. Plus, we play NC State, Kansas, and Tennessee that season. What's so bad about that?

The Tennessee game is the turning point of our season. We play them for the first time in history on January 16. They are ranked No. 1 and we are ranked No. 2. It is a Monday afternoon, and the place is packed, and everyone is rocking and rolling. They have, I think, a minimum of ten high school All-Americas on their roster. We have Nykesha Sales and Rebecca Lobo. But we beat them, 77–66.

Walking into Gampel Pavilion that day is surreal. The whole student section is full and they are wearing T-shirts that say, "Best of the Best." It is an electric atmosphere, and the intensity is unbelievable.

When I get home afterwards, I want to watch a tape of the game. I can't even hear what the announcers are saying on the television because the crowd is so loud.

What I remember most about the game itself is Jen Rizzotti hitting a big three from the wing late in the game. At the time, Rebecca has fouled out. Obviously that makes you really worried, but Jamelle is a huge figure in that game because she is so tough. They can't really seem to guard Jen, and Kara plays really well in that game, too. She makes some big catches along the baseline, and when I look on the tape afterwards, I wonder how she was able to hang on to the ball.

After Jen hits that three and we win, the fans stay in the stands. Nobody wants to leave. The place is turned upside down. It's bedlam, inside and out.

It is the pivotal moment of our program.

Usually the polls come out on Monday with the weekly rankings, but they hold the poll for the outcome of this game. Obviously, the next day we are ranked No. 1.

So it's nine-thirty in the morning, and I'm not out of bed yet. Kathy comes in to check on me, because it's not like me to sleep so late. She says, "G, you've got to get up." I say, "No, I'm never getting up, I'm becoming the Howard Hughes of college basketball," and I put the covers over my head.

After that, there is no turning back.

By the time we play Kansas on January 28, we're 16–0 and I really want Rebecca Lobo to be the national Player of the Year. I really feel how she does in the Kansas game will determine it. We are on CBS television, playing a doubleheader with the men. Kansas has a terrific team. They have Angela Aycock and a bunch of perimeter players like Tamecka Dixon that scare me half to death.

But we beat them. Jen makes a number of big plays, and Rebecca is Rebecca. She scores 25 points in 36 minutes, grabs 12 rebounds, has six assists, two blocks, and one steal. That's the day she puts a stranglehold on her reputation. People who doubted us before don't doubt us anymore. Everyone wants to know about Rebecca Lobo now. The funny thing about it is that Kesha plays really well in that game, too, but it kind of gets overlooked. She is 5 for 7 from the three-point line. I turn to Chris at one point in the game and say, "She's not playing like a freshman. She's a veteran now."

The craziness of this amazing season starts to take over. Everything changes. Everyone wants a piece of us. The interview requests are just pouring in for Rebecca, and she's getting a little overwhelmed. We all are. It's not just *Sports Illustrated* and the national print media. It's *Good Morning America*. It's the *NBC Nightly News*. We couldn't have prepared for what happens to us that year. Who would have ever guessed it would become so big, so fast?

I can see it's wearing on Rebecca, and that worries me. I walk into our locker room one day and I say, "I have a question for you guys. How many of you in this room wish you were Rebecca Lobo, so you could play 30 minutes every night, be on the cover of magazines and newspapers, have every TV station clamoring to talk to you, and have the whole state of Connecticut thinking you walk on water?" They all start saying, "Sure, great. Pretty cool." Then I turn and point to Jill Gelfenbien, a kid on our team who is a walk-on, a soccer player who is with us to stay in shape. I say, "How many of you want to be Jill? She comes to practice every day for two and a half hours and busts her butt knowing the only way she's getting into the game is if we're up by 30. Pretty hard, right? So which one do you want to be?" They're all looking at me like I'm stupid. Of course they all want to be Rebecca Lobo.

Then I say to them, "Now think about this. How many times does Jill have to face the media and explain why we lost? Never. Does Jill go home at night and say, 'If I don't get 20 points and 10 rebounds tomorrow night, we're going to lose'? Never. If Jill makes one bad play, or has one bad game, is it headline news? No. So how much fun is it really being Rebecca Lobo every night, when, if you don't put up certain numbers, or if you don't produce a certain way, not only might you lose, but you have to stand there in front of everyone and say, 'It's my fault. I sucked'?

"So, whenever you think this one has it much better than that one, or this one has it much worse than that one, remember we are all in this together. And realize that on this team, Rebecca Lobo will be treated exactly like Jill Gelfenbien and everyone in between, and will enjoy all the things that come with winning, and suffer all the things that come with losing."

I try to deflect as much of the pressure off Rebecca as I can. It isn't easy. She has become an icon overnight. Sometimes, you can see the tension in her face. I remember playing Boston College that season, when everything is sort of at its peak in terms of attention and publicity and madness. Rebecca plays poorly. We win the game, but as she's walking off the court, I can see it on her face. She knows she should—and expects to be—criticized for her performance.

She has been manhandled the entire game by the BC players. They are coming at her two and three at a time, and they are beating her up. I am ticked off by their tactics, but I also know I need to do something to deflect some of the attention away from Rebecca.

I go off on the officials and BC's coach, Cathy Inglese, in my press conference after the game. I get fined and reprimanded by the league for my comments. I don't regret what I say, but I guess I regret the timing a little bit.

I guess I do that a lot. I choose the wrong time to voice my opinion on how Cathy Inglese coached her team that day. I like Cathy. I respect her. I just didn't like the way she coached her team. You've got to remember that when it comes to Boston College, there's a certain level of arrogance that goes along with them. I wouldn't mind if that arrogance came from their ice hockey team, because they've won championships, but for anybody else at that school to be arrogant is just out of the question. What have they done? If you're the Duke men's basketball team you can be arrogant. Or the Tennessee women's team. But BC basketball? Hey, how about winning a national championship first?

But that isn't really what it is about. I am protecting my

player and deflecting some of the heat that is coming her way. I'll do that anytime. That's not a tough decision. When Rebecca does face the media, the questions are now about my outburst and the beating she takes in the game, instead of why she didn't play well.

We get into the tournament, and we are rolling. We beat Maine, Virginia Tech, and Alabama by an average of 35 points to get to the East Regional championship.

We're playing Virginia, my old school, against the woman who gave me my first big break in women's basketball, Debbie Ryan. Debbie is the exact opposite of me. She is very detail-oriented. I'm more of a seat-of-the-pants coach. But I know one thing we share: a burning desire to win.

Virginia is really, really talented. I'm watching their team play Louisiana Tech knowing we'll play the winner, and I'm trying to figure out which team I want to win the game.

I watch for a while, and I realize, "Man, we don't want Virginia. They have too much offense. If we play Lousiana Tech, we'll have an easier time guarding them."

Of course Virginia wins, and I'm a nervous wreck. They have Wendy Palmer, who is a money player, and Jenny Boucek, a tough little point guard who played in the pros for a while. They have Tora Suber. They have Monick Foote, who we pass over in the recruiting process when we decide to go after Nykesha instead.

I can't sleep the night before the game, which means I'm a mess the next day. We're 32–0, we're playing on our home court for the chance to play in the Final Four, and I'm a freaking wreck.

Once again, the doubts creep in. Have I prepared them well enough? What did I overlook? Are we mentally tough enough to win a game like this?

One minute, I'm convinced I'm not a good enough coach to get us there. The next minute, I'm convinced I have nothing to worry about. I absolutely torture myself like that for several hours leading up to the game.

We start out strong. It's back and forth for a couple of minutes, and the next thing you know, we're blowing them out. We go on this killer run, and Jen is the one orchestrating it, and all of a sudden I look up and we're ahead by 19 points. I can't believe it.

Next thing you know, we're in big trouble. I'm watching it happen like I'm in a movie theater and the plot takes a bad twist and I am powerless to change the story line. Our guys start thinking, "Ho-hum. Another blowout." I'm watching it happen, but I can't seem to do anything about it. Before you know it, Virginia has tied it up. I turn to my assistant, Tonya Cardoza, who played at Virginia, and say, "Weren't we just up by about 18?" She says, "No. We were up 19."

I am mad. Mad at myself, and mad at my players. We got up and we got careless, and that never should have happened. Virginia, who comes out tight as a drum, gets down by 19 and figures, "What the hell, let's go down having some fun." They're loose, they're not running anything, and they're scoring all over the floor. They're hitting threes from the lobby of the arena.

For the first time, my team has been hit square in the mug, and they're stunned. We are in the middle of this incredible scoring drought and they don't know what to do. When halftime finally rolls around, we're down by seven points, 44–37.

I've always said that if halftime hadn't come when it did, we never would have won a national championship, because we would have been down by 19 ourselves, and we wouldn't have had time to recover.

We go into the locker room, and I don't have to say anything. Jen and Jamelle step up and say, "Now look, dammit, this is how it's going to be. Here is what we're going to do." And they take over. They are not going to let us lose this game.

Jamelle, I remember, makes some big shots in the second half. Kara Wolters makes some huge plays. She hangs on to some impossible passes in the second half and scores some big baskets. Virginia has to concentrate so much on Rebecca and Kara because of their size, that Jamelle and Kesha and Jen are free to make shots.

It's a nip-and-tuck game all the way, but we end up winning 67–63. Down the stretch, Rebecca blocks two big shots and Nykesha steals a pass. As good as we are offensively, it is often our defense that comes up with the biggest plays.

So now we are in the Final Four, and nobody is going to stop us. Kara Wolters is growing up before our eyes. She has a monster game in the semifinals, scoring 31 points and grabbing nine rebounds against Stanford.

Kara is a unique player. She, Rebecca, Carla Berube, and Jamila Wideman, who ends up at Stanford, all play on the same AAU team together. They are tremendous, and they are fun to watch. Rebecca and Jamila get all the attention, and Kara is the afterthought. Everyone says, "Oh yeah, and they have this big kid, too."

People shy away from recruiting Kara because they say she is immature. I say, "She's a little kid in a big body." Hey, if you were a 6-foot-7-tall woman, it would be easy to walk around being bitter. Kara takes it as, "Hey, this is fun."

A lot of people miss the boat on Kara because she needs

so much work. She's slow, she's overweight, she can't jump, blah blah blah. But we all underestimate how competitive Kara is, and how much she wants to prove everyone wrong.

Her father, Willie, is a big part of her life. He sees a world of potential and wants her to reach that. We hear some stories about him while we're recruiting her. He's one of those parents who gets caught up in the moment and starts yelling and has to be removed from some gyms along the way. I have my share of battles with him, but I'm telling you right now: I don't think Kara ever becomes an All-America without her father's help. He knows the game, and he teaches her a lot. She gets a lot of her competitiveness from him. She ends up having some of the best hands and footwork of any center in college.

There's no question we take a chance by recruiting her and signing her. Her dream is to go to Boston College, but they won't touch her.

I'm glad we don't feel the same way.

Thanks, in part, to Kara, we are in the national championship game. We don't even have to ask who we are playing, because in the back of our minds, we've known all along: it's Tennessee.

The officiating is horrendous in the first half. We have three kids sitting on the bench with foul trouble: Rebecca, Kara, and Jen. I'm saying to myself, "This is insane. How can you call a national championship game like this?" The funny thing about it is the second half is called completely differently. Somebody must have walked into the officials' room at halftime and said something to them. I promise you, it wasn't me.

So we're down six, 38–32, at halftime, and I am pacing in our locker room. I say, "So this is how it's going to end? We're 34–0 and we're going to finish 34–1? We're going out with a whimper? Do you realize how badly we just played in that first half? Let me ask you a question: we played about as badly as we can play, and we're only down six. If someone played that poorly against us, how much would they be down?"

"They'd be down 26," answers Jen, who is all fired up. I say, "That's right. So I've got to believe the second half will be different. Look, there is no way they can beat us. Does anyone doubt us?"

I look around the room, and you should have seen the look on Jen's face, and Jamelle's face, and Rebecca's face. They are so intense. I walk out thinking, "We're going to win."

So what happens? Right off the tip, Tennessee nails a three, and we're down nine. So much for my rousing speech about how everything is about to change.

The key is we never let Tennessee build the lead to double figures. We just keep chipping away and chipping away. Rebecca takes over. She starts making shot after shot. She's incredible. Up to that point, she is spending all her time worrying how not to lose the national championship, instead of how to win it. Now she's all about winning.

The biggest possession of the game is when Rebecca and Jen are both on the bench late in the second half with foul trouble. We need a bucket really, really badly. There's a scramble for the ball. Kesha somehow comes up with it, and gets it to Jamelle. She posts up Dana Johnson, who is a huge kid. Jamelle drop-steps and scores, and I think to myself, "Here we go."

On the next possession, Jen is back in the game, and there's a long rebound off a Tennessee miss. Jen gets the ball, goes coast to coast, and we have the lead.

It comes down to this: we're up four with 10 seconds left. If we can inbound the ball, and they foul, and we hit the free throws, it's over. So Tennessee calls a timeout, and as my players are jogging over to our bench, my mind is going a thousand miles an hour.

I'm thinking to myself, "If we inbound the ball, and they steal it, and make a three, and call timeout, we have to inbound it again, and suppose they steal that pass, and hit a three, and we lose?" I'm out of mind at this point. I'm not saying any of this out loud. I'm saying it to myself as my players are coming toward me for the timeout.

Now the players are sitting in front of me, and I'm thinking, "This is going to be a bitch." I'm wondering who I want to inbound the ball. Rebecca is pretty strong. She has a good arm. But who should catch the pass? Jen? Jamelle? Can Jamelle make the free throws?

That morning at shootaround, we had gone over our out-of-bounds plays to make sure we had it right. I'm thinking we should use the same play we ran that morning, which is a long pass. But then my mind starts racing again. I'm thinking, "If we throw a long pass to the other side of the court, even if they do steal it, they won't have much time, but if they do launch a shot, it will be a three. If we inbound it closer, it would only be a two-point basket if they steal it. Now, what if we throw a long pass out of bounds and no one touches it, and they get to inbound it right under our basket?"

I decide to have Rebecca inbound the ball for the long bomb. I send Carla Berube for the long pass. Now, Carla is a sophomore. She never speaks. She doesn't ever say boo. But she's got a lot of guts.

So Rebecca throws the pass and Carla catches it, and she gets hit, so she goes to the free throw line. I turn away. I don't want to look. How could I have put this sophomore, this quiet kid who never says a thing, in this position? I'm waiting for the ball to hit the rim, but I don't want to look. I don't hear anything. I say to CD, "What happened?" She says, "It's in." The ball never touches the rim. The net barely moves. The second one: same thing. They are two of the purest free throws ever made, and two of the biggest clutch plays in the history of our program.

That night in Minneapolis, we have an unforgettable celebration. Everyone is there: school officials, parents, our players, the coaches, our fans, my brother Ferruccio, my sister Anna. Everyone is there except my parents.

My dad hates to fly. There's no way he's getting on a plane, and there's no way my mother is coming without him. They are watching on television back home. As the game is winding down, and we take the lead, he can't watch anymore, because he's afraid we're not going to do it. When we finally do win, he's in the bathroom, all choked up. You don't think he's actually going to let anyone see him crying over a basketball game, do you?

I call my parents after it's over. My father, who never seems to care much about my team, is really excited. Now he has something to brag to his friends at the Italian club about.

We celebrate into the night. It's about two or three o'clock in the morning, and there's just a small group of us left. I'm sitting on the couch with my arms around the two seniors, Rebecca and Pam Webber. Jamelle is there, and Jen and Missy Rose, who are both wearing cellophane on their heads, and a few others, and someone says, "Let's watch the tape of the game!" They put it in, and we cheer for every big shot, every big stop on defense. Of course, as I'm sitting there watching the tape, I'm seeing things I don't like. We make a bad pass against their pressure. We get beat on a pick-and-roll. Next thing you know, I'm rewinding the tape, saying,

"Look at that right there. Do you see how bad that is?" They all start laughing at me. Missy turns to me and says, "Coach, stuff it. We just won the national championship."

Yes, Missy. We did.

FOUR

Almost four years have passed since we have won the 1995 NCAA championship, and I'm sitting under the bleachers with my head in my hands.

My team is on the floor, waiting for me, but I don't have anything left to say. I cannot reach them. I cannot make them understand what I am trying to teach them. I don't think I've ever felt this frustrated in my entire life.

The thing is, we've got all sorts of talent. We've got Svetlana Abrosimova, this amazing offensive player who has come to us from Russia. We have Shea Ralph, a high school legend. We have Swin Cash, and Asjha Jones and Tamika Williams and Sue Bird, and they have been lauded as the best recruiting class in women's college basketball history. Sue Bird is hurt, but we still should be able to beat everybody and win a national championship.

But we're too busy beating ourselves.

So we're in practice midway through the 1998–99 season, and I'm trying to teach them something. I don't even remember what it was. Maybe it is how to make a cut without the ball or how to close out your man when we need a stop. It is something basic. Something they should know.

I'm trying to talk to them, and all I'm getting is these blank stares. Nothing I am saying is registering. It is so important for me to communicate with my players in practice, and one of my faults is I get very, very frustrated if I think my players aren't getting it.

I say to them all the time, "We've got two issues here. Either you are bad learners, or I'm a bad teacher. Which is it?" In this case, I'm not sure. We've got all these new players on our team, and I'm not connecting with them.

I'm having these tremendous bouts of self-doubt. I've had my ups and downs with various kids, but one thing I always prided myself on is being able to reach my players. I've never had a problem reaching them—until now. I go home every night and say to Kathy, "What the hell am I doing wrong?"

I look at them standing there, knowing they don't have a clue what I'm talking about, or what I want from them, and it just kills me. So I tell them, "That's it. I can't take this anymore.

"I tell you the same thing every single day," I say. "I tell you the same thing, and you still don't do it. I am having a nervous breakdown right here in front of you. You are watching me have a breakdown."

I am shouting. I mean to say it quietly, but I am shouting.

Suddenly, I feel very tired. Instead of walking out of the gym, I take a right, sit down under the bleachers, and lean against the wall.

Nobody knows what to do. The players are standing there. CD and Jamelle and Tonya are throwing up their hands.

They aren't worried about me. They are worried about the kids, and what they'll make of this.

Nykesha Sales has already graduated, but she is there that day practicing with us. She comes over to the bleachers. Kesha sticks her head under and says, "Yo, Coach. What are you doing under there?" I say, "This is where I want to be. Leave me alone." She says, "You've got to come out of there." I say, "Why? I don't want to talk to you guys. I want nothing to do with you. I just need some peace and quiet right now. Leave me alone." She says, "Coach, you're making us a little concerned. Are you okay?" I do not answer her.

Everyone stands around for a little while longer to see if I'm coming out. Nobody knows what to do. Finally, they all just file out and go home. I'm sure it shakes them. I'm sure they are wondering what the hell is going on.

I don't know how long I stay there before I finally pull myself out from under there and go home, too.

That day really drove home for me how stressful coaching is. I don't realize the toll it takes on me sometimes. It's so much work, and your whole job is dependent on these young college kids who are having trouble with their boyfriends, or at home, or with school, or in their dorm. At the same time, who is going to feel sorry for a guy like me, who is living the life I'm living, enjoying the benefits of this job? When you look at it that way, what toll has it taken? But that day under the bleachers, I'm not sure it is worth it.

That night I tell Kathy, "I'm really frustrated. I don't have it. When we're really good, I have all my players right in the palm of my hand. I can play them like a violin. I can pull the string, and they respond. But this time, I'm asking them to do things and they're looking at me with this vacant stare and I'm wondering, 'Where are my guys?'"

Every season I'm used to having three or four guys who are my core guys.

Right now, I don't have any.

That night, the freshmen call up one another and they meet in Tamika's room. They are rattled. They stay up most of the night talking about what happened. Swin calls her mom and says, "You aren't going to believe what's going on here." Her mother tells Swin, "You better work this out with Coach Auriemma." Tamika is the most upset of all. She tells Asjha and Swin, "We're the worst. How could we do this to Coach? All he wants is for us to be great, and now we've made him have a nervous breakdown under the bleachers."

Everyone shows up the next day waiting to see what happens. Will I be there? What will I say? Are we going to get blasted? I show up, I blow the whistle, and I say, "Let's go. Let's practice." And that is it. The truth is, it isn't as bad as the players think it was. They like to tell people I had some kind of breakdown. What I had was one of those tremendous bouts of self-doubt that came and went.

They practice really hard that day. They always do. That is never the issue. But by the end of the season, I have no idea about the team. We're getting ready to start the NCAA tournament and I'm thinking, "Okay, what are we going to do?" For the first time in my life, I don't know.

The strange part about that 1998–99 season is we start out on such a high. The reason for that is mostly Sveta. She becomes what I always thought she'd become—the best player on our team. We play UCLA at Pauley Pavilion in our third game of the season, on November 17, and she's awesome. She scores 39 points on 17 shots. That's impossible. And the best part about that game is that Diana Taurasi, the best high school player in the country, is watching the whole thing, sitting right behind the UCLA bench. We win the game, 113–102.

From that point on, I say to myself, "This is the future of women's basketball, right here. We're going to play in a way that is going to blow people away. We've got all these athletes that can run and defend and score and press. We can beat you in a hundred different ways." The UCLA game is a perfect example. The score at halftime is 60–54. I don't want to walk off the court. As we're leaving, I turn to Chris and say, "I can't live like this. How in God's name am I going to be able to coach like this?"

We went to the Final Four in 1991 and scored 55 points in a loss to Virginia. We won a national championship in 1995 and we scored 70 points. Now we're scoring 60 points at halftime? I turn to Jamelle and say, "Who plays basketball like that?" But finally you realize, "Okay, *we* do. If this is how it's going to be, let's try to score a hundred every night." And we do—for a while.

We have Sveta, who has been waiting her whole life to play like this. She has been butting heads with me since the day she arrived, because she wants to shoot, and shoot some more. We have Shea Ralph, who just physically wears people down. We have Sue Bird, who is starting at the point as a freshman, because Rita Williams has graduated. We've got Asjha and Tamika and Swin, who can rotate in and out almost anywhere.

So we're off. We beat Washington 101–81, and Holy Cross 107–56, and Notre Dame at their place 106–81. We score 100 points in nine out of our first 13 games, and we are 13–0. In our second game of the year, we score 100 against Arkansas in a game in San Jose, and we're up by 40, and a woman starts yelling from behind our bench, "Stop running up the score! Put the subs in!" I turn around and tell her, "Those are my bench players. You should hope I put my starters back in. They're not as good." That's because I have Swin and Sue and Asjha and Tamika on the floor, four freshmen who go on to be first-round WNBA draft picks.

We are really good. We are about to be something special, but then it starts to fall apart. Sue tears her anterior cruciate ligament in practice. Nobody is near her. She's coming down on the break, pulls up to take that little 15-footer that you see her make all the time now in the WNBA, and bam! She falls down. She says, "Ooohh." She doesn't scream or yell or grab her knee. Just a little "ouch." We send her to the training room, and she comes back and starts running up and down the floor and says, "Coach, it doesn't feel right." She gets some X-rays, and she has a torn ACL, and she's done for the season. Then Swin ends up with a stress fracture in her leg. Amy Duran, our senior, breaks a bone in her hand.

I thought we'd get the leadership we needed from Shea Ralph. We do, eventually, but not during the 1998–99 season. I'm sure it is the longest season of her life. She is coming off a medical redshirt year, and she just isn't ready yet to step up and take over the team.

Shea was recruited by a ton of big-time schools. Everybody wanted her. I thought it was fifty-fifty that we'd get her. So one day I'm talking to her on the phone and she says, "Coach, what kind of role do you see for me if I come to UConn?" I tell her, "Shea, I don't know. If you are really, really good, then you'll have a chance to play a lot. But if you suck, you won't play at all."

A couple of weeks later, I get a call from Shea's mom. They want to move up their visit from October to September. I say, "We're not ready. We're just getting back to school.

What's the rush?" Her mom says, "Well, Shea wants to get this whole thing over with, and she wants to visit Connecticut, and if she likes it, she'll probably commit."

We move Shea's visit up a month, and she comes up for a couple of days. It's pretty quiet on campus. There's not much going on. I drive her to the airport and she says, "Coach, I'm not much into this recruiting stuff. If you want me, I'd like to come to Connecticut." I say, "Shea, we'd love to have you, man."

She commits to us and goes out and has an incredible senior year in high school. She's the USA Player of the Year, and someone from *USA Today* is interviewing her, and they ask her why she chose Connecticut. She tells them, "Well, Coach Auriemma was the only coach that told me if I was really good I'd play a lot, and if I sucked I wasn't playing."

I almost fall off my chair the morning I read that. I call her up and say, "Geez, Shea. Did you have to say that in the paper?"

In Shea Ralph's freshman year, 1996–97, we are the best team in the country. Shea's problem is she's used to having the ball every time down the floor. So, in practice, whenever Shea has the ball things go pretty smoothly. But when Shea doesn't have the ball, she just stands around. And, to compound that, she does not defend, and she does not rebound. She does not do anything. She feels her job is that when she has the ball, she should do what she's always done—go to the basket.

I try to impress upon her, "This isn't high school. You're not going to take 40 shots, you're not going to score 50 points." I am trying to get through to her that she needs to be less selfish, while at the same time I am admiring her tremendous ability, desire, and will to win.

In her very first game, against Western Kentucky, I put her in the game at the 15-minute mark. I don't make a habit of starting freshmen—and that includes Diana Taurasi—but the really good ones, like Dee and Kesha and Shea, go in at the 15-minute mark.

So Shea is in the game, and the first time she touches the ball, she happens to be standing out at the three-point line. She catches it, turns, and bang! She drills a three. And that isn't even one of the strong points of her game. But just the fact that she has the confidence to take it really impresses me. When she drills it, I remember saying, "Boy this kid has a lot of heart and a lot of confidence."

As time goes on, Shea struggles with the concept of equality. I don't know whether it is just Shea, or growing up and having everyone telling you that you are the best. That can be hard on a kid—really hard.

Early on in the season, we're playing Tennessee, and Shea is a nervous wreck. She's awful. We're in the middle of a timeout and I say to her, "You know something? You're scared to death. I thought you came here to play in a game like this. And here you are in the situation you've always dreamed of, and you're scared to death. You know what? Maybe you're not cut out for this. Maybe I should take you out."

The whistle blows, Shea goes back out there, and she scores something like eight points in three minutes. She gets the message. She understands that when I put her in at that 15-minute mark, we need something good to happen.

One day in practice, she gets me so frustrated I stop our team in the middle of a scrimmage. I say, "Shea Ralph. We have just practiced for two and a half hours, and do you know how many shots you've made? None. How can someone who scored 4,000 points in high school go through a practice that is two and a half hours long and not make a shot? And, even worse, you don't have an assist, and you don't have a rebound. You've done nothing."

Shea says nothing. She just looks at me with this blank stare.

Our next game is against Rhode Island. The game starts. I always put her in at the 15-minute mark. The 15-minute mark comes and goes, and Shea is not in the game. The clock ticks down to 14, 12, 10, 5, and now it is halftime, and Shea Ralph hasn't played at all.

We go into the locker room and everyone is sitting there looking at Shea. I don't know who is more stunned, Shea or her teammates. I say to her, "Shea, how many points did you score in that first half?" She's turning red. She wants to kill me. "None," she mumbles. I ask her, "How many rebounds did you get?" She says, "None." And then I ask her, "How many assists?" Now she's so pissed her eyeballs are popping out of her head. "None," she answers.

I look at the team for a minute, then I say, "You know what, Shea? You just played that first half the way you practiced the other day." Now the steam is coming out of her nostrils. But she says nothing. What can she say?

At the 15-minute mark of the second half, I put Shea Ralph into the game. She is possessed. She almost gets a triple double. She is all over the floor. After the game, I refuse to allow her to talk to reporters. The first seven questions they ask me are why she didn't play. I say to the writers, "Are you shitting me? We just won a game, and eleven other kids played great, and all you want to know about is one kid who didn't play in the first half?" They answer, "Yes." So I say, "Well, tough luck. She didn't play because I didn't want her to play." The writers keep pressing. "Why?" one of them asks. "None of your business," I tell him.

I figure that is that, but what does Paige Sauer, Shea's roommate, do? She tells the reporters everything. She tells them the whole story. I go to Paige and I say, "Who made you the spokesperson for Shea Ralph? If I want Shea Ralph to say something, I'll let her say it. No one talks for Shea Ralph except for me."

Naturally, everyone is in an uproar. Shea was the top recruit in the country, and our program is scrutinized so closely that everything we do is big news in Connecticut, especially when it's mildly controversial.

I don't care. All I know is from that day on Shea Ralph's work habits are terrific. There are only about five kids in the history of our program whose practice habits are beyond reproach. If you told me in Shea's freshman year that she would be one of those kids, I would have told you you were crazy. But it happens. It takes a while, but by her final season she becomes the symbol of our toughness and perseverance. God only knows how good she would have been if she hadn't had so many serious injuries. The poor kid has torn the anterior cruciate ligament in her knee five times, and has battled an eating disorder much of her life.

Shea's problems start in high school. They are well documented—after the fact. I didn't know she had a problem when I recruited her. I knew she was a workaholic and a perfectionist. I knew she was an excellent student, and someone who was very, very motivated, but it didn't really dawn on me, honestly, until she had her first knee injury in March of her freshman year.

When kids have eating disorders, they can hide it from those around them pretty easily. But now all of a sudden

Shea has to rehab from a torn ACL. Now she's around the training room all the time. Now people are keeping an eye on her, and starting to notice her eating habits.

One day, one of our coaches says to me, "Do know what Shea has for breakfast? A bagel and a diet Coke. Her lunch is a diet Coke and yogurt. For dinner she has, maybe, two diet Cokes and some raw vegetables."

I'm thinking to myself, this kid is playing three hours a day on that? I'm no expert on the relationship between nutrition and knee injuries, but I've got to believe that if your eating habits are that poor, and your nutrition is that bad, it can't possibly contribute to rehabilitating an injury properly. In fact, I've often wondered if that's why her first surgery didn't take. She worked very hard to get back, and everyone kept saying, "Are you ready? Are you ready?" She wanted to be playing so desperately, but then the first time she really goes hard on it, boom! It goes again.

I call Shea into my office. How do you say to someone, "You have an eating disorder"? You don't. You just try and surround her with the right people, like trainers and doctors and nutritionists. You say, "Shea, I'm no expert on this, but I'm going to tell you what I see, and what other people see, and why it concerns us.

"The way you are preparing your body to play on this team is wrong. A regular person trying to play college basketball takes in thousands of calories." Then I ask her, "Shea, what did you eat today?" We added up her intake, and it's well under 1,000 calories. I think we get her to see for herself that that kind of diet simply isn't healthy, and she starts taking steps to fix it.

I don't know how prevalent eating disorders are in sports.

I'm sure there have been girls on my team that had them that I did not know about.

We do have to watch Kara Wolters closely for a while, although she certainly doesn't have any chronic problems. Even so, I weigh her every Monday. I do that because she needs to keep her weight at a certain level, and she keeps falling below that weight.

Kara comes to Connecticut as a heavy player. She works really hard, gets into shape, loses a lot of weight, and says, "Ooh, if I lost this much weight and feel this good about myself, imagine how much better I'd feel if I lost even more weight." She wants to get too thin, but we won't let her. We tell her, "Kara, once the trainers, the nutritionist, you, and I agree on a weight that is comfortable for you, we're going to keep you there. If you try to fall too far below that weight, you're going to have a problem."

Shea works really hard at keeping herself healthy at Connecticut. She misses all of the 1997–98 season with knee trouble, and maybe, in retrospect, I am expecting too much when she comes back healthy the following season. It's just that we need leadership, and I'm looking anywhere I can to find it.

You'd think with all the drama and disappointment that the season is a total disaster, but the truth is we're still one of the top teams in the country. We're 27–4 heading into the NCAAs. That is mostly because of what Sveta does for us. She loves the pace of pushing the ball. She can play forever without getting tired, she can score from anywhere on the floor, she can make threes, she gets to the basket, she steals the ball, gets offensive rebounds. She's the best-conditioned athlete in the country.

We win the Big East tournament, and I make a calculated

decision. I'm going to start hammering these guys to get them ready for the NCAAs. I tell myself, "Like a fresh, hot piece of steel, I'm going to take this, and I'm going to work on it until it becomes a sword." So I start. I bang, bang, bang away at them. By the time we get to the Sweet 16, winning is so far removed from what we are doing, it's ridiculous. They aren't responding. I'm trying to make them do something they just aren't ready to do.

I am very hard on them. I'm questioning their toughness and their ability, because every single time that season when adversity hit, they'd all look around and say, "I don't know. Not me."

Shea wants to be a leader so bad, but she doesn't know how to do it yet. She's got to screw up a couple of times first. Sue Bird hasn't been on the floor enough because of her injury to have an impact. Swin is a tremendous leader on the court, but not so much off the court. Tamika and Asjha aren't saying a word. Sveta is still learning to speak English and express herself. So what we've got is a void, and nobody knows how to fill it.

I'm up nights trying to figure out what I'm doing wrong. It's gotten to the point at Connecticut where I'm getting a lot of publicity and a lot of accolades, but I don't feel comfortable in the role of some kind of savior.

Because I know it's not true. We all have our flaws, which is why I have no interest in writing a book saying, "If you approach things the way I do, then you too will be successful." That's a bunch of crap. We are held hostage, all of us, to our players.

If Diana Taurasi had gone to another school, if Swin Cash or Rebecca Lobo or Jen Rizzotti or Sue Bird had gone somewhere else, who knows what would have happened to me? If

Red Auerbach hadn't coached so many Hall of Famers, maybe he wouldn't be considered one of the greatest coaches who ever lived. It's the people you surround yourself with that dictate your success. If you are fortunate to surround yourself with the right people, then you reach a level of success that other people only dream about.

I've never been stupid enough to think my ideas or strategies are the only way to go. At the same time, I do believe you can go to school and study painting, music, or how to coach, and you can do it exactly by the book, but that doesn't mean you'll be better than someone who has an inherent feel for how to do it.

I've always had that feel. From the time I was a little kid, if I set my mind to something, I could do it. The things I wasn't good at, I stayed away from, because I hated to fail. So I stayed away from math, science, things that required a level of thinking that was very rational.

Anything that required a formula was a problem for me. My mind didn't work that way. Can you train your mind to work that way? I assume you can. I couldn't.

During that 1998–99 season, for the first time, this innate ability I've always had, to reach kids and get the absolute most of them, has failed me. And I feel like I have failed them.

One game I am so frustrated, I fling the water bottle I have in my hand and it hits CD. As the players note later, it splatters "all over her beautiful Nordstrom clothes."

One of the problems is the players are having trouble telling me what's on their mind. They are too intimidated. It used to be that someone like Meghan Pattyson would just come in and sit on the couch and tell me what's up. The players are always welcome to come see me, but there's one rule they all have to follow: I won't talk with them about another player. The last thing you ever want to do is get into a situation where you bring players in and pump them for information about their teammates—unless it's in fun, because you want to get a dig in.

I don't pry into my players' personal lives. I care about what they are doing in school. I care about anything that is going on in their family that I should know about. If you don't want me to know, I don't have to know. Your professor doesn't know everything, right? If I feel there's something going on that's affecting your play, I might ask some questions, but I don't want to hear about why your boyfriend is a jerk, or that this player is mad at that player. No girly girl stuff is allowed. This is not a junior high school team. We don't have time for that.

I also don't have time for a group of players that don't buy into our program. I have my share of outbursts with that 1998–99 group because they aren't buying what I'm selling. Part of it is an issue of trust. The players don't trust me enough to believe I know what is best for our team. There is a lot of sneaking around that season, and that's something we haven't dealt with before.

The Big East tournament is at Rutgers that year, and we have a curfew at the hotel the night before the first game. CD does a room check, and everybody is where she is supposed to be.

I'm coming in after having some dinner with friends, and I hear some noise coming from Shea and Asjha's room. My door is right across the hall, and I can tell they have visitors. I call up Chris and tell her what's going on. I tell her to go down to their room. CD is pissed. She's pissed because I'm making her go down there and she is already in her pajamas.

She's also pissed because it's a big game for us tomorrow, and two of our players have broken team rules. Chris is very big on rules.

She goes down there and knocks on the door, and there are three or four women in there. They're Asjha's friends. CD blasts our kids. She tells Shea, "You're supposed to be a leader. This is how you lead us?" Then she turns to Asjha. Her nickame is "Precious II" because we never—ever—get on her for anything. Nykesha Sales is the original Precious. We never raised our voices with her. Asjha is the sequel. This time, though, Precious II is going to get it.

"Asjha," CD says, "you should know better. Don't you think this game tomorrow is important? What could you possibly be thinking?" Chris recognizes one of Asjha's friends in the room. She's a player for Wagner College. She tells her to leave, then snaps, "This isn't Wagner. This is the Big East."

Shea and Asjha are shaking. They're crying, because they know they're in trouble. I don't think either one of them sleeps a single minute that night. I tell them how disappointed I am. Then I say, "You better play your ass off tomorrow."

The next morning, I don't say much. They both look like hell, but they play great during the entire tournament. We end up beating Notre Dame by 21 points in the final, and Shea has 19 points, 10 assists, and six rebounds. Asjha scores 21 points in 29 minutes.

Even so, I know we have no chance of winning a national championship with this group the way they are. We are rudderless. We almost lose to number eight seed Xavier. We are down 40–36 at halftime, and Tamika hits two big free throws in the final minute to win it for us, 86–84. All that does is postpone the inevitable. In our next game, we lose to Iowa

State in the Midwest Regional final, and we finish the season with a 29–5 record.

It is a traumatic experience for all of us. We let everybody in the state down because we lose five games. You have to understand that by that point, we are so big that five losses is unacceptable. I think that's a little unfair to those kids.

A lot happens that year. The injuries are crushing to our season. We are missing four starters against Boston College in January, so we lose, and they start celebrating like they've won the national championship. I understand it is a big thing for them, but it's not exactly like we were at full strength. That's like me playing Tiger Woods in golf and saying, "Okay, Tiger, you play left-handed." When I win, should I go around yelling, "I beat Tiger's ass"? No, I should go around saying, "I beat him, but he was playing left-handed."

But the thing we probably don't understand at that time is, "Guess what, guys, this is how it's going to be. They beat Connecticut. They don't care who was wearing the uniform for us. It's a big deal, no matter what, and unless we understand that, we're screwed. So don't be mad at them, just don't let them beat you." We play Boston College one more time that season, and we bury them.

Our coaches go to the Final Four that spring, and it's weird because we're not playing in the game. While we are there, Jamelle gets a call that her mom has been killed in a fire. That puts things in perspective in a hurry. We turn around and head back home and gather up the players and make sure everyone is there for the service. Jamelle needs the team's support, and we make sure she gets it. That kind of news sets us all back. It's like a huge blow to the gut.

We go to play in Europe that summer, and the first two games over there, it's the same old crap. We look horrible.

We're in Rome, and I take them to this outdoor court. It's about 85 degrees outside. I say to them, "We're not leaving until we get this right." We're standing there in the hot sun and we keep working at it, working at it, working at it, and we're there almost three hours.

We've lost the first two games over there because, like usual, no one has stepped up. Sue is back, and she's starting to find her way, but everyone else is wandering around. We've got three games left, and they are tired of losing tight games. They are tired of me getting on them.

So we're in the middle of a game and Shea makes a pass, and Swin is trying to get open. She fakes one way, then the other, and makes a cut. Shea throws her the ball, and it flies out of bounds.

Timeout. I'm livid. I say to Shea, "What kind of crappy pass is that?" The first words out of her mouth are, "I thought she was going backdoor." I say, "You know something? That's what's wrong with you, and that's why we can't win right now. You're blaming Swin for that pass, but you know what? If you thought she was going backdoor, why wasn't the pass thrown toward the backdoor cut? Why was it thrown over here? So let me tell you what the right response should be, Shea. When I say, 'What kind of crappy pass is that?' you should say, 'Coach, that was a lousy pass. That's my fault. Sorry, Swin.'"

Everyone is pretty quiet. But I'm not done. I say to Shea, "When you start taking responsibility for your own self and stop pushing it off on somebody else, then we're going to get it."

I was talking to Shea, but they all understood. It was a message for all of them.

We're playing in Paris, and it's our last night, and we go out to dinner as a team, and then back to the hotel. Kathy and I are coming down the elevator to go have a drink in the lobby, and the door opens and a couple of our players get on. They are dressed up, ready to take on Paris. When Kathy and I get to the lobby, we go sit on a couch near the entrance. The players go to the other end of the lobby. We watch as all the players come down and gather together. Then they turn and walk right past us out the door. They don't ask permission. They just go.

I can't believe it. Kathy and I are sitting there, and my mind starts racing. What if Sue Bird's mother calls me up and needs to speak to her daughter, because it's some kind of emergency, and I have to tell her, "I have no idea where she is. We're in Paris, and the whole team has gone out, but I don't know where they are"?

We sit and wait. The longer we sit, the madder I'm getting. Why didn't they ask me? Why did they openly defy me like that? Two of the players, Christine Rigby and Kelly Schumacher, come back because they've forgotten something, and CD grabs them and tells them to get the team back to the hotel—immediately. Schuey runs down, grabs everyone, and says, "We better get back. Coach is not happy."

I sit my team down. They all look like they've just robbed a bank. I say to them, "What made you think this was okay? What made you think it was okay to sneak out of here in a foreign country where you don't know the language or the customs? What made you think that was smart? And the funny part is, if you had asked me, and told me where you were going, I would have said yes. But now I can't trust you. You just walked out of here, and now I can't trust you."

The players don't say much. One of them makes a feeble attempt to explain that since I saw them leave they weren't really sneaking out. They figured I hadn't stopped them from leaving, so that meant they were free to go.

Right.

Before the next season begins, I call Shea, Stacy Hansmeyer, and Paige Sauer to my house. They will be our three seniors. Normally by that time, we've already named the captains, but as we sit there in my living room I tell the three of them, "You haven't proven to me you should be captain. Any of you. You have between now and October 15 to change my mind and prove to me you can be the leaders of this team."

Shea looks as though someone has shot her right between the eyes. She wants desperately to be our leader. At that point, I think she finally understands, "Man, Coach wants to treat us like adults. He wants to give us responsibility. He wants to trust us. All we have to do is live up to his expectations."

They all know it won't be easy.

It never is.

FIVE

You know what everyone is saying at the end of that 29–5 season: "He supposedly recruits the best class in women's college basketball history, and they can't even get to the Final Four?"

The truth is, most kids need time to develop into the player they are going to be. It's as much about maturing as a person as it is about maturing as a player.

When coaches recruit players, we have to figure out a way to project what these kids will be like as they mature.

I'll be honest with you. Recruiting is the worst part of my job.

It is also the most important part of my job.

It doesn't work the way people think. Everyone has this idea that because Connecticut and Tennessee are the two biggest national powers, we must be falling over each other recruiting the same kids every year.

In fact, we rarely recruit the same kids because our recruiting methods are so different.

Take Ann Strother, for instance. Ann is everyone's high

school player of the year—Gatorade, *Parade Magazine, USA Today*. She is Ms. Colorado Basketball. It turns out that Tennessee and Connecticut are her two biggest suitors. We like Ann because she typifies what we want in a player. She's unselfish, she's talented, she can shoot the ball, and she works hard.

I have Ann on a Junior National Team one summer. Her only weakness is the same thing that causes her to struggle in college initially, and that is that she can get overpowered physically. Her competitiveness is what stands out. She's not afraid of anybody.

When she comes for her visit, we show her the real deal at Connecticut. She comes to my house and meets my family. We introduce her to our guards, Diana Taurasi and Maria Conlon. Now, there are two kids who are totally opposite. One is this brash kid from California who is just oozing confidence and talent, and the other is this quiet kid from Connecticut who has worked for every single thing she's gotten. You couldn't meet two people who are more different. But that's what we have here.

Ann hangs out with my players. She watches practice. I'm sure we take her to dinner somewhere, but I don't remember. She sits in on some classes and she meets other students. So I say to her, "Ann, are you coming here or not?" We know each other a little bit from me coaching her, and she has grown up watching Connecticut on television.

She's interested, but now she's going on her visit to Tennessee. They pick her up at the airport. She goes to Pat Summitt's house. The entire team is there. The entire team is at Pat's house wearing T-shirts with Ann's baby picture on it.

They take Ann to the arena, and they have a jersey with

her name on it hanging in a locker. Inside the arena, they have the PA system and the big screen hooked up, and they announce her name and put it up in bold letters on the screen. They have this indoor blimp that flies through the arena and drops a national letter of intent at her feet.

That kind of stuff just doesn't do it for me. But it does for a lot of kids.

Ann never says anything about her trip to Tennessee until long after we've signed her, and she's part of our program. Once I hear about it, I start kidding Ann. I tell her, "You sure you don't want to change your mind and go to Tennessee? Because, you know, Ann, that could be you next year, or the year after, sitting in a house wearing a T-shirt with someone else's baby picture on it."

Look. Everyone has his or her own deal. There is no right way or wrong way. Both Pat Summitt and I have been successful recruiting. I'll do it my way, and get whoever I get, and she'll do it her way, and get who she gets.

We know of this one recruit who ends up going to the University of Florida. She is picked up by a motorcade of Escalades. There is a TV set in the car. When she gets to the office, they have a full-size cutout of her next to the door. They take her to a restaurant where they have a special menu with a steak named after her. Pretty cool, huh? Hey, when you are eighteen years old, that stuff will turn your head.

But what that kid doesn't realize is that is the last time she will ever be in that restaurant. It will be the last time she will ever see an Escalade. Actually, in the case of some schools, it *won't* be the last time she sees an Escalade, but that's a whole other issue.

I know of one school that books a hotel room for a recruit,

and before the kid arrives they fill it with all sorts of gear. They load up the room with sneakers, T-shirts, sweats, balls—all sorts of stuff. Now, the kid isn't supposed to take it. That's an NCAA violation. They're just supposed to look at it—wink, wink. But who would ever know if they do take something?

I guess I've just never been a gimmicky person. We don't have names on the back of our jerseys. There's no bullshit with our program. We don't wear headbands or armbands. Don't get me wrong. We've got the best of everything. I'm as conscious as anyone about getting the kids what they deserve—as long as they deserve it.

I remember Tamika Williams telling me Ohio State was sending a plane to pick her up for her official visit. She lives in Dayton, Ohio, and they fly her to Columbus in a private jet. After that visit, I send her a note in an envelope with one of those little wooden planes enclosed. The note says, "Sorry, Tamika. This is the best we can do."

Sometimes, you recruit a kid, she signs with you, and you figure, "Great. We're all set." Well, not always. We recruit this kid from New York, Kathy Green. We figure she has a chance to help us. The summer before she comes, in 1989, she's out one night and sticks her head out the window of a moving car to make fun of one of her friends. She slams her head into a tree. She's lucky to be alive. Of course we honor her scholarship, but she can't play at all after that.

As good as our program has become, recruiting is still a unique challenge for us. Let's face it: Storrs, Connecticut, doesn't exactly recruit itself. Some places are easier to close the deal than others.

The way I see it is, your campus is what you want it to be.

If you drive onto our campus, and you're coming down the hill and the horse barns and the big fields and all those other rural scenes are on your left, you might say, "Man, this is Hicksville. I might as well be in the middle of nowhere."

Now you look to your right, where the campus is. Now you say, "Hey, wait a minute, 20,000 people live in this community of students, faculty, and others, and it's a place that's alive, full of energy, and there's an incredible amount of stuff going on."

So it's all in how you choose to look at it.

When we go to a player's house for a home visit, we sit down and show them. We show them pictures and say, "This is what our campus is like. Here's where we're located. Don't be surprised when you come up here." Then we tell them, "Decide on what you want to focus on. Are you going to get fixated on the cows and horses to the left, or the two gorgeous lakes in the middle of campus?" I make it clear to these kids that if they are looking for a campus like Boston College or UCLA, it's not what we have here.

We're not going to be able to present ourselves the same way a Big Ten school does. We can't show our recruits a Saturday when 80,000 people are watching our football team play. I remember in 1993 when we are recruiting Nykesha Sales and she goes on her visit to Ohio State. I know they are taking her to the Michigan–Ohio State football game. I turn the game on, and it's snowing. I turn to my wife, Kathy, and say, "Yessss!!!"

When we are after Tamika Williams, Notre Dame is recruiting her heavily. She is heading out for her visit, and it includes a ticket to the Notre Dame–USC football game. I tell her before she leaves, "Now, Tamika, when you're at the game, I want you to zero in on the linebackers for Notre

Dame, because I think two of them are seniors, and I know the football team is going to be a big part of your decision. Oh, that's right, you're a basketball player, not a football player."

It used to be the only time we allowed recruits to visit was during basketball practice in October. We wanted them to experience the intensity of our program. Our campus is pretty in September, but there's no Ohio State–Michigan football game going on. But now, while we're waiting around for these kids to come watch practice in October, other schools are pressuring kids to make a commitment. So we have to allow the kids to come earlier.

We take them down to the stadium. Our football program has really been upgraded, and now we play Syracuse and Pittsburgh, and we can put 40,000 people in the seats. Our team went to a bowl game in 2004, and they will only get better. But I still say that shouldn't be the reason kids come here.

I think what we offer is a unique opportunity to be entrenched in an environment that fosters studying, closeness with the student body, a bond with your teammates, and a place where you always feel safe. And guess what? There's always something to do every night if that's what you want.

You want to get out of Storrs? Get in a car and drive twenty minutes to Hartford. If you have a weekend off, you can drive a couple of hours into Manhattan, or head up to Boston in an hour and forty minutes. Go east for forty-five minutes and you've got the ocean in Rhode Island. How many campuses can say all that?

I really believe our location has contributed to our success. Some campuses are so big and spread out, I'm not sure the kids develop the kind of strong bonds that our kids do.

We usually pair our freshmen with other freshmen on the team, but nobody has to room with a player if they don't want to. The reason we put them together in their first year is we don't want them to end up with someone from campus who we know nothing about, who might be a little whacked, or might not understand the commitment of a student-athlete.

If players end up not getting along, they can switch. That's fine with me. My only comment is, "Figure it out. I don't want to hear about it."

Rebecca Lobo and Pam Webber roomed together as freshmen and stayed together all four years. Jen Rizzotti and Jamelle Elliott came in together, roomed together for two years, and the fights were so bad, and the arguments so loud, they moved away from each other. Having said that, you probably couldn't find two teammates who were closer, or more competitive. They remain very close friends today.

Because of our success, we are the targets of a lot of negative recruiting from other programs. That happens a lot more now than it used to. Other schools love to kill us. They tell kids, "You want to play in cow country? You want to go up there and play with all those white girls?" We also get a lot of, "You want to go play for that maniac? You think you can get along with that guy up there, that screamer?"

What you don't hear anymore is, "Do you really want to play for a man?" That's because 90 percent of the players we recruit have played for men. If I walk into an AAU tournament next week, I'll guarantee you that of the fifty teams, about forty-five of them will be coached by men.

After we've recruited and signed a kid, they'll tell us sometimes what other programs say about us. I've never confronted another coach about it. What's the point? It bothers me that they use negative recruiting, but my feeling is they're not going to get a kid that way, and if they do, that's not the kind of kid we want.

We definitely have recruited kids we would have loved to have in the program, but who got away. I loved Semeka Randall. I thought she'd be a terrific player, and she was a great kid. It was one of those unusual times when Tennessee was also going after her very hard, and we were battling head-to-head for her.

We know Tennessee has the upper hand, but Semeka agrees to visit Storrs, so we pick her up at the airport and bring her onto campus. We have something to eat with her, and she spends time with our players. She's a great kid, very intense. When she leaves, I feel like we aren't going to get her. I get the impression her high school coach is bullshitting us the whole time. That's always a bad sign. Sure enough, Semeka signs with Tennessee. Still, I respect the way Semeka handles herself. She calls me and tells me her decision, and I wish her luck.

One of the other players I hated to lose out on is Jamila Wideman. She played AAU basketball with Rebecca Lobo and Kara Wolters and Carla Berube. I love everything about her. We give it our best shot. It comes down to Stanford and us. She picks Stanford.

What can I say? You want me to tell her, "You're making a big mistake"? Was I going to tell this kid she was stupid for choosing Stanford? They had a better program than we did at the time. We hadn't got it going yet.

That one really stung, because Jamila spent a lot of time with us, and she was just such a wonderful kid, and her family was so awesome. She ended up doing really well at Stanford, although we played them and beat them while she was there. We also won a national championship during her four years, and they didn't, so it's kind of ironic.

The ones that make you mad are the kids who don't have the guts to call you themselves to tell you they've chosen another school. They have their coach do it. The character kids like Randall and Wideman pick up the phone and say, "Coach, I admire your program, but I've chosen so-and-so because it's the best place for me."

Sometimes I get mad at kids. Sometimes I get into altercations with them because they're not telling me the truth. Kids will tell me, "I'm going to this school," and I'll say to them, "Are you sure? Because two days ago, you told me this is where you want to be." So often the kids aren't making the decision themselves. It's the parents or the coach that's doing it for them.

Then you have kids who tell you their goal is to win a national championship. They say, "I want to play at the highest level." So that's when we say, "There's only one school in America that sells out every women's game. That's us. So it's not like you have a choice to go ten other places."

We've sold out every game at Connecticut since 1997. People are outside every night trying to get tickets. I tell kids, "If you are a performer, this is Broadway. Not that the other places aren't good, but this is the big stage. If you are really good, you are going to be great here. And if you aren't any good, you will be exposed here."

So the kid leaves talking about winning a national championship, then signs with a school that has never been in the tournament, or hasn't gotten out of the second round. So you say to yourself, "What's that all about?" Well, obviously someone changed their mind about what it was they really wanted. That kind of stuff can drive you nuts.

There is a kid out of Scarsdale, New York, named Hillary Howard. She is a point guard. I see her play, and she has everything. She is smart, full of fire, can shoot, can see the floor, and can handle the ball. She isn't the fastest kid in the world, but she is so savvy, and she is an absolute pure point guard. Jen Rizzotti is graduating, and I want Hillary to replace her.

Her coach and I get to be good friends. His name is Paul Celentano, and he brings her up in the summer. She tells him she wants to go to Connecticut. I tell her, "Look, Hillary, with Jen graduating, you've got a chance to play." We end up talking a lot, and we get very close. We just click.

But there are a couple of problems. Her mom is a North Carolina graduate, and her dad is a Duke guy, a Wall Street guy. Hillary keeps telling me, "Don't worry about it. It's my decision." I say, "Are you going to make an official visit?" and she assures me she will.

First we go down for the home visit. Her parents are very cordial. They love basketball and they love their daughter. They're good people. But they do not want their daughter at UConn. That is obvious to me as I leave their house.

To make a long story short, Hillary never visits Connecticut. She commits to Duke without ever seeing us.

I'm really, really upset. I call her up and I tell her, "Look, if you told me all along, 'Coach, Duke is my number one school and you have to knock them out,' I would have understood we were fighting an uphill battle, and I would have given it my best shot. But you never gave me that impression. All you ever said to me was, 'Connecticut, Connecticut, Connecticut.' You told me this was *your* decision."

She is upset, but not as upset as I am. All I want is for her to be honest with me.

That whole experience teaches me a lesson. I can't ever forget that these kids are only seventeen and eighteen years old. Some of them can't make a decision that big on their own. Some of them say what they think you want them to hear, not what they are feeling.

I know it is hard for Hillary to call and tell me she is going to Duke. I didn't stay mad at her. She is such a great kid, how could I? Before she signs with Duke, and we still think we have a shot, I start kidding her. I tell her, "If you don't come to Connecticut, I swear, you'll never score against us. If we ever play you, forget about scoring, you won't even get a shot off against us. We'll track you down every inch of the floor."

So Hillary goes to Duke. We get Rita Williams to play point, and she turns out to be a great guard for us. We don't play Duke—until Hillary's senior year, the 1998–99 season, when Duke is ranked No. 4 in the country in the preseason poll. We play them in November, our first game of the season.

We have Sue Bird, Swin, Asjha, Tamika, Svetlana, and Paige Sauer and Kelly Schumacher. We are loaded. This is before everyone gets hurt and our season gets away from us.

Hillary Howard is starting at the point for Duke. I don't get a chance to talk to her before the game. I want to, because by this point there are no hard feelings, but we have pregame stuff I need to take care of. We destroy Duke, 104–74. We embarrass them. Their coach, Gail Goestenkors, is distraught. They have a really good team, but we just have it going that day.

Poor Hillary Howard. She makes one shot, I think. She is

out of it. It's not like we do anything special to her. Maybe she is thinking, "Oh no, I'm playing Connecticut." We'll never know. But she is not herself.

Duke ends up going all the way to the Final Four with Hillary at the point that season, and they lose to Purdue in the final game. So she gets there. I was glad for her. I still hear from Hillary now and then. I'll always wonder what it would have been like to coach her.

That's the funny thing about recruiting. You never know how it will end up. You might think you've lost out but find out just the opposite later on.

That is exactly what happens with Brittany Hunter. She's the number one high school post player in the country in 2002. Her mom is a very nice person, but her stepfather is someone I know I'm going to have a problem with. I know it's going to be a hard sell because I can tell neither of them wants Brittany to come to Connecticut.

I go for a home visit and the stepfather doesn't ask a single question. He barely looks at me. The mom is a little antagonistic. I tell her I'd be happy to answer any of her questions, but she doesn't really have any. Instead, she tells me all the doubts she has about Connecticut.

Still, Brittany likes our program, so she agrees to come for an official visit. She spends some time with our players, she has a blast, and she tells our kids, "I'm coming to Connecticut." Naturally, my players tell me this.

So Saturday night rolls around and we take the mom out to dinner. Brittany isn't there. It's CD, Jamelle, Tonya, Kathy, and me. We're talking about schools and different opportunities, and somewhere along the way, the mom makes a comment about how some schools guarantee more success than other schools.

I jump in and say, "Not really. Just because you go to Duke doesn't mean you're going to be successful, and just because you go to Connecticut doesn't mean you won't be successful. I'm pretty successful, and I didn't go to Duke. Gail Goestenkors and (Duke men's coach) Mike Krzyzewski are pretty successful, and they didn't go to Duke."

Brittany's mom is undeterred. She doesn't realize it, but everything she's saying is incredibly insulting to our program, and to the people sitting around the table with her. Everyone is uncomfortable. She keeps ripping on our school, and I have to excuse myself and go to the men's room before I explode. I compose myself, come back, and she starts in again.

I can see where this is all leading, so I say to her, "I'm just going to ask you this, point-blank. Are you going to be okay if Brittany says to you, 'Mom, I want to go to Connecticut'?" Her mother says, "She's going to have to prove to me that's the best place for her." So I say, "Okay, what if she says to you, 'Mom, I want to go to Duke.' Does she have to prove to you that it's the best place for her?"

The mother says, "No." So I say, "Well, you know what? Then this is the worst situation to be in, because you're not giving us a chance. We're not playing on a level playing field here, because no matter what we do, we can't win. Even if we convince her this is the best place for her, and even if she tells you this is the best place for her, you're still not going to let her come. So what is the point of this visit? Why are you here?"

By this point, my voice is raised quite a few decibels. Within minutes, we're in a full-blown argument at the Depot Restaurant, which is right off campus. We are causing a scene. We're both yelling and screaming at each other, and everyone is looking. Tonya leans back in her chair, catches Kathy's eye, and says, "Stop him."

But it is far too late for that. Brittany's mom and I are so loud, I end up paying for the dinners of the couple seated next to us. As we are leaving, a number of people sitting at the bar grab Tonya's arm and say, "I guess she's not coming here, huh?"

I do admire Brittany's mom. She was standing up for what she believed in, and she wasn't about to back down. We both finally calm down a little, and after we do, I give her a hug and I tell her, "I don't agree with you. Brittany told my players she wants to come to Connecticut. You should let her come."

I see Brittany the next day before she leaves, and she tells me, "This is where I want to be." The next weekend, she goes to Duke for a visit and commits to them. She calls to tell me and I say, "Why are you going to Duke?" She answers, "I think it's the best place for me." I say, "No you don't." There is dead silence before I say, "You're making a big mistake."

A few days later, there is a report in the newspapers that Brittany Hunter is going to Duke. She is quoted as saying she loves the kids and the coaching staff at Connecticut, but she chose Duke because she felt she'd be better off twenty years down the road.

Our local reporters ask me about it and I say, "When is the last time you heard a kid talk about twenty years down the road? Who is putting that idea in her head?" I tell our writers, "There are just as many kids from Duke waiting tables as there are from any other school. They just happen to work at better restaurants."

The funny thing about that is a couple of years later, Ann

Marie Person, who worked in our media relations office, leaves to take a job in the Atlantic 10 Conference. She's at a bagel shop one day, and she's wearing a UConn women's basketball sweatshirt. The guy behind the counter says, "I hate UConn. Their coach is arrogant." Ann Marie says, "You mean Geno Auriemma?" He says, "Yeah, that guy. Where does he get off saying that thing about the kids from Duke waiting tables? Who does he think he is?" Ann Marie says, "Oh, so you went to Duke." The guy answers, "Yeah, I did. That guy has a helluva nerve. He doesn't know what he's talking about." At that point Ann Marie says, "But aren't you in a restaurant about to serve me a bagel?"

Obviously Brittany's family doesn't find my comments very humorous. Meanwhile, Brittany calls me up, and she's crying. She says to me, "How do I get out of this?" I say, "Tell your mother and stepfather you don't want to go there." But she can't. She can't do it.

Brittany calls me five times that week. Her stepfather sends me an e-mail saying, "I understand you are harassing my daughter. Stop calling and writing her." I write him back and say, "Hey. We're not contacting her. She's contacting us."

What can you do? She chose Duke. It's a very fine school, but she made a mistake, because it was obvious to us her heart was with Connecticut.

In the spring of 2004, shortly after we have won our fifth championship, we receive a phone call from Brittany's mother. It turns out Brittany wants to transfer to Connecticut. We're glad to have her. She comes to us with a badly damaged knee, and ends up having major surgery. She will be eligible to play for us in the 2005–06 season, but at this moment, we're not sure if she'll be able to play again. I hope she gets the chance. She's got a lot of her mother's spunk.

After more than twenty years of recruiting, it's obvious to me that kids aren't always going to be straight with you. For years, Chris and I took it for granted that kids were going to tell us the truth. I always give everyone the benefit of the doubt until they prove me wrong. I'm getting burned today because kids and their parents look at me straight in the eye and lie to my face. But if I ever did that to them, they'd expose me for being the worst guy in the world.

Here's the way we used to recruit. Let's say we have four spots open, and we have around eight players we think can fill those four spots. We don't like those eight players the same. Now, most programs have backups. We don't do it that way. We identify the four we want, and we spend all of our time on those four. My staff and I get together and I say, "What do you think?" We'll go over the kids and we'll agree, "We really like this kid," then we'll go to her and say, "Where are we on your list?" She'll tell us, "You're really high on my list." Now we have to, as a staff, go back and say, "Is she bull-shitting us, or telling us the truth?"

When we are looking at Nykesha Sales, she and Monick Foote are the two best players coming out at their position. We have home visits scheduled for both of them. Monick is from Delaware. Nykesha is from Bloomfield, Connecticut. There are some tournaments late in the year, and they're both playing, but they are in two different places. I've got to decide which one I'm going to see.

Now, Nykesha has already gone public in the papers saying, "I am not going to Connecticut. I like Geno and Chris Dailey, but I don't want to stay in my home state." Her top choices are Ohio State and Virginia. We're number three. We're also in Monick's top three.

I make a decision. I call up Monick's coach and I say, "We're canceling our home visit." My feeling is, how could I go into Nykesha's house and say, "Kesha, you're the one I want," then go the next day and tell Monick, "You're the one I want"? Obviously I would be lying to one of them, but that's college recruiting. Well, not anymore.

Now I've got all my eggs in Nykesha's basket. I go to her and tell her, "You're the one. I've canceled my home visit with Monick Foote." She says, "Yeah, okay." Very subdued. It sure wasn't like, "Wow, thanks, that's really cool, Coach."

Nykesha comes on her visit, and she has a great time. CD does a great job with Kesha. She just talks and talks with her, and finds out what is really important to her. In the meantime, Kesha isn't saying too much. She isn't leading us to believe she's coming here.

But I know we have her when, on her official visit, we take her to Margaritaville, a Mexican restaurant near campus. We take her out with a couple of our players and I say, "You guys like sweet peppers?" Kesha says, "No, I hate peppers. They're too hot." I say, "No, no, these are the really sweet ones. Try one." I throw a couple in my mouth.

Then I give her some. I've given her some jalapeño peppers, the really hot green ones, and she pops them in her mouth. She immediately turns about ten different shades of red. I just want to see her reaction. The kids and the coaches are laughing hysterically, and Kesha can't get enough water and soda in her mouth. She is really having trouble.

Before long, she's laughing with us. The way she reacts, and how much fun she has, leads me to believe, "You know what? This kid is in her environment." Jamelle Elliott is there that night, and she really connects with Kesha, and she agrees. She tells me, "I think we've got her."

At the end of Nykesha's visit, we're sitting under the stands, and she says to me, "Coach, if I come here, do you think I can wear number 42?" Her number in high school is 24. She is already respectful enough not to ask for 24, because that is Kerry Bascom's number, and she is our all-time leading scorer at that point. I tell her, "I'm sure we can get you number 42."

We get Kesha. Virginia gets Monick Foote. Both schools end up happy.

Obviously not all the endings are happy ones. After we win our third consecutive championship in 2004, two of our kids announce they are transferring. People are shocked. They want to know what's going on. To break it down most simply, it is bad recruiting by us.

I like to think we do the best job we can of getting to know our kids on a personal level. We have three freshmen come in the summer before the 2003–04 season. One of them, Kia Wright, stays two weeks and leaves. She's homesick, she's from New York, and she's overwhelmed with the schoolwork and the workouts, so she transfers closer to home, to St. John's. She's one of their top players in 2004–05. She's a great kid. I'm glad it works out for her there. Our only problem is our campus isn't in New York City.

The other two kids, I believe, have a chance. Kiana Robinson is a guard who has some potential, some athletic ability. She comes to summer school and plays after camp. Now, we've just won two national championships in a row, but she shows up and wants to show our guys how to play. That doesn't go over too well. Our guys spend the next couple of months whacking her around, which she kind of deserves. Kiana is on her heels now, and she can't seem to use her abilities to get the most out of her talent. I say to her in January of 2004, "I don't think you are going to be here too long. You don't seem to like it here." I encourage her to leave. She isn't fitting in. She transfers to Syracuse.

The other kid, Liz Sherwood, is about 6-foot-5, and I think she has a chance to be like Kara Wolters. She is a high school teammate of Ann Strother, and has great hands and great feet. But we are in a battle with her father, who never really wants her to be here. He feels she should have gone to Notre Dame or Vanderbilt. While we are recruiting Liz, he calls our program "a basketball factory." I say to him, "I don't know what you mean." He says, "What are your graduates doing these days?" I look at him and I say, "Well, you've got a point. Let's see. Sue Bird is making half a million dollars playing for Seattle, Swin Cash is on the cover of every magazine in Detroit, Tamika Williams is starting for Minnesota in the WNBA and getting her master's degree at Ohio State. Asjha Jones is playing pro ball and going to graduate school in Maryland, so I guess they aren't doing as well as those twenty-two-year-olds who graduated from Notre Dame and Vanderbilt and are making $45,000 a year."

I guess you could say we get off on the wrong foot.

To Liz's credit, she wants to come here, and she seems to like it here until she has a problem with her knee. She has to have a little surgery, and that's when I tell her, "Liz, you need to lose weight. Now, will that help you be a better basketball player? Yes, but I also think down the road, after you stop playing, you will be glad you did this." I tell her if she commits to working with the trainer and the nutritionist and our strength coach, not only will she be in the best shape of her life and become a great player, she will have a different way of life when her career is over.

I have this conversation with her at the end of October. Between October and April, there is little or no change. Then her father and I get into it at the end of the season. Liz says, "I'm not happy here." I say, "You loved it for three months until I said you weren't playing until you lost some weight. Now you don't like it? What do you want me to tell you?" She says, "I'm never going to get to play here." I say, "You're right—unless you do what I ask you to do." She says, "Even if I do those things, I'll never play." I say, "Who told you that?" It's her father. So I tell Liz, "Okay, here's the best thing for you. Go someplace where you won't have to do any of the things I'm asking you to do, and you can play anyway. Good luck."

I probably make a mistake with her. You can't ever say that the coach is right, the program is right, and the players are right, and if you don't make it here, you're wrong. That's not the case at all. I have made tons of mistakes with kids. Sometimes it can work even after you make those mistakes, but that only happens if you and the parents are on the same page.

I never bond with Liz Sherwood or Kiana Robinson. I never make a connection with them. Is it their fault? My fault? You'd have to say it's a little of both. All the tradition we have, all those championships, they don't mean anything to Liz or Kiana because they don't feel connected. In the end, kids want to feel like they know you and you know them. They want to feel appreciated. Those two kids never feel that way, and it's as much my fault for not making them feel connected. I hope they both find what they are looking for.

In the meantime, I have changed the way we look for players. In the past, we've always given kids the feeling that we'll wait as long as we have to wait. For ten years or so, that never failed. We always got the kid we wanted. But now, in the age of Internet access, coaches can spend days and nights e-mailing recruits and establishing "friendships" with the players.

I don't want any eighteen-year-old friends. I don't need any. I have no intention of playing Instant Messenger with some recruit at two o'clock in the morning.

Starting now, if you visit Connecticut, I don't care when you come up here, whether it's spring, summer, or fall, I'm going to ask you, "How do you like the school? Do you feel comfortable with the coaching staff?" If you say yes, then I'm going to ask you, "Do you think this is a place where you can be successful?" If you say yes, then I'm going to say, "What is your plan going forward?" You are probably going to say something like, "Coach, I really love Connecticut, but I have four other schools I want to see."

So then I'll have to ask you, "Now, wait a minute. You are going to compare us to four other schools? Does that mean there's something here you don't like, or don't see?" You might say, "Well, I haven't seen the other schools yet. They might have something I like better. They might have something I haven't even thought of yet. I might like the other coach better."

That's fine, but that will be it for you at Connecticut.

Consider if it is the other way around. Suppose I say to a player, "I really like you, but I'm putting you on hold until I see what a couple of these other players are like." In the meantime, there could be a coach that says, "You're the one

I want." Kids don't like to hear, "Just wait while I look at these other four players."

Coaches don't like it either. We're the ones putting $30,000 on the table, giving you the opportunity to travel all over the country, to play in a top program with the best players. Everything is in the players' hands. Why should they hold all the cards?

My new approach is, "Here's what we have. Either you want it, or you don't." I equate it this way. You walk into Nordstrom's department store. You're looking for shoes. You see a pair you like. They are the color you want, the perfect size, and the price you want to pay. Are you going to tell me you're going to put them back and look in three other stores for something better? If you are, you're not the kind of person I want.

So we're taking a proactive approach. This is what we have. This is who we are. Take it or leave it. We're not getting any better after you leave. The facilities won't be better two months from now. Neither will the coaching staff or the players.

We recently had a kid who made a campus visit and said, "Coach, I love it here. You know what? I'm going to call you in about a week and tell you I'm coming here, but first I've got to make another visit." She goes to a school down South, and you know what they tell her? There are more black people down here, and you'll feel more comfortable.

Are you kidding me? That's not an issue. It wasn't an issue when you were here telling me how much you loved this place. I'm at the point where I want kids who know what they want, and nothing and no one will talk them out of it. I've made a commitment to you. I've watched you play, and I'm offering you a scholarship.

The alternative is, "I like you a lot. You're pretty good. But you know what? You're not quite good enough. There's another kid I want to see. So hold on, and I'll get back to you."

It can be done that way.

Just not by me.

SIX

I am still recovering from my first season with "the best college recruiting class in history." I look at Sue, Swin, Asjha, and Tamika and I can't believe we struggled as much as we did in 1998–99. I am worried about my team.

Kathy keeps telling me they are going to figure it out. "G," she says, "you've got to believe in them. Once you do that, they'll be fine."

Kathy knows what she is talking about. She is very much a part of our program—not in a meddling way, but in a way that is very supportive to the players on our team. Many of them when they come to Connecticut are far away from home for the first time, and Kathy has a way of helping them feel comfortable. They also know that even though she is married to me, she doesn't always agree with me. Many times, when I am being a hard-ass, if you ask her to choose sides between the players and me, she's with the players.

I meet Kathy in college, in 1972. I'm going to Montgomery County Community College, and in some ways, my first encounter with her is pretty typical of how I do things. I'm on the basketball team, and one of my teammates, Dave McEvoy, says to me, "Listen, two girls are coming to the game tonight. I'm going out with one of them, and the other one is her friend."

The "friend" is Kathy. Dave's girlfriend is Robin Friedman, who is Kathy's best friend from high school and college. So we play the game, and we shower, and I guess I take kind of a long time, because I come out and there's Kathy, standing there all by herself. I look around, and everybody else is gone—including Dave and Robin. I say, "You must be Kathy. How are you getting home?" She says, "I guess you are taking me."

It turns out Kathy lives in a town called Cheltenham. She tells me this, and I say, "Where the hell is that?" It turns out it's about half an hour away, right down Route 73. It's where Reggie Jackson and Craig Littlepage, the athletic director at Virginia, are from.

I drive Kathy home. Now, I've never been to this area before. There's this term called the Philadelphia Main Line. There's a train that runs from the city out toward Villanova. The part where Kathy lives is a different section of the Main Line. It's the high-rent district. It's a place where people like me have no reason to go.

So I'm driving through this neighborhood in my 1968 Barracuda and I feel like I'm in the middle of a Currier & Ives picture. Everything is perfect. Each house is bigger than the next one. It's really a spectacular sight. As we pull around the circle, I look at the top of the hill, and I'm thinking to myself, "This isn't bad. Look at that car in the driveway. Look at that pool. Maybe there are some benefits to dating a rich girl. I think I can hang out for a couple of years with all this." I turn to Kathy and I say, "Which one is your house?" She points to the drugstore and says, "My mom and I share an apartment on the top floor there." I say to myself, "Oh well, so much for the easy life." I kiss her good night, and she goes home.

Only that isn't the end of it. She is nice to be around. She is pleasant, very smart, and very down-to-earth. She isn't all caught up in herself, and she isn't too girly girly. The next day, I see her in school. I meet some of her friends and she meets some of mine. I go to some parties with her, and the next thing you know she's coming home with me to have dinner with my mom and dad.

I fall in love with her. I find myself thinking about her all the time. She's very supportive of what I'm doing, and we spend all our time together.

Six years later, we get married. I can't find anything wrong with her. We're very compatible. There is never any bullshit. She never gets on my nerves. I've always been the kind of person who needs a lot of space, and she has no problem with that, because she's so independent herself.

We've been married more than twenty-five years, and I bet we didn't have our first argument until about three years ago. She's always right. So, lately, I'm getting pissed off because she's always right, and I'm trying to fight her, and it causes arguments, because I'm not right, and she is. I guess I've got to live with that.

The thing about Kathy and me is we've been through it all together. She is teaching when I first start out in coaching, and we don't have any money. While I am going to West Chester, Jim Foster hires me to coach the junior varsity girl's team at Bishop McDevitt School. I'm driving from West Chester to Glenside, Pennsylvania, for an hour, and driving back the same day. I make $400 for the year. It costs me more than that in gas money. My car only costs $400. It is a Volkswagen.

Some women would have been hounding me to get a "real" job. Kathy is never like that. She knows how much I love the game. In fact, when Phil Martelli hires me to coach at my old school, Bishop Kenrick, Kathy hooks me up with one of her friends, whose dad owns a supermarket. I stock shelves from eleven at night until seven the next morning. The guys I work with blast Led Zeppelin all night so I don't fall asleep. Then, after I get done, I go to a couple of classes, take a quick nap, and coach in the afternoon.

Kathy and I get married in 1978. Neither of us has a job. Her teaching job is through a federal grant, and when the grant dries up, so does her job. I'm coaching at Kenrick with Phil, and trying to do all these odd jobs to make some money. When the Virginia job pops up, we pack up one carload of stuff and move there for a job that pays $13,000 a year.

I'm sure I have died and gone to heaven when Connecticut agrees to pay me $29,000 in 1985 to be their head coach. I can't believe my luck. Kathy feels the same way. She adopts the players on the team like they are part of our family. I'm really, really fortunate, because when I come home, if I'm on top of things and doing my job, we're not going to celebrate like we've won the lottery. But when I am wrong, I'm going to hear about it every single day. Kathy isn't afraid to let me know I'm screwing up.

It's Kathy who assures me the 1999–2000 season is going to be fine. She is right. My team shows up in preseason with a new resolve. All of a sudden Shea doesn't care about scoring points. She doesn't care about her own stats. She just wants to make sure our team wins. She becomes the consummate team player.

Sveta also has a certain look in her eye. She has become more acclimated to the United States, and she has grown to accept the way our team plays basketball.

You have to remember what Sveta has gone through to play college basketball here. We find out about her from a friend of ours, Boris Lelchitski. Chris scouts her in Brazil and gets very excited, and says we should get her. We convince Sveta to sign. She comes to this country not knowing anyone—not even me. I have never met her. She flies over to the United States from Russia and she's in the airport, and all of a sudden it hits her. She starts saying to herself, "What am I doing? I don't know these people. I don't even know who to look for when they pick me up at the airport."

Chris Dailey picks her up. She makes sure everything is perfect. She has every detail planned down to the second. That's CD.

The first thing I do when I get the Connecticut job is hire Chris. I know her from serving on a couple of committees with her when we are assistants—me with Virginia, CD with Rutgers. When I hire Chris, I end up getting three people for the price of one assistant. I get someone who is really talented at what she does, an incredibly hard worker, and someone who is incredibly organized. At that time, CD does a little bit of everything, because we have no other help. Her job evolves into being an associate head coach, an administrative assistant, and a head recruiter. You name it, and Chris has done it. There are a whole bunch of associate head coaches in the game today, but I believe Chris is the first.

She's like a pack mule. She thrives on work. She's devoted twenty years of her life to this program.

She doesn't have to worry about a lot of the day-to-day stuff anymore. Jack Eisenmann and Robyn Danahy and Peg Myers (who is really Peggy Walsh, my star player from my first season) handle a lot of the administrative things. We hired Sarah Darras to run my life for me, and she has become invaluable. If we lose Sarah at this point, you might as well cancel the program.

The extra people free Chris up to do what she loves most—deal with our players and our recruits. She prides herself on being able to communicate with our athletes and help them become great players. When Sveta Abrosimova steps off the plane in America, CD is there, and Sveta is in good hands.

Sveta's English is not very good when she arrives. She has an enormous challenge in front of her. She is in Connecticut about a week before she comes to see me. She walks into our offices and she can't believe it. She sees my assistant coach Tonya Cardoza's office and she thinks, "I wonder who she is. Her office is so big. She must be very important." In Russia, the coaches all cram into one room. She almost falls over when she sees my office, which is twice the size of Tonya's.

Sveta is one of those people who would prefer not to rely on others. She wants to do it herself. That is great—but it can be difficult when you are in a strange country speaking a strange language and using a strange currency. One afternoon, she spends forty-five minutes standing in front of a washing machine trying to figure out how to use it. It would have taken five minutes if she just asked someone—but she doesn't.

There are days Sveta loves me, and there are days Sveta

hates me. I do not give her many breaks. I am like that even though she doesn't know anything about NCAA basketball. I am like that even though she spends every spare moment of her time in her room studying, because she is struggling so much with the written and the spoken language. Most times, she writes her notes in Russian, then translates them into English afterwards. But by the time she leaves here, she is a dean's list student.

After practicing with us a few days, Sveta realizes our program is very team-oriented. Every time she takes a shot, I'm on her case. She immediately starts to get concerned. She doesn't want to lose her identity over here. Then there are those crazy no-look passes that she just loves to throw. I can see we are going to have our share of battles.

One day, after she throws this ridiculous pass through three people, I tell her, "You do that one more time and I'm sending you back to Siberia." Sveta starts laughing. It turns out one of her club teams actually *was* in Siberia.

She is extremely talented. She is quick and she can run all day and she can score all over the court. She makes it all look effortless. She is the happiest person on this earth when we are pushing the ball up the floor and running the lanes. I tell her that is how I hope to play during the entire 1999–2000 season.

Swin comes back healthy and she isn't about to forget what we just went through. She tapes in her locker a picture of herself crying on the bench after our loss to Iowa State in the NCAA tournament the season before. I ask her why she has the picture up there. She says to me, "I don't want to ever feel that way again. I don't want to ever forget what that felt like. Look at me. I look pathetic."

Swin Cash has never looked pathetic a day in her life. She

is the ultimate diva. While she is at Connecticut, her team-mates put a sign above her locker that says, "Drama Queen." She loves it. I have to admit I have some reservations when we recruit Swin. How many kids send you their prom picture, then call you up and say, "You better have that picture on your desk when I come up there"? Who the hell does that? Swin does. She's a prima donna, all right, but she'll rip your heart out on the court.

We actually almost stop recruiting Swin. I am trying to call her, but she wants everything to go through her high school coach. He gets so overwhelmed by all the schools contacting him that he just shuts us all down. We don't hear anything, and we figure she is no longer interested.

Swin, meanwhile, doesn't hear anything from us, and she's starting to get bummed out. She wants to come to UConn. Finally, she gets her courage up, and calls me and says, "Don't you want me anymore?" I tell her we do. She says, "Good. Because I've been talking with Tamika Williams, and we're both coming there."

One of the more rewarding moments I've had in my career is when I get a call from Carol Callan, who is on the Olympic selection committee for the 2004 Games. It's the summer of 2003, and she says to me, "Listen, we're thinking of adding some people to this foreign tour we're doing this summer to give them the experience of playing with a national team. We're taking a mix and match of people. Swin Cash's name has come up. I'm wondering how you think Swin will react to being on the tour." I say, "What do you mean?" Carol says, "Well, do you think she'll be okay with not being the star of the team? How will her attitude be?"

I know where this is coming from. It is the whole diva thing. I tell Carol, "Swin's attitude will be the same whether she gets 30 minutes or three minutes. I guarantee you she will be fine." She says, "Okay, then. Good. We're looking forward to taking her, and we hope it works out." I say, "Oh, it will, Carol, but can I tell you one thing before you go? Whoever's job is on the line here because you are taking Swin, they don't know it yet, but they're done."

Carol is a little taken aback. She says, "What do you mean by that?" I say, "I'm just telling you that once Swin goes on this tour, she will force you to put her on the Olympic team. Unless you are prepared to have Swin Cash play for you in the Olympics in 2004, don't take her, because she'll outwork everyone to earn a spot on the squad."

The U.S. team goes on tour and they play great. They come back and Carol calls me up. She says, "You were right. Nobody competes harder than Swin Cash. Nobody brings more energy, and nobody has more pride."

Swin Cash makes the Olympic team and earns herself a gold medal to go along with her two national championships.

Now, there's no question Swin is high-maintenance. She knows it. We all know it. But she's also very bright, and she's absolutely stunning. I wish I had a dollar for every guy who comes up to me and says, "I can't believe how beautiful Swin Cash is." Swin shows up at the 2004 NBA All-Star Game, and she turns heads everywhere she goes. She is hanging out with Minnesota Timberwolves forward Kevin Garnett, who is the MVP of the NBA in 2004, and they are the talk of the town.

When I see that, I can't help but think, "That's one diva who has come a long, long way."

Even though Swin and Sue and Asjha and Tamika are only sophomores, they've already been through so much, they act and feel like upperclassmen.

Paige Sauer and Stacy Hansmeyer know they are good, but they realize they aren't as good as some of the other players who are behind them. Even so, when the season starts, I give them their minutes. They are seniors. They have earned them.

But later, as we get deeper into our schedule, I make a decision. I go to Paige and I say, "I appreciate all you have done for this team. But I need to start Schuey (Kelly Schumacher) now." Paige is okay with it. She understands. She could destroy our season right there if she doesn't, but she's absolutely great about it.

Now I pull Stacy aside. I tell her, "Stace, I don't know how many minutes you are going to get the rest of the way. You are a senior, I understand that, but Tamika, Asjha, and Swin need to play." She looks at me and says, "Coach, that's not a problem. I just want to win a championship." Stacy is such a great kid. Her nickname is Bam Bam, because she's so hard-nosed. She's from Oklahoma, and she plays ball like she's playing for the Sooners football team. But get her away from the court, and she's a striking, attractive individual. I hate like hell to ask her to sit, but I do it because I know she has it in her. She sings the national anthem on Senior Night, and there's not a dry eye in the place.

What Stacy and Paige do for our team that season shows me more of what it is about to play for Connecticut than maybe any other kids I've seen before or since. Of course they want to play. Of course what I ask them to do is incredibly difficult. But they make the ultimate sacrifice in their senior season, and I will be forever grateful for it.

Our team goes 36–1 in 1999–2000. We lose one game—to Tennessee by a point—and run the table on the rest. That includes a 19-point win over Tennessee to win the national championship.

It's mostly the same kids from the year from hell, only they are a year older, a year wiser, and a year closer to understanding what it takes to be champions.

Chris, Tonya, and Jamelle believe our team had to go through the 1998–99 season for them to realize what it takes. My coaches' feelings are, "Hey, you think you're such hot stuff, and just walking onto the floor at Connecticut is enough. Well, guess what? This is what happens to kids at Connecticut, because everyone is out to get you. That leaves you with a choice—fight back, or give in to all those people who are against you."

By suffering like we did, by not getting to the Final Four, by not even getting to the Elite Eight, we have an opportunity the following season to dust ourselves off, come back, and say, "All right. No more."

We start the season with a really solid win at Iowa. Then we come home and play in the Coaches vs. Cancer tournament at the Hartford Civic Center. We have Kentucky in the first game. It is a good test for us, and in the first few minutes of the game, we are failing.

They are beating us badly. I'm pissed off. I don't like the way the referees are calling the game, and I tell them so. They toss me. The kids are convinced I did it on purpose. I assure you I didn't. Nothing that happens with me during a game is calculated. I'm far too intense to plan something like that in advance.

Anyway, I'm gone, and Chris takes over. The kids are a bit wide-eyed, but they are also saying, "Man, I can't believe Coach got tossed for us." Then they take the next step, which is to say, "We know exactly what he wants us to do. We have to do this without him."

And they do. They play great down the stretch. Sue Bird is at the point, and she is barking out orders, making sure everyone is where they are supposed to be. It is exactly the kind of on-the-court leadership we are missing the season before. Shea and Sveta are playing like veterans. Our team wins 68–62. They prove to themselves what I've been telling them all along. When nothing is going right, that's when you find out what kind of character you have. After they win that game against Kentucky, they celebrate like they've won the national championship, because they have taken responsibility for what happens out there. They have done it without me. They have learned to rely on one another.

The next night, we play Old Dominion in the championship of the tournament, and we kill them. We score 109 points, and we win by over 40 points. We are taking out the disappointment of the previous season on everyone in our path.

The only teams that give us trouble are Tennessee and Rutgers. We play Pat Summitt and her team in Knoxville on January 8 and win, 74–67. Then they come to our place on February 2 and we lose by a point, 72–71. Semeka Randall hits an incredible shot for them down the stretch, and Sveta passes up a shot in the final seconds that might have won it for us. It is a great basketball game, but I am on Sveta afterwards. I can't understand why she chooses this time of all times to pass the ball.

In early February, we go to Rutgers, which has always been a very difficult place for us to play, and we hang on for a 49–45 win. It is one of those days when nobody can score. We miss every open shot. Asjha Jones bails us out in that one. She's the only one who can get the ball in the hole.

By the time March rolls around, this team is as hungry and as focused as any team I've had. I am pushing them to the limit, and they are looking at me as if to say, "Is that all you've got?" I am routinely having the starters play five-on-seven in practice. They are too good to play five-on-five. They want a bigger challenge. Like I keep telling them, "If you can score like this against seven defenders, imagine what you can do against just five of them."

We breeze to the Final Four. We beat Hampton in the first round by 71 points. We beat Clemson by 38 and Oklahoma by 22, and LSU by 15, and Penn State by 22.

My slogan for that Final Four is "Get on the bus." The game is going to be played in Philly, the city where I grew up, and I can't believe how much fun it is. It is the night before the championship game, and we are going to this place called Finnegan's Wake, and we've rented a bus, so everyone I see that day, I ask, "Are you on the bus? Get on the bus!" They have a microphone on the bus, and I'm doing my own tour of Philly for our fans, our media, my family, and anyone else that gets on that bus.

I can't help but think about my father that weekend. We are playing in his backyard, and he really would have enjoyed it, I think. He only saw me coach once before he died. It was in 1991, and we were playing NC State and Clemson in the Palestra for the chance to go to our first ever Final Four. The Palestra was only twenty minutes from our house in Norristown, so my dad had no choice. He had to go. I remember he was holding my son the whole game. Michael was about three, and he fell asleep in my father's lap.

My father got cancer in his kidney, and then it spread to his lungs. He was a smoker. It was his only vice. He didn't drink anything but coffee. He didn't gamble. He didn't womanize. His deal was to smoke a couple of packs a day.

When they discover the cancer they take out his kidney and we think they get it. But then it pops up in his lungs. He comes up to our house in Connecticut for Thanksgiving in 1996. He looks pretty good. I remember thinking, "He's got a chance." But then just like that—poof. He goes the other way.

On that Thanksgiving night, it is pretty chilly. We have just eaten and I grab a cigar and say to my dad, "C'mon, let's go for a walk." My dad can't smoke anymore, but he is dying to, so I light the cigar, and blow the smoke toward him so he can suck in the aroma. We walk around for a while, and we talk. We don't talk about anything in particular. We're just a father and a son enjoying the holiday. It is one of those perfect nights when we finally get there. I finally feel like we connect.

I have a lot of great memories of my father. I loved the summers we worked together doing construction. He was with his buddies, all these Italian guys in their late forties, and I was this young twenty-year-old guy, and every day I'd bust them because I spoke English, and they had an accent, and I was in college, and they didn't finish grade school. They were on me all the time, giving me jobs they knew I couldn't do.

When I think of my childhood in Norristown, I think of my father coming home every Friday night with these sandwiches we called zeps. They are like hoagies, only wider, long like zeppelins, and they are loaded with oil, onions, Italian cold cuts, and provolone cheese. He'd bring them in the house wrapped in wax paper, and we'd share them.

When I am a senior in high school, my father takes my

mother back to Italy for the first time since they have moved. They come back from that trip, and my father gives me a gold chain with a crucifix. Ever since then, the chain has not been off my neck. Not even for one minute.

When I go to college, I work in a steel mill to help pay my tuition. It is so hot I wear an asbestos jacket and asbestos pants. I wear a bandanna around my face saturated in water so I can get oxygen, because that's how bad the sulfur fumes are. One night, I get home and take a shower, and my crucifix snaps in half. The heat from the steel mill breaks it. Eventually, my parents replace the crucifix for me. The chain remains the original. I wear it every single day. It is a great reminder of where I have come from, and how I have gotten to this point in my life.

Even though my father isn't there to see us win it all in 2000, my mother and Ferruccio and Anna are there. They have always supported us. They all come to my party the night before the final. Jen Rizzotti and Rebecca Lobo are there, acting as my bouncers. They are checking IDs at the door. I send out this little card in the mail before we leave for Philly that serves as the invitation to the party. If you don't have the little card, you don't get in—at least for a while, anyway. By 2 a.m., there are all sorts of people there I have never seen before. I don't care. I'm having the time of my life.

We play Tennessee for the national championship, and we completely dismantle them. We beat them 71–52, and it really isn't close. We are ahead by 13 at halftime, and we never look back. It's not like we play the perfect game. We are 1 for 9 in three-pointers. We get outrebounded by a few. It's our defense that wins it. Tennessee turns the ball over 26 times, and shoots 31 percent from the floor. Semeka Randall, the recruit that got away, shoots 1 of 11 from the floor that day.

Kelly Schumacher is immense. She has nine blocks. The two best games of her career are this one and the game the next year in the national semifinals, when we lose to Notre Dame. Those two games get her tons of exposure, and she is drafted in the first round of the WNBA.

I always thought Kelly could be really, really good. She is 6-foot-5, can run and block shots. But she lets a lot of things get in the way of her being good. Every little thing that happens to her is a big dramatic event. When she has a fight with her boyfriend, she can't play well for a week. She has a hard time sustaining things, but when she gets it going like she does against Tennessee in the championship, you think "My God, if she could ever do this on a regular basis, forget it. She'd be unstoppable."

Kelly has gone on to a nice WNBA career. I don't hear that much from her. She's separated herself from the program, for whatever reason. I don't think there's anything wrong, or any hard feelings. I think it's just the way Kelly is. Sue Bird sent me a text message from Russia wishing me Happy New Year. Kelly's not going to do that, which is fine. That's just Kelly. Without her, we don't beat Tennessee for the 2000 championship.

There are a couple of things that bother me about Tennessee in that game. One is when we inbound the ball under the basket, right in front of our bench, and Asjha is acting dopey. She's playing like, "Maybe I want the ball, maybe I don't." Tennessee forward Michelle Snow is guarding her, and I know Asjha can score on her. I'm going crazy. We have to inbound the ball again, and I start yelling, "Asjha, take her! Asjha, take her! Asjha, take her!"

At that moment, Michelle Snow turns around and swears at me.

I can't believe what I'm hearing. Nobody on our bench can either. So I go nuts. I'm shouting to the referees, "Did you hear what she just said? Did you hear her?" They're shaking their heads no. I tell them, "She swore at me. What are you going to do about that?" The refs turn blue when I tell them what she said. Our players are sitting on the bench with their jaws to the floor. I don't think I've ever seen CD so disgusted in my life. But the refs can't really do anything, because they didn't hear it themselves.

So we win the game, and we are going through the line for the traditional congratulatory handshake, and Al Brown, a Tennessee assistant, gives me the classic cold fish. He barely looks at me, then he gives me this limp half-ass shake that is just so unprofessional, it is unbelievable. Now I'm hot at Al Brown. I'm going after him. You never—ever—do something like that, and I'm going to tell him all about it. Chris grabs me before I can get to him. She says to me, "Geno, we just won the national championship. Let it go."

Sorry. I can't. It's one of the worst cases of poor sportsmanship I can imagine. And I'll tell you one thing—Pat Summitt would never do that. Win, lose, or draw, she understands how it works. I bet she's more disappointed than anyone in the history of basketball when her team loses, but she's never going to show that in public, or belittle the other team's accomplishment by walking down there and acting like some spoiled brat.

When you win as much as Pat and I have won, you better learn how to accept losing, too. If you lose, the first order of business is to congratulate the people who won, and allow them to feel how they should feel—that they did something great. Now, after that, if you want to go into the locker room and throw chairs out the window and swear and scream and act like an idiot, that's fine.

I've always said hockey players are the ones who have it right. There's nothing I love more than watching them at the Stanley Cup finals, lining up to shake hands when it's all said and done. Look, I'm not saying you have to bring a bottle of champagne over and pour it on their heads. But it's not going to kill you to go over and shake hands.

After we win the championship in 2000, the state goes wild. I am so happy for Shea and Sveta. I have put them through a lot, and now they can celebrate. Now they can call themselves champions.

I wish I knew then what was to follow. I wish I could have told Shea and Sveta to savor every minute of that feeling. I guess at the time, I figured we would come back and do it the next year. Why not?

There was no way of knowing how heartbreaking it would end for those two players in their final seasons. Both of them would suffer injuries that would end their Connecticut careers—and our NCAA title chances—prematurely.

Sveta has always had back problems, but she has never had a serious injury. How ironic it is that the following season we are at Tennessee, and she goes up for a layup and she feels something pull. She's got some immediate pain. She comes out of the game. At the time, I don't think it's anything serious. We put her back in, and it's obvious she can't go. It turns out she has a torn ligament in her foot in an area where the odds of it happening are something like 1 in 150,000. It's such an unusual area of the foot, and it's a total freak thing. But Sveta is done.

Her parents have never seen her play. She has been saving

up for three years to fly them over here to see her play in her senior season. Everyone knows she comes from a poor, poor environment in Russia, so fans start sending money to our offices so Sveta's parents can come. Of course we can't keep any of the money. It is an NCAA violation. I will tell you this: the people of Connecticut sent enough money to have her parents come over three or four times. It is just another signal that our program has gotten very, very big.

Our kids do something very sweet. They chip in and hand Sveta an envelope of their own money at Christmas. They want to make sure her parents get here. It is their secret. We coaches don't know about it until long after Sveta's parents have come and gone.

It is just awful when Sveta gets hurt. I think up to that point, she may be the most complete player we have ever had. She is a three-time All-America. No one else in our program had done that before, and Diana Taurasi is the only one who has done it since. For Sveta, who took such terrific care of herself, to have a season-ending injury like that is cruel. It is a cold twist of fate. It makes me want to cry every time I see her, because I know how much it means to her to have her family see her play.

After she finds out she's done for the year, Sveta calls her parents and tells them not to come. They don't listen to her. They come anyway. I go with Sveta to the airport to pick them up and give them both a big hug. I had never met them, but I feel like I've known them forever. They keep calling me "Mr. Auriemma." I keep trying to get them to call me Geno. The most touching moment for me is when Sveta introduces me to her parents as, "This is my second father."

I wish Sveta's career could have ended differently here. She captures the hearts of every single fan in Connecticut.

She used to tell me, "Coach, you can yell and scream at me all you want. I don't mind. Just don't take me out of the game, okay?" My mother absolutely loves Sveta. I go home to Norristown to see her one weekend, and she has one of those life-sized posters of Sveta tacked on the door. Meanwhile, there isn't one picture of me in the house. My mother gets really angry with me when I yell at Sveta. "You leave her alone," she tells me. "I think that Sveta is such a sweet girl."

She isn't the only one who thinks so. Everyone adopts this girl. Everyone. If you only have one name, that's how you know you've made it big. Like Dee. Or Sveta.

Or Shea. Poor Shea. Her career here ends the way it starts—with an injury. We are playing Notre Dame in the Big East final in 2001 when, about 15 minutes into the game, she tears her ACL again. We know right away. We've seen it so many times before. It is just so sad. None of us can believe it. They cart her off to the trainer's room, and I am just sick about it. At halftime, I grab my team and say, "C'mon, let's go see Shea." I don't realize she is already back in the locker room with us. The look on her face says it all.

I would say Shea Ralph spent one year too long here. Because of her injuries, she stayed five years. She probably should have left after her junior season, because it was going to be hard to duplicate that storybook ending, but I wasn't going to tell her that. When she said, "I want to come back," I said, "I support you 100 percent."

Looking back, Shea's five years here were incredibly dramatic. I would say she probably had the most unbelievable experience of anyone. She comes in as a freshman and has to learn to play without the ball in her hands, which she's never done. She has to learn to play with other good players, which she's never done. She has to come off the bench, which she's never done.

So she has this incredible learning curve, and then, just when she's got it all figured out and is playing the best basketball of her life, she gets injured and it's all taken away from her. Then she wants to come back so badly, and she works so hard, then boom! She's hurt again, and misses back-to-back seasons. Then she comes back again, and is playing, and has no idea how to lead, and meanwhile we really need her to lead. But because she's missed time, and because she's so into her workout, her rehab, her own issues, she has no idea how to step up. So it's a year wasted, because she just doesn't get it.

Even so, she has moments where she is brilliant. And, eventually, it all comes together. In 1999–2000, she has maybe as good a year as anyone has ever had at Connecticut. We win the championship, she's the Final Four MVP, she's a first team All-America. She's on top of the world. She's tough, she's strong, she's got it all going, like a gladiator coming out with blood all over him saying, "Until you kill me, watch out."

For her senior year to go the way it did was a tremendous letdown for all of us.

We can't win without Shea—not after losing Sveta, too. You look back, and you are just so glad things worked out in Philly for those two.

For the rest of us, I feel certain there will be other chances.

SEVEN

When you win your second championship, it puts you in a little bit of a different category. When you win just one, people can write it off as good luck, or maybe a fluke. When you win a second one, they start saying, "Hmmm, he must know what he's doing." And by the time you've won five of them, they've elevated you to some kind of genius level, which is obviously ridiculous. It drives me crazy. All of a sudden I've got all the answers? I don't think so.

Sometimes I read stories that have been written about me and I wonder who it is they are talking about, especially the ones that call me a born leader. They couldn't be further from the truth.

I wasn't a natural leader as a kid. I was a natural follower. I was playing catch-up all the time, trying to keep up with the language and the style and the culture. My son is a natural leader, because from the time he has been ten or eleven years old he walks around like he knows more than anyone else. He has enough confidence in himself to take control of the situation, so people gravitate toward him. Well, when I was his age, I didn't have that luxury. In the first place, I didn't know the language well enough, so I was always so indebted or beholden to all these people for helping me and teaching me. I was always the guy in the back.

The good part about that was it taught me how to be a great team player, and how not to focus on individual rewards. It wasn't really an issue with me since I didn't stand up for myself. I was content to be one of the guys. I didn't strive for anything individual.

When you get older, you realize individual goals aren't bad. In fact, they are quite meaningful if you've worked hard to attain them. Our program is built around playing the ultimate team game, so our players can reap the ultimate individual rewards.

Certainly Nykesha Sales could have received more individual attention if she went elsewhere. Almost any other program in the country would have started her as a freshman, but we had a bunch of veteran players that deserved that honor. Kesha is a gifted offensive player. She has a way of taking the ball and doing things with it that look almost effortless. I love to watch her play.

Off the court, she is one of the most sensitive kids I've ever coached, but she is also one of my all-time favorites. She is just a sweet, sweet kid. That's why the players nicknamed her "Precious," because I rarely yelled at her. I just thought she was one of those kids that wouldn't respond to that.

I probably did her a disservice. I should have been harder on Nykesha when she was here. Maybe I could have changed her personality. She is a little too laid-back.

Kesha is well on her way to setting a new scoring record at Connecticut when, in the second-to-last game of the regular season in her senior year, she tears her Achilles' tendon. It happens on February 21, 1998, against Notre Dame and I am just sick about it.

I'm feeling horrible for Kesha. She only needs two points to become our all-time leading scorer, and now she's done for the year and headed for surgery. Here's a kid who has been so unselfish her entire career, who has sacrificed her own numbers to make the team better, and now she's going to come up short. So I'm talking to Villanova coach Harry Parretta. We play Villanova in our final regular-season game. He agrees to let Nykesha score the first basket of our game. Now I call up Kerry Bascom, who holds our all-time scoring record. I explain to her what we're thinking about doing. "But I won't even consider it if you're not comfortable with this," I tell her. But Kerry is fine with it. I knew she would be. She says, "Coach, you and I both know if Nykesha hadn't gotten hurt, she would have destroyed this record."

Just to cover our bases, we call Big East commissioner Mike Tranghese and tell him what we'd like to do. He signs off on it.

I go to Kesha with the idea, and at first she's hesitant. The last thing she wants is for people to think she cares that much about the record. I say to her, "Please let me do this." She finally agrees.

The game is in Philadelphia. Kesha is in uniform, behind the bleachers. She comes out, and Villanova lets us win the tip, and Rita Williams gets her the ball. She scores an uncontested layup. We then allow Villanova to score a basket uncontested on the other end so they are not at a disadvantage. The crowd goes crazy. They love it.

I figure everyone will understand the spirit in which this decision is made.

I have never been so wrong in my life. The backlash is so

vicious and so ugly and so unfair I can't believe it. And, worst of all, they attack Nykesha for her part in it.

Here's the point I was trying to make. The kid is going to break the record. She gets hurt. Now, let's say she is in line to break Sarah Behn's Big East Conference scoring record. You aren't going to screw around with that. Let's say Kesha is going to break an NCAA record. You don't mess around with that either. You are never going to impact another kid in another program.

But now we're talking about the University of Connecticut. Who cares? It's ours. This program belongs to us—no one else. People come back to me with, "What about the integrity of the game?" Well, I understand that. That is a valid point. But my point is, we play this kid 24 minutes a game for her entire career, because most of the time we are blowing out teams and we don't want to run up the score. Kesha could have scored 3,000 points if I let her.

The part that still mystifies me is that there are about 5,000 people at the game the night we play Villanova. The minute they see and understand what is happening, they all jump to their feet and give her a standing ovation. These are not our fans. These are Villanova fans. Their first instinct is to cheer for this incredible player whom they respect. Now, the next morning, they wake up and read the paper and see the TV and realize what idiots they are. They should have been throwing stuff at her because everyone is saying what a horrible thing it is that has happened.

I don't understand that. The minute people start criticizing me, the incident becomes a lightning rod for men versus women, and how they approach sports, and how a men's program would never do that. Oh really? That's not how I remember it. Seems to me I remember Green Bay Packers quarterback Brett Favre allowing himself to be tackled so Michael Strahan could have the sack record. That was fine, because it was Brett Favre, this bastion of pro football, so the whole thing died down after three days. I don't remember George Will weighing in on that one, do you?

I realize in the wake of the controversy how truly naive I was. I thought I could have a logical discussion with people about issues. I thought I could say, "Can't you see my point of view?" Some can, but there's another half that can't see your point of view, and never will. It's taken me a very long time to come to grips with that—in everything. I'm talking coaching, recruiting, my personal life, and business. As much as you want to believe, "Well, of course they will consider my side of it," some people won't. They don't want to see it.

You also have to get used to the idea that some people are never going to like you, either. The first year we go to the Final Four in 1991, I get a stack of congratulatory mail that fills up my office. But after we win the national championship in April of 2004, I can fit the number of letters I get in one drawer. Nobody wants us to win anymore. That's just the way it goes.

The person I feel the worst for is Nykesha Sales. None of it is her idea. She's not the kind of kid that gets off on individual glory. But I talk her into it, and then the whole thing blows up. I feel badly when I see Kesha quoted that sometimes she worries it's the only thing she'll be remembered for. That is just absurd. She is one of the great college players of her time. She is a WNBA star. If that is all people remember her for, they are not paying attention.

I am very, very disappointed in how the whole Nykesha Sales event was handled. I don't understand why every time something happens, it's necessary to treat it like the event of the century and to have it dissected and examined to death by everyone. After we let Kesha score that layup, it seems as though everyone in the country feels this need to step up to the podium and voice their opinion on it. And God forbid there is any gray area in discussing it. Either it was the best or the worst—nothing in between.

Don't they understand that life is gray? Coaches have a tendency to live in that black-and-white world, too. We tend to say, "No, you're doing that wrong," but the truth is that you could be doing it wrong and moving toward doing it right. It's conceivable you could be passing through that gray area. What is there in life that you can say, "That's wrong and it will always be wrong," or "That's right, and it will be always right"?

When Mets pitcher Pedro Martinez throws a one-hitter and strikes out fourteen batters, that doesn't make him the best pitcher there is. That doesn't make him the surefire Cy Young winner. Treat the event for what it is. What it means is that when Pedro Martinez has his stuff he's as good as anybody.

The truth is, most of us are not the best or the worst. We're somewhere in the middle. We may have moments of brilliance and, every once in a while, moments that land us in the gutter. The trick is not to wallow in the gutter so long that you can't get out. The trick is also not to ever get so delusional that you believe you are going to stay on top forever, because that won't happen either.

I have my share of critics. They all come out of the woodwork after the thing with Nykesha, and they reappear during the 2003 season. We are in the midst of the longest winning streak in women's college basketball history when we lose to Villanova. We play badly. I'm not happy.

———

After the game, I'm addressing the media, as I always do. There's a student reporter there named Amanda Allnutt. She works for the UConn paper. She is a kid who has been a sore spot with our players for most of the season. They don't like her line of questioning. They find her to be very negative— a pretty difficult thing to do when the team you are covering hasn't lost a game in almost two years. She bugs me a little bit, too.

So here I am, talking about this loss to Villanova, and how my team will react to it. I start to say, "Well, we'll either bounce back, or we'll lose in the first round of the NCAA tournament." Before I can finish, she interrupts me. She says, "What are you going to do to make sure that doesn't happen?"

Now I'm pissed off. We've lost one game—one game— and she wants me to guarantee it will never happen again? How the hell am I supposed to do that? So I snap at her. I say, "You ask a lot of questions that really piss me off, and you're too young to ask those kinds of questions. Older guys can ask questions like that, but not you. You're too young. It's just a goddamned game. It's not the end of the world. But every question you ask is like we should cancel the season because we just lost. Relax."

I know right away I've screwed up. She asks a couple more questions, and I pull back a little bit and I answer them. I'm trying to turn this into a lighthearted sparring match, but it's not working.

Of course, the only part ESPN shows on *SportsCenter* is the first exchange. It makes me look like some ass who can't handle losing and picks on a student reporter because of it.

I regret what happened with Amanda Allnutt. I never should have berated her like that in front of everybody. What

I should have done is waited until the end of the press conference, motioned her aside, and expressed my displeasure privately. It is a mistake on my part to take her on in front of all the other journalists. If I could do it over, I would do it differently. She is a student reporter who was trying to do her job, and I lost my patience with her.

Naturally, the sound bite on *SportsCenter* causes a big commotion. I'm getting killed. What are you going to do? Nobody wants to hear my side of it.

The day after it happens, I get a phone call from Michigan State men's coach Tom Izzo. Now, I don't know him at all. He sees the clip on ESPN and he calls to bust me. He says, "You win 70 straight games, and then you finally lose one, and this is what you get? I thought it was only like this up here at Michigan State when you don't make it to the Final Four." We have a good laugh. I really appreciate the phone call.

Obviously I've got to make things right with Amanda. The next few press conferences after our exchange, she doesn't ask any questions. She's gun-shy. I've scared her half to death. She doesn't say a thing. Finally, during one of our press conferences, I say, "Don't you have any questions?" She says, "No, not really." I tell her, "Don't stop doing your job because of me. I said what I needed to say. It's over with." She nods her head. I'm looking at her and I realize, "Hell, she's just a kid."

I can't fix what happened between Amanda Allnutt and me. The damage is done. In that situation, you have to be big enough to say, "I'm sorry. I blew it."

Of course, people who didn't like me in the first place are having a great time with it. They love it. Sometimes when you have some of those dark days, you say to yourself, "I don't need this. I should get out of here."

I've never seriously considered leaving Connecticut. Of course, it's not like I've been inundated with offers or anything. These days, I make too much money, and everyone assumes I'm not leaving. But you'd think ten years ago I might get one offer. Maybe this is the only place in the country where they like me. Maybe everyone else in the country is saying, "You can keep that dope. We don't want him out here."

What else would I do? Part of me would love to give the men's game a try. I think it's probably too late for me, now that I've hit fifty years old, but strictly from a competitive standpoint, I really, really, really would love to sit across the sidelines from some of the guys I've never coached against but have tremendous respect for, like Phil Martelli, like Bobby Knight, like Roy Williams. Give me a level playing field, and let me see if I can adjust to that game. Part of me would love to do that.

Then there's another part of me that despises the entire culture. You can't get guys to play hard anymore. If a player jogs, the coaches clap, because it passes for working hard. If a guy makes an attempt to do something, it's cause for celebration. What happened to doing your job because you're supposed to? It's the culture. From the time those kids are thirteen, someone is kissing their ass and telling them how great they are. So the entitlement level is so high that coaches have to worry almost more about staying on their star's good side so they don't turn on them, because they're so used to having their way. I'm not sure I'd want any part of that. Of course, it's not like I've turned down all these opportunities. No one has ever offered me a men's job.

————

The other thing about the men's game is when someone makes a good offensive play they act like they have won the lottery.

I love watching Richard Hamilton play. He went to UConn and now he plays for the Detroit Pistons. He's a very nice kid, and better yet, he's a Philly guy. His team, the Pistons, won the 2004 NBA championship, and Richard was a big reason why.

Nine different announcers went absolutely berserk every time Richard got on the floor and moved without the ball. He's very good at it, but they were acting like they'd never seen it before. The fact that so few people in the NBA game do an essential skill is bizarre. It is absolutely bizarre. It would be like in baseball saying, "Wow, look at Alex Rodriguez pick up that ball and turn the double play." Well, that's what he gets paid to do. But in pro basketball, anyway, basketball has become something other than it was intended to be.

Maybe I'm too old-fashioned. I don't accept the way they play the game today. There's nothing wrong with individualism. Elgin Baylor certainly was one. Michael Jordan was an individualist, and so, clearly, was Wilt Chamberlain. But there is still a time and a place for a cut and a pass and a screen and helping your teammate get open, something that may not show up in the box score. Like in baseball, when someone moves the runner over. How does that get you on *SportsCenter*? It doesn't. It just proves you are a good teammate.

I watch the Connecticut men play all the time, but I watch from home. It's too hard to go to the games, because people come up and start talking to you, and you end up missing huge chunks of the game. What I like is how the women's team and the men's team get along so well. There is a really nice camaraderie there. Sue Bird was telling me the other day she loves it that Ray Allen is in Seattle where she is playing, so they can support each other.

A lot has been made of my relationship—or lack of relationship—with UConn men's coach Jim Calhoun. The stuff that goes on between Jim and me isn't that much different than what goes on at other schools. But we've both been national champions, so people really pay attention to us.

Someone once told me the biggest mistake we made was getting successful before the football team and the men's basketball team did, because now everyone resents us. I think there's some truth to that. Because no matter how much everyone at the university wants to hold you up as a model and say, "Hey, look what the women have done!" what they are really saying is, "Geez, I wish our football and basketball programs were at that level."

I'm glad we're at a school where all the teams are national contenders. Having said that, no matter where you are, there are always little competitions within schools. Programs vie for who is getting the most money, the most attention, and all that other stuff. I guarantee you there aren't a handful of women's basketball coaches in America who have a great relationship with their men's coach—unless they are losing. Every coach of the women's team who is just okay, or losing, will have the support of the men's program. The men's coach is going to say, "Oh, she's a great kid and she works so hard. I help her any way I can." But the minute that women's team goes to the tournament seven times in a row, and starts getting to the Final Four, and the men's team doesn't, then see what happens.

Jim Calhoun and I do a lot of things together for the

school. It's been okay. We just travel in different circles. We don't really have that much in common. I am happy when the men succeed. It's good for us.

But somehow people want to pit us against each other. I was at a black-tie event for Coaches vs. Cancer a few years ago. Calhoun and I were hosting the event together at the Basketball Hall of Fame in Springfield, Massachusetts. I am going around trying to hobnob with everyone, and I haven't had anything to eat, and I start to feel a little nauseous.

I'm not that sharp. I don't feel that good, so I'm not paying enough attention. I'm up on stage talking and I crack a couple of jokes, and people take offense to it. They think it's a cancer event and nothing should be funny.

Before the dinner, there had been an article in the paper saying that this big change had come over Jim Calhoun, that he was a kinder, gentler coach. I make a comment saying, "You know, I've been reading all this stuff about the kinder, gentler Coach Calhoun, and let me tell you something. Come a month from now, after practice starts, he'll be an ass like the rest of us."

I should have known better. I was trying to make a joke, but nobody thinks anything I say about Jim Calhoun is funny. Somewhere along the way, people have decided Jim and I are mortal enemies and there is this heated competition between us. Really? Whenever people say there's tension between us, it always lumps the two of us together. Even our former school president, Harry Hartley, insinuated it was mutual. He told *Sports Illustrated* there was "dynamic tension" between the two of us. Well, where did that come from? I've never felt slighted by anything that's happened with the men's program. It only enhances what we're doing. I think a lot of that tension is one-sided.

Anyhow, after I make my little comments about Jim, a week or so after the dinner it gets back to me that someone is spreading the word I called Jim an ass at a public event. Now, Jim was there. He heard it himself, and he knew the context of it, and he never said anything to me, nor did he seem bothered by it. But that doesn't matter. It quickly turns into, "There goes the women's coach up there cracking jokes at an event that's not supposed to be funny."

Now, you've got to remember there's a small Jim Calhoun contingent attending the dinner, and a small Geno Auriemma contingent attending the dinner, and the other 90 percent of the people are there because they love both of our programs and they want to donate their time and money to a good cause.

Someone gets a bug up their rear end and decides, "I'm going to make an issue of this." I have no idea what Jim thought. He never said anything to me about it. The whole incident is about to hit the papers until everyone realizes there isn't much of a story.

I learn a lesson that night. I am stupid for trying to have fun like that, because it isn't my crowd. Know your audience. I won't make that mistake again.

I just wish people would stop looking for trouble between us.

A lot of women's coaches badger their athletic director to be paid the same as the men's coach. Their feeling is, "I do the same job as the men's basketball coach, therefore I want the same money." Bullshit. You don't do the same job. They are two different animals. I have never compared myself to Jim Calhoun, financially or otherwise. When my contract has been up, I've compared myself to other women's basketball coaches.

I don't like getting into the money thing. It bothers me. If I am already the highest-paid women's basketball coach in the country, then when my contract is up, what is fair to pay me? When do you get "what is mine" and when do you cross that line to the point where you are just being a greedy son of a bitch? When there's a market out there, and fifteen people are making what you are making, and you want to put yourself above that group, that's one thing. But what if there is nobody out there making what you are making? Then how do you decide what to ask for? You have to say to your athletic director, in my case Jeff Hathaway, "Hey, Jeff, what do you think is fair?" He throws out a number and I say, "Fine."

I don't know how Jim Calhoun does it. I don't care. I'm tired of talking about him, to tell you the truth. We've made it work here. We don't have to be best friends—and we're not. We both work here. We both support the university. That's all I'm going to say about it.

Besides, I don't think either one of us is going anywhere.

I have heard from the WNBA a few times, but I haven't really been tempted to do that. I don't like the pro game nearly as much as I like watching the college players.

One day Ernie Grunfeld, who was the general manager for the New York Knicks and the New York Liberty at the time, calls me up. He says, "We want to hire you to coach our women." Jeff Van Gundy is the Knicks' coach, and he is making around $3 million, which makes him one of the lowest-paid coaches in the league. You figure he coaches about 100 games a season—82 in the regular season and, if he's lucky, some playoff games. The WNBA is only about 50 games a season. So I say to Ernie, "Okay, the WNBA plays about half the schedule that the NBA plays, so just pay me half of Jeff's salary and I'll come." Ernie just laughs at me.

He says, "You're out of your damned mind," and I say, "I know. I know."

The one goal I have left is to be the coach of the Olympic team. I don't know if that's something that will ever come about, but I'd like a crack at it. I've coached at almost every level of USA Basketball. But the circumstances surrounding the Olympics are different than they used to be.

For instance, in order to coach the 1996 Olympic team, Tara VanDerveer had to take a year off from Stanford. I'm not sure that's something I would do. In 2000, they were looking for the same kind of commitment, so they got Nell Fortner, who had only been at Purdue one year, to take it. It's easy to leave a program after one year, because you haven't established a real connection yet. Obviously my roots run pretty deep here at Connecticut.

I think, too, the WNBA is a big factor now. I get a sense that from now on, the Olympic coach will be chosen from the WNBA coaches. They are the "pros," and they coach the best and most experienced players, so I have a feeling that is the new trend.

I still remember my first USA Basketball event. It is the Olympic Sports Festival in San Antonio in 1993. We walk into the opening ceremonies at the Alamodome and there are 60,000 people in there and I'm thinking, "Geez, this must be what it's like to coach football. This is unbelievable." It is an amazing rush.

The other moment that stands out is when I am coaching the USA Junior National Team in Argentina in 2000. At the time, I'm thinking it's a lark. We play Argentina, then Mexico, then all of a sudden we're in the semifinals and we're playing Brazil, and they're really, really good. They are much better than I expect, and we do beat them, but then we are getting ready to play Cuba for the gold medal. I walk in and I see the poles where they put the flags of the winning country at the end of the day and then all of a sudden I am scared shitless. All of a sudden I think to myself, "What the hell am I going to do if we lose?" It's an unbelievable pressure situation, because everyone knows you can't lose if you are the United States and you are playing basketball.

It's funny, but I didn't feel the same way when I was an Olympic assistant in Sydney. Maybe it's because I knew we were going to win. It was almost impossible to imagine us not winning in that situation. I did love watching them put the gold medals around our players' necks, and I always love it when they play the national anthem. It affects me a little more, I guess, because I wasn't born here, and I've always put a tremendous value on representing your country.

I become an American citizen while I am coaching at Connecticut. The reason I do it is because we go to Italy to play in 1994 with Rebecca Lobo's group, and I don't want to go in there with an Italian passport. I start thinking, "What if they stop me and say, 'Yo, bud. You know that two-year service requirement in the military that we have? You haven't done that yet.'" That scares me enough to go down to the courthouse and take the naturalization test.

I wish they would make that citizenship test harder. I wish they'd require you to have some working knowledge of how the government operates. I wish they would ask us what it means to be an American. It's too easy. It's almost like getting your driver's license.

My naturalization ceremony is the worst. It is in Hartford, Connecticut, and we all just stand there while some guy reads my name off a piece of paper.

My mother's ceremony is really cool, though. She does it

in 1976, on the two hundredth anniversary of the Constitution, in Philadelphia. They have it at the old Independence Hall. She is nervous for a month. She is saying Georg-a Washington and Abraham-a Lincoln every ten minutes. I think she feels as long as she knows those two guys, she'll be okay.

My father never becomes an American citizen. I remember one summer when the two of us are working construction together in Norristown for a friend of his. We are helping to put up an office building. He says to me, "The Republicans are killing this country." I answer him, "How you do know? You can't even spell 'Republican.'" He just keeps railing on. His friends at the Italian club have told him Ronald Reagan is a bad man, so he hates Reagan, and he's just waiting for Mussolini to come back any day now and take over America.

After my dad's brothers come over to this country, and my dad is alone in Italy, he hooks up with some guys and he goes around singing all these fascist songs. He is delayed being allowed into America because of it. I'm sure the U.S. government takes one look at him and says, "We're not letting this nut in."

I ask my mother once about it and she says, "Oh, you know your father. He had a big mouth. He didn't know when to keep quiet." I laugh out loud, because I know exactly what she is saying. One day, when I am a teenager, my dad is hosing down our garage door and he starts singing all these Italian fight songs from the war. It's 1968, and my mother is looking around worrying that someone might hear him. I tell her, "Don't worry. They'll just think he's just another crazy Italian guy."

Even so, my father loved this country. He was proud of his

row home, which was so close to the guy next door that when he flushed the toilet, you knew about it. He loved his little house and his tiny backyard, where we hung all the clothes because we didn't have a dryer.

At the end of our little piece of yard, he had a garden, where he grew parsley, onions, tomatoes, cucumbers, basil, and carrots. He'd tend to it, weed it, and make sure we had fresh vegetables all summer to eat.

After a few years, he put a little aluminum porch on the back of the house. He'd go out there, sit back, have a cigarette, and convince himself he was in heaven. He would take a big, deep, satisfied sigh and say, "This is my life. This is my garden, this is my yard, this is my dog."

We had a great dog. His name was Rocky, because we got him in 1976, the year the movie came out starring Sylvester Stallone. Rocky ate only Italian food. He'd look at dog food and spit it out. He ate everything we ate. He finally died of high cholesterol.

My father loved that dog. He loved to watch him run around the back of his little yard.

The only time my dad strayed too far from his house was to get dressed and walk down to the Italian club. He'd walk straight through the worst part of town carrying a wallet full of money he didn't need. We never got him to use a check or a credit card. He always just had a big wad of money he was never going to spend.

He would never have believed what Kathy and I did a year or so after he died. We are talking about a way we can give back to the University of Connecticut, and after I sign my first big contract with Nike, we decide to make a donation to the library.

I've always admired Penn State football coach Joe Paterno

and former Indiana basketball coach Bob Knight for the generosity they showed their schools. They are always working to make the university a better situation for everybody—not just the athletes.

Both Kathy and I feel that if someone wants to look at me as a role model, then what I'd like to impress upon them is that if you enjoy school and enjoy basketball, the way to keep enjoying both is to make sure our academic structure is second to none. I choose the library to make my point. I make a $125,000 donation. My mom can't read or write, and my dad barely made it through the fourth grade. Meanwhile, my daughter Alysa has read more books by the age of seventeen than just about anyone I've ever met.

If anyone ever asked me the one thing that stands out in my life, it would be the ability to read and write. It's the one thing my parents couldn't do, and it's the only thing my daughter can't live without.

We don't want our names attached to the donation. We just want to do it quietly. But Mark Emmert, who used to be our provost, and is now the president at the University of Washington, wants to acknowledge it, because he is hoping it will spur on other people to give. We say fine. They have a little plaque inside the library that says the Auriemma Family Reading Room. I'm pretty sure my girls don't ever go in there. I think that would be a little too weird for them. They do an excellent job of keeping the fact that they are Geno Auriemma's daughters separate from the fact that they are UConn students.

Sometimes that is a challenge. The bigger our program gets, the bigger we get. Sometimes it seems Connecticut women's basketball has become almost larger than life, and it becomes difficult, especially if you are like me and you are convinced you are going to fail at any moment.

I read something really cool once. Someone was doing a story on Cary Grant, the actor. They wrote, "Everyone wants to be Cary Grant, including Cary Grant." He used to say all the time, "I wish I was me." He was a big star with the talent to pull it off, and he was comfortable with who he was, but even he knew nobody was that great.

You have to figure out what you can live with. You have to decide what makes you happy. Phil Martelli, who is one of my best friends, is a big star in Philadelphia, especially after taking St. Joe's to the Elite Eight in 2004. He is the number one candidate for the Ohio State job after that, but he doesn't want it. He wants to stay in Philly. He tells Ohio State and its $800,000 salary and its glamour and its Big Ten cachet no because he won't leave Philadelphia.

He handles himself really well in front of people. I'm not so good at it. The assumption is you should be able to handle the constant attention. It supposedly "comes with the territory." But if you ask most coaches, they didn't set out to make all this money or get all this notoriety. They just love to coach, and the rest comes along with it. So I've got to deal with having people watch me all the time.

I've never gotten used to it—especially during a game. Our locker room used to be down the other end of Gampel Pavilion. When we walked out of the locker room toward our bench, we used to have to walk all the way across the court. I hated walking across that court. I always felt like I was naked. Everyone is looking at you. I used to grab either Jamelle or Tonya just before we'd go out there and strike up a conversation with them, usually about nothing. I'd make things up, just so they would walk with me and I wouldn't have to do it alone. After a while, they caught on. One night, I grab Jamelle and start blabbering to her about nothing, and she turns to Tonya and says, "Here he goes again. He's using me."

I don't know why I hate walking across that court so much. I guess I don't want anyone thinking, "Look at that guy. Who the hell does he think he is? What makes him think he's so damned important?"

Coaching is a very difficult trade to measure. It's not like the bricklayers I worked with as a kid. They were like surgeons. They'd take the bricks, one at a time, and use their spade, their trough, and their hammer to make that brick fit exactly where it is supposed to go. They'd do that all day, brick by brick, and when they were done, they'd stand back and look at it and say, "That is my work. I'm really proud of it." Imagine being one of the workers who helped build those spectacular cathedrals in the Middle Ages. They had a tangible reward at the end of their job.

As a basketball coach, you really don't have that opportunity. You look back on your season and say, "Okay, we are 39–0, we won a national championship," or "We are 37–1 and won a national championship." And . . . what? That means you're good? I guess.

The problem is you start to look at other things. You start saying, "I wish I could have influenced this kid this way," or "I wish I could have taken this kid." After the Villanova loss, I remember thinking, "Why didn't I prepare us better?" You do that enough and it probably isn't healthy. That's the way I've always been, someone who can't fully enjoy success. I'm not too thrilled with myself that I can't reflect on my accomplishments and gain more satisfaction from them.

But I'm also not too thrilled with how people react when

you don't do things exactly the way they would like you to do them. I've had that happen with writers. They write something about me and I say, "That son of a bitch, I thought he was my friend," but then you learn that writers aren't your friends. They can't be. They have decisions to make based on what is going on, and they look at it and they say, "Should I go this way, or that way?" and if their integrity tells them, "I have to write this," they do. And me, being a little thin-skinned, I get on the phone and say, "What the hell are you doing?"

It happens a lot during the whole Nykesha Sales incident. The local writers are killing me, these guys who I call friends. Mike DiMauro, who is a columnist for the *New London Day*, writes some stuff that really bothers me. I say to him, "Mike, you don't understand," and I don't talk to him for a few days. But then I get over it.

The one that really ticks me off during that whole thing is Jeff Jacobs of the *Hartford Courant*. I don't talk to him for six months after he rips me in the paper for letting Nykesha score that layup. His story isn't just a differing opinion. His story is sarcastic and demeaning—not just to me, but to Kesha. He calls her "Soupy Sales." He is ridiculing her for a decision I made. I think Jeff is a great writer. He also writes for the number one paper in Connecticut, and obviously that means I have to deal with him, because if I don't, it causes other problems. At the time the controversy is going on, I swear I'll never talk to him again. He knew—and so did I— that I couldn't do that. I'm the coach at the University of Connecticut. I have to talk to him.

But I wait until August before I do. I finally call him up and say, "Look, I know you've been trying to reach me. Let's clear the air." It is pretty tense for a while, but we've both said our thing and moved on.

While all of that is going on, my assistants are really supportive. They circle the wagons. I tell them, "See? This is what you have to look forward to when you are a head coach."

When I do leave Connecticut, which I don't have any plans to do in the immediate future, most people assume Chris Dailey will be the next head coach. I'm not sure she wants it. I've talked to her about it, and I don't know if at this point in her life she's interested in being a head coach. I know Jamelle Elliott would be interested, and I think she'd be perfect.

I'm so lucky to have Jamelle on my staff. Sometimes assistants are too close to the situation and they always take your side. Sometimes you resent them because they always take the players' side. But here's the unique thing about Jamelle. She can walk into my office, or walk into a staff meeting before we meet with the players, and say from experience, "This is what's going on. You may not know this, or you probably do know this and don't want to admit it, but here's the situation and you're dead wrong, and you better do something about it."

CD will do that, too, but it's different. She'll tell me when she thinks I'm out of line. But that's coming from one professional to another and it doesn't hold the same weight as one of your players who was on the other end of things. Jamelle can say with authority, "Coach, I remember when you came in and said this or did that, and you may have forgotten, but here's how we felt about this after you did that, so you need to fix it."

I have a lot of ex-players out there coaching. If you had

---

told me back in college that Jen Rizzotti would be a head coach, I'd tell you, "You're nuts." It didn't fit her personality. But she's turned out to be a helluva coach at Hartford. Tamika Williams is an assistant at Ohio State, Shea Ralph is an assistant at Pittsburgh and Paige Sauer is an assistant at Fairfield, and Stacy Hansmeyer is an assistant at Oklahoma, and Carla Berube is the head coach at Tufts, and Wendy Davis is the head coach at Western New England. I'm proud of all of them. They are out there spreading the gospel, so to speak, of how we do things.

We're pretty big at keeping things in the family, but I also think you have to be careful about that. You don't want to eat yourself alive. You don't want, all of a sudden, for the only ideas to be your own. You don't want it to be that you throw stuff at people and they throw you back the same stuff. Bringing someone in from the outside is a good idea. I'm not saying a head coach, necessarily, but if we ever had an opening for an assistant, you'd like to think about getting a person from the outside.

Of course, the problem with that is if Shea calls and says, "Coach, I really want that job," how are you going to say no? If Stacy Hansmeyer says, "I really want to come back to Connecticut," what would I say? But here's the thing: they will never do that. They will never ask.

Everybody has his or her own calendar when it's time to go. Tonya seriously considered the Boston University job a couple of years ago. She's from Boston, and she spoke to Nicole Wolff's dad, Dennis, who is the men's coach there. She starts thinking, "Wow, that would be cool, to go home to Boston," but then, right or wrong, reality sets in. Then she starts thinking, "Financially, it's only a little bit more than I'm making here. Number two, I'd have to live an hour away from campus because it's so expensive in the city. Number three, I'll have to leave Connecticut, where I have tremendous responsibility, where I coach in front of a sellout crowd every night, where we have a private chartered plane, where we have the best athletes in the country. I'm going to trade that for a place where there are four hundred people in the stands on a good night, where you have to bus to upstate Maine for your games, where nobody really cares about women's basketball?"

I admire my assistants more than I can ever tell you. I think their job is as tough as anything I've ever seen. It's so hard for them to have a life outside of our program. They work fourteen-hour days, they work weekends, and they are traveling, and God forbid they might want to settle down and have a family.

Let's say you are a minority woman who is twenty-five or twenty-six years old. You had a great playing career. You're bright and you're articulate, like Jamelle and Tonya. Do you know how many opportunities you could have? Thousands. Business, entertainment, sales, you name it. They could make a ton of money and have a nice lifestyle. So they look in the mirror, and they say, "Why am I coaching? Why do I need this crap?" It's because they love the game.

That's why we all do it: because we love the game.

EIGHT

There are some gifts in life that you learn to appreciate almost immediately.

When Diana Taurasi signs with Connecticut, I know she is one of those gifts.

Sometimes, when you recruit a top player, you really don't know how it's going to go until the final days. I know that's how I should feel with Diana, because she's the most highly sought-after player in the country. But I feel like we have the inside track after the first phone call.

My assistants aren't as sure. They have a strong sense that UCLA, which is half an hour from her house, is the front-runner.

That may have been true. All I know is the first time I talk to Diana we just click. I talk to her very pointedly, and she talks to me the same way. There is no bullshit, no sickly-sweet "Oh, you're the greatest" kind of nonsense. Obviously Diana is a terrific player. The first time I see her, I know. She has it all—the talent, the confidence, the presence, the toughness. She scores 3,047 points for Don Lugo High

School in Chino, California. I watch her play at an AAU game, and she is amazing.

So I call her up to let her know we are interested, and at first she sounds kind of blasé. Bored, even. She is the best player in the country and she's getting calls from absolutely everybody. I tell her a little bit about our program, and then I say, "Diana, if you work really hard, and do what we ask of you, you have a chance to be really good."

All of a sudden, it's like a light switches on. Suddenly she becomes very animated and conversational. She starts asking me all sorts of questions about Connecticut. Later, Diana tells me she is tired of everyone telling her how great she is and how special she is. This is a kid from California who could turn around tomorrow, sign with UCLA, and start as a freshman. In fact, she probably could start anywhere—except Connecticut. "Coach," she tells me later, "you were the first person who didn't guarantee me everything. You were the first person who said I'd have to work to be good."

We go for the home visit, and it goes very well. Dee's parents are immigrants. Her father, Mario, was born in Italy, in a village not unlike mine. Lili, her mother, was born in Argentina, and met her future husband when his family moved there when he was a young boy. Just like my parents, the Taurasis speak in broken English. Their primary language at home is Spanish.

As I'm talking to Dee, I realize we have gone through some of the same experiences. When your parents are in a new country, and they don't know the language very well, you find yourself doing things for them most kids don't have to do. Dee talks about having to help pay the bills, to make sure her parents aren't getting cheated, having to order the meals in a restaurant because her parents can't read the menu. Things like that sometimes can be a little embarrassing when you are a kid, because everything embarrasses you anyway. Just like me, she had responsibilities most kids her age didn't have to contend with.

I understand exactly what she is talking about. I can still remember as a little boy in Norristown walking through town paying the bills for my parents. They don't have a credit card or a checking account. They hand me these envelopes with wads of cash inside, and send me on my way. So I walk around the corner to the bank to pay our mortgage, then over to the electric company to pay our lighting bill, then to the corner market to pay for our groceries.

Her parents relate to these stories. It is a time and a place and a culture they identify with. I can see they like me, but Dee's mother still doesn't understand why her daughter needs to go all the way to the other side of the country to play basketball. She has developed a comfort level in her community in California, and she can't imagine leaving that safe environment.

This is something I understand as well. My father never leaves Norristown after he moves here from Italy. He stays in the very first house he bought, right up until the day he dies. He learns to drive only when he is fifty-five years old, and the only place he ever goes is to the Italian club, to play cards with his Italian friends. If he had ever moved, he would have had to learn a whole new way, and that was just going to ruin everything.

I always used to joke with my brother and sister it was lucky my father wasn't a world leader, because if anyone ever wanted to assassinate him, it would have been the easiest thing. He did the same thing every day. He took the same route to where he was going and never wavered from his routine. He also walked around with a bunch of cash. He never spent any of it, but there were always big wads of bills tucked carefully into his wallet.

My father never understood how this coaching stuff works. I remember back in the early nineties, I was buying a house, and I was talking with him about how expensive they were in the Connecticut area, and he says to me, "Well, how are you going to pay for this house?" I tell him, "Well, my contract is pretty good. It will help me pay for it." He cannot understand this. He bought his house for $13,000 and paid it off, just like that. I'm about to buy a house for $200,000, and I'm only making about $55,000 at the time, and he can't make the math work.

He says to me, "What do you mean, a contract?" I explain to him that they pay me to coach my team, and we agree on a number of years ahead of time for how long I will be at the school. He says to me, "But what happens when there are no more games?" I say to him, "What do you mean?" He says, "What happens when they decide not to play the games anymore?" I finally realize what he's getting at. That's what happened to him. He worked in a factory for twenty-five years. One day they called him in and told him, "We're closing the factory. We don't need you anymore." They stopped making the bricks. They stopped needing my dad. So he figures Connecticut is going to walk in one day and say, "Okay, you can go. There are no more games." I try to tell him that's not going to happen, but he doesn't believe me.

I tell stories just like that one to the Taurasi family. They tell me their own stories. I feel a real connection to these people.

On my home visit, we talk all day. I get to Diana's house at eleven o'clock in the morning, and I don't leave until nine o'clock that night. I really like her parents. I think they like me, too, but I know it is going to be very difficult for Lili, Dee's mother, if she comes to Connecticut. She wants her to stay home and go to UCLA, so they can see her all the time. If I had a dollar for every time Lili says, "It's just that Connecticut is so far away," I'd be swimming in cash.

People made a big deal about my connection with Dee's parents, because of our common experiences coming to this country and trying to make a go of it. There's no question that gave us all a comfort level that other people may not have had. But I could have dinner with Diana's mother and father every day for six months, and if we didn't have the kind of basketball program we had, it wouldn't have made any difference. We wouldn't have gotten her. Did I use where her family was from as a building block? Of course I did. But just because we are all immigrants does not mean you are automatically going to become best friends.

It becomes pretty apparent Dee's decision will come down to UCLA and us. Stanford doesn't even recruit her. Dee says it's because her grades aren't good enough.

I can't stop thinking about Diana Taurasi. We are in our office, and I look at my watch, and it's 10:20 a.m. That means it's 7:20 a.m. on the West Coast. I tell my staff, "Let's call Diana. We know she leaves for school around 7:30, so let's get to her before she leaves." We know when she eats lunch. We know what time she practices. We know what time she comes home and goes to the beach for a pickup game. We know everything.

The Taurasis come for Dee's official visit. I take them to dinner at my home. I find a bottle of Italian wine with the Taurasi label on it, and I pour them a glass.

When Dee visits our campus, Shea Ralph takes her

around. Dee is just so impressed with Shea, how tough she is, how nice she is, how loyal she is. Shea tells her playing at Connecticut was the best decision she made in her life. "But it's not going to be easy," she warns Dee.

Dee already knows that. That's why she comes. She isn't looking for something easy. It had already been too easy for too long. Everything she does is perfect. She can score at will. Nobody ever challenges her, on or off the court. It's far too much of, "Whatever you want, Diana. You're the best, Diana."

Diana also likes the challenge of playing for Connecticut. By this point, we're among the elite programs in the country, and it would be easy to look at our roster, see all our talent, and say, "There's no room for me there." A lot of players look at our team as unreachable. In fact, a lot of good players are afraid to come to Connecticut, because they have doubts they are good enough. But Diana looks at it the opposite way. She sees a roster that has Sue Bird, Swin Cash, Shea Ralph, Svetlana Abrosimova, and Asjha Jones on it and says, "That's where I want to be. I want to play with the best. I want to be the best."

We have won our second national championship the season before that, beating Tennessee in Philadelphia. We've already signed Diana. I am holding the Sears Trophy up in the ballroom and I look out at the crowd, and I see a couple of my ex-players, and then I see Dee. She is smiling. She can't wait to get here.

When she does, I sit her down like all of my top players, and I ask her what she wants to be, just like I had done with Rebecca and Nykesha and Sue Bird. Dee wants to be the best—it's really that simple.

I say something to her I have never said to anyone else: I

tell her, "If you come to Connecticut and do what I tell you to do, you're going to be the best player who ever played this game."

She looks right at me. She doesn't blink. She believes me, because she's already thought of that herself.

So Dee commits to Connecticut, and we get her here, and she's very strong-willed. She's very, very confident and very composed, and that is her strength, but maybe her weakness, too. I ask her what number she wants to wear and she says, "00." I tell her, "You want to wear 00? Then you're an idiot. Nobody wears 00 in college. That's just a way of drawing attention to yourself. Pick a real number."

She thinks about it for a second, and then she says, "Okay. I'll wear number 1." Now I'm getting pissed. I say to her, "You are not wearing number 1. Nobody is wearing number 1. You haven't done anything to earn the right to wear number 1."

Now she's ticked off. She's giving me this song and dance about why she's good enough for it, but I'm not budging. I tell her, "Look, pick number 3."

She says, "Why?" I say, "Because if you do this right, if you do what I tell you, then you are going to be the Babe Ruth of women's basketball."

Now, this is how I get myself in trouble. I see all this potential in Diana, and I set these incredibly lofty goals for her, and then I say to myself, "There's no way anyone can be as good as I think she is." I'm starting to doubt my strategy. I start worrying. "I know she's really good, but will she understand how hard it's going to be to get to the next level?" Just because Shea Ralph and Rebecca Lobo responded, it doesn't guarantee Diana Taurasi will.

I make it very, very difficult for the good players. Shea

warned her. I challenge them, and I challenge them again. Because, for most of them, it's the first time anyone *has* challenged them. They don't get it from their peers or their coaches in school. Nobody gets after them the way I do.

I've set the bar so high for Diana, I feel like I have to warn her. I tell her, "Look, this isn't going to be any fun. This isn't going to be like, 'Okay, I'm going to Connecticut, here I am, Coach, when am I going to be a first team All-America like you said?'" I tell her, "I'm banking on the fact you are going to go with the program I am laying out for you."

Diana does do that—eventually. But we have some very stormy times before we get to that point. Her first year, in particular, is really rocky at times.

For starters, Dee is used to doing whatever she feels like doing out on the court. She loves to freelance. She feels like she can score at will at any time, so why should she go through all these screens and cuts and passes when she can just take it to the hoop and get two points whenever she wants?

And then there are her passes. She loves to fire these no-look passes to our players. She thinks nothing of driving the lane, then throwing this bullet over her right shoulder and expecting one of the kids on the baseline to catch it. Well, the problem is the kids don't catch them. I stop practice, blow the whistle, and say, "What the hell was that?" and she looks right back at me and says, "She should have been looking."

No. Wrong answer. Like I tell my players all the time, a good pass is one that gets caught and results in a score. Anything else is a lousy pass. We went through this with Svetlana, too. She'd try to make these impossible passes, and when the ball bounced off someone's head she'd put her hands up in disgust. I'd say to her, "What do you think you are doing?" She'd answer me in her broken English with, "She no cut." I'd say to her, "What do you mean she no cut? You are supposed to get her the ball in a place where she can catch it. If you don't, it's *your* fault, not her fault."

That is the responsibility I give all the really good players. For a while, that is a real struggle for Dee.

Dee has another big problem, too. She's not that interested in the defensive end of the floor when she comes to Connecticut. She is an excellent defensive player—when she applies herself. But that's not happening on a regular basis.

There's a drill we do in preseason where we've got two lines. One line is on the wing and the other across the court on the other wing. We put a defensive player in the middle. The idea is to simulate being the "help" defensive player. Your man doesn't have the ball, so, in essence, you are responsible for guarding both people, because you don't know who will end up with the ball.

I have the ball, and when I pass it to one of the players on the wing, your job is to sprint out there, close out, and guard that guy. That guy is going to try and score on you, so you've got to contain the dribble, contest the shot, block out, and rebound the ball. When you do all those things, the possession is done. If you don't do all those things like I want you to, you've got to stay in there. Then I pass the ball to the other wing, and you've got to defend her, too.

If you don't do it the first or second time, you're dead. By the third time, you're tired, by the fourth time, you're frustrated, and by the fifth time, you hate me.

The first time Dee does the drill, she's in there for a very, very long time. We are counting off, five, six, seven, eight, nine, ten, eleven times, and by then, she is a ghost out there. She can't move anymore, nor does she want to move. She's mad at me, most likely mad at herself, and she's embarrassed.

She is, after all, supposed to be the best player in the country.

She keeps looking over, expecting me to tell her she can stop. I don't. I tell her, "Keep going. You're staying in there." I use this great line that former Green Bay Packers coach Vince Lombardi used on one of his players, Paul Hornung. Lombardi was running his guys into the ground making them do this difficult football drill until Hornung turned to one of the other players and said, "Man, how long are we going to do this?" The other player answered, "We're going to do this until he's tired of watching us do it."

So that's what I tell Dee. I'm going to keep her in there until I'm tired of watching her. So she quits. She stops trying, and then I throw her out of practice. I say to her, "Get out of here. You're an embarrassment to this program."

She has been practicing with Connecticut a grand total of two weeks.

Dee shows up the next day, ready to go. She is fine. She doesn't harbor bad feelings, or wonder why I'm picking on her. She knows. We don't even talk about it. We don't have to talk about it. We just keep going.

But neither one of us forgets about it, either. That's why when she gets to her junior year, and she's taking over the team, and making other kids accountable, I'm smiling inside, because it starts right there, with that humiliating, wonderful drill. It's one of my favorite drills, because I get to decide when you are done.

I get a kick out of these coaches who say, "I make a deal

with my best players. I don't bother them, and they don't bother me." I'm totally the opposite of that. I bother my best players. I poke and I prod and I push and I cajole and I irritate, because I want to find out, right from the opening day, how they are going to react under stress. They are going to have to handle the most stress of anyone on the team.

There's one undeniable quality about Diana, and it's that she is fearless. She doesn't care. That is her biggest strength, and her biggest weakness. Her mind-set is, "I'll shoot the ball ten times. I don't care if I miss all ten, because I'll make the next ten." Sometimes, before a really big game, I cruise up next to her and say, "Hey, Dee. What do you think? This is a really big one. Are you worried about anything today?" She just looks at me and says, "No, it's just a game, man."

When Dee is a freshman, the other players hate that part of her. They don't hate her personally, because she's an impossible person to dislike, but they hate her nonchalant attitude about everything. She has moments where she is thinking, "I'm going to throw this pass through five people, and whether it gets there or not, I don't really give a damn." So then she throws the pass and I say, "What the hell kind of pass is that?!!" and she just shrugs.

Defensively, a player is dribbling the ball up the court against her, and she takes a swipe at it, and they go by her for a layup. She takes the inbounds pass, goes up the floor, knocks down a three-pointer, and figures that makes everything all right. I blow the whistle and say, "Whoa, whoa, whoa. What do you think this is, some pickup game in California, and whoever makes the last three-pointer wins? That's not how we play here."

She just shrugs. Then I get even madder than I was, and I make the team run. If one kid screws up, they all run. The other kids start to say, "Man, she's killing us. She's making us run because she doesn't give a damn." They start riding Dee hard. Now *they* start making her life miserable.

They start calling her "Little Dee" or "Baby Dee." They want her to grow up. When Dee is being really stubborn, they call her "Little Geno." They tell her she should be my daughter.

Swin is so exasperated with her that one day she tells Diana, "Listen. We won't deal with you anymore. Do you understand? We won't deal with you until you act like you have some sense." Dee just looks at her. She doesn't care. She just does what she wants.

Even so, after all that, if you pull those same kids aside and ask them privately, "Who's the best player on the team?" they will all say the same thing: "Dee. No doubt about it." Dee can easily start for us, but that would mean sitting Shea or Sveta. They have just won a championship the year before. One is a three-time All-America and the other is the MVP of the Final Four. Now, Dee may be the best of all, but how do you justify that? I can't. Dee comes off the bench.

Dee spends a lot of time on the exercise bike on the sidelines. Every time I throw her out of practice, I look up a few minutes later and there she is, pedaling the bike. She isn't going anywhere. That is her message to me. She isn't going anywhere.

The kids who really get to know Dee, like Morgan Valley, who is one of her closest friends, realize the person on the court is really just the shell of Dee.

The inside of Dee is an intensely private person who wants to be viewed as the best at everything. She's being interviewed once, and she makes this ridiculous comment that she could play on any of the sports teams at Connecticut.

She stresses *any* team, including the men's team. People come up to me saying, "She's kidding, right?" Well, part of her is. And part of her isn't.

We were someplace once, and the team starts playing Ping-Pong. Dee watches for a while, then takes the paddle. That's it. No one can touch her. She beats everybody. If you ask her a question, she has to be right. If what she says is wrong, there's a reason for it. If you call her on it, she says, "Well, that's what I meant." You press her on it and say, "Dee, what you said is wrong." But she dismisses you. "That's what I meant," she'll say again.

Diana only deals in positive self-talk, and that's not a bad way to go. That's why she wants the ball in her hands late in the game. She has convinced herself she's going to do the right thing with it. Her goal on the 2004 Olympic team was to make everyone on that team think, "You know what you heard about me? It's not true. I'm the best teammate you'll ever have." Because she commands so much attention, people come in expecting her to be a prima donna, like some of the other top WNBA stars, but that's not Dee.

Some of these women who play in the WNBA couldn't carry her shoes. If you ask them, they'll tell you how good they are because someone told them along the way, "Man, you're awesome. You're the best." Meanwhile, you look at what they've won—nothing—but that doesn't stop them from prancing around like they're something special.

So here comes Diana Taurasi, and they get their backs up, just the way they did when Rebecca Lobo was at her peak. They see Dee and they think, "Oh, Diana Taurasi, poster girl for college basketball, we'll show her." Well, what are you going to show her? She's the nicest kid on the team.

She's one of most unselfish kids on the team. And she's the best on the team.

I think Rebecca Lobo went through that a little bit when Tara VanDerveer coached the 1996 Olympic team. For whatever reason, everybody wanted to knock Rebecca down a few pegs when she left Connecticut. There were players on that Olympic team who really loved watching Rebecca being denied a big role. Part of it was they were jealous. Part of it was because they didn't like our program. They liked being able to say, "What's the big deal about her?" What you want to tell them is, "You can never be Rebecca Lobo. You can never be that good, with that much pressure on you, and still smile, sign autographs, and treat everybody with respect."

You try not to get too mad when things like that happen. I tell Rebecca it is just the insecurity of others, some kind of built-in animosity, and that's part of growing up. Not everyone is going to love you. If that's the worst thing that happens to you, you're doing okay.

Diana has already proven she can handle that aspect of her career. She's actually a pretty quiet person. She rooms with Morgan at Connecticut, and their big thing is to stay home, order some pizza, watch a movie or play *Madden Football*.

At the end of Dee's senior season, she wins the Naismith Award, but all the other Player of the Year awards go to Duke star Alana Beard. So you ask, how can that happen? Here's how: because people are ignorant and jealous, and they go by numbers and stats. Alana Beard is a great player, but she's not Diana Taurasi. To no one's surprise, Dee is the number one pick of the Phoenix Mercury in the 2004 WNBA draft. She plays on the 2004 Olympic team that wins the gold medal. She has it all—except her degree. I make it very clear I expect her to get that, too.

Donato and Marsiella Auriemma. One of the few times out to dinner. Photo courtesy of the author.

Me; my mother; my brother, Ferruccio; and my sister, Anna, right before we sailed to America, November 1961. B.S. (before smiles), real happy campers, wouldn't you agree? Photo courtesy of the author.

First holy communion in Montella, Italy, 1960. Praying for a good call from the Big Official in the sky. Photo courtesy of the author.

Graduation from Bishop Kenrick High School in 1972. I look ready to tackle the world. *Right!* Photo courtesy of Marsiella Auriemma.

Me and Kathy. Wedding day, October 28, 1978—best recruit I ever got. Photo courtesy of Marsiella Auriemma.

Kathy, Michael, Alysa, and Jenna, Christmastime 1993. Santa has been very good to us. Photo courtesy of the author.

Michael, Kathy, Alysa, Jenna, and Marcie at Meghan Pattyson's wedding. Meghan played ball here 1989–92. Alysa sang. The girls cried. Michael ate. Photo courtesy of Pamela Benepe and Co.

At the Hall of Fame in Springfield, MA. They have my sneakers and clipboard from Minneapolis. Photo courtesy of Bob Stowell/Basketball Hall of Fame.

Jamelle Elliot, the heart of a champion. She "carried" us in the regional final! Photo courtesy of the University of Connecticut.

Sue Bird and Diana Taurasi. Best backcourt since Goodrich and West. Photo courtesy of the University of Connecticut.

Asjha Jones, Sue Bird, and Nykesha Sales, WNBA Finals 2004. Three of the best ever to play at UConn. Photo courtesy of the WNBA.

Asjha Jones. Solid in every area, great person, great student, great player. She's "Precious." Photo courtesy of the University of Connecticut.

NCAA Champions 2003. This group knew how to win! Photo courtesy of the University of Connecticut.

Diana Taurasi 2004—that's a lot of points for someone who loved to pass the ball. Photo courtesy of the University of Connecticut.

I've never looked better holding the NCAA championship trophy, surrounded by Chris Dailey, Willnett Crockett, and Doris Burke. Photo courtesy of the University of Connecticut.

The best team ever, 39–0! In Governor Jodi Rell's office right before the parade. Photo courtesy of the University of Connecticut.

At the mall making a Christmas card, 1990–91. I love being Santa! Photo courtesy of the author.

The Auriemmas at the Coliseum in Rome. These guys used to be referees. Photo courtesy of the author.

National Championship parade in Hartford, CT. Two teams, two titles, one crazy state. Photo courtesy of the University of Connecticut.

At the New York Stock Exchange, 2002. We got to ring the bell, thanks to our friends Rob Kimble and Kumar Ramanan. Photo courtesy of the NYSE.

President George W. Bush and I talking about raising daughters. Not bad for an Italian kid from Norristown. Photo courtesy of the White House.

Thrill of a lifetime, 1995. Jenna and me with President Clinton. Photo courtesy of the White House.

This picture says it all. We've left room for a few more. Photo courtesy of the University of Connecticut.

The moment every coach lives for. I'm saluting every player who was there in the stands or at home watching. Photo courtesy of the University of Connecticut.

My former players are always welcome to come back to our program and practice occasionally with us. It's a great chance for the current team to see the success stories, not to mention a great chance to compete against some of the best talent in the world. I love it when they come back. It's also a great way to build a long-standing tradition and connection between these women.

I would love Dee to come back and remain part of the Connecticut program, but I've already told her she is not welcome back on this campus until she graduates. She knows I mean it.

It's not Dee's fault she didn't finish. The WNBA screws up women's basketball. They start their training camps in April, and if you are someone like Diana, who has played international ball for most of her career, you can't make up courses in the summer. If you have to start your pro career in April, then you're not going to be able to graduate on time. That means a kid like Diana has to come back in the fall or the winter to finish. I told her if she doesn't, she'll never be allowed on these courts ever again. Her parents deserve that. I went into their home and told them her daughter would graduate with a degree.

In January of 2005, Dee took me at my word. She came back to Connecticut and enrolled in classes to complete her degree.

Our graduation rate is pretty good. I guess it depends on who you ask. If you ask the NCAA, any kid that has transferred out counts against you, so that's a zero graduation rate for that kid. I think it's more realistic to rate the kids that played here four years. If you use that standard, every single kid that has played here for four years has graduated.

I make sure our kids take their academics very seriously.

Part of that is probably because I didn't do that when I was young. I got by. I didn't bother to excel, and I regret it. I don't want any of my players to look back and say, "I should have studied more. I should have gotten more out of my classes."

One afternoon when Nykesha Sales is a freshman, she comes into my office. I know something is up, because she can't look me in the eye. She is bothered about something, but it takes us a while to get to it. It turns out her grades that semester aren't great. She isn't flunking or anything, but she doesn't do as well as she thought she should, or what she thought I'd expect her to do.

Truth is, Nykesha is pretty conscientious about her work. It just takes her a couple of months to realize what that means on a college level. After that first semester, she snaps out of it. She is a 3.0 student the rest of the way.

That happens to these kids sometimes. They come into college, and they convince themselves grades don't matter—until they see them on their report card. The best example of that is Meghan Pattyson. She is a good high school student. So she comes to Connecticut, and I would venture to say that by the end of September, if she doesn't know the name of everyone on campus, she at least knows what everyone looks like. If she doesn't know where every party on campus is, she knows most of them. Every place I go, people are commenting to me, "What an unbelievable kid that Meghan Pattyson is. What a great personality. She's everywhere." I'm thinking to myself, "Hmmm, I'm not sure if this is good." But I wait.

Well, her first report card comes, and she takes one look at it and she absolutely flips. Now, we've already seen it, because we get it before they do. I don't know who kills her more: her father, or me. When her father and her mother and I see that report card, we all go ballistic.

I don't expect my incoming freshman to get all A's. It's a big adjustment coming to college, and playing a Division I sport and getting used to a different schedule and environment. Even so, some of them do. Rebecca Lobo, Wendy Davis, Pam Webber, I'm not sure they ever got a B. Nicole Wolff had a 4.0 her first semester here.

Who knows what Meghan thought? I guess she figured she was going to get a 2.5 or 3.0. But when the grades come out, she is barely a 2.0. I tell her what I tell all the kids when they come: if you screw up the first year, it's a bitch getting it back. Now it's a constant uphill battle. Now even if you get an A it won't matter. It's so important getting off on the right foot.

Meghan comes into my office to talk about her grades, and I rip into her good. I am all over her. I tell her, "You think this is Camp Connecticut? You think you can just come here and have fun and goof off?" I get her dad on the phone and we both make it clear to her: it has to stop.

I want her to understand why it matters. I tell her, "You can pretend to be anything you want. You can bullshit people all you want. But guess what? When your transcript goes to your potential employer, you are what the paper says you are. When you go into an interview and say, 'Well, that's not really me. Let me tell you what happened,' you better be prepared for someone to say back, 'Well, no. I'm not interested in what happened. Here are your numbers. Here is your bottom line.'"

Nobody has to say anything to Meghan Pattyson after that first semester. She is so mad at herself she is hell-bent on fixing it. She does really well the rest of the way.

In fact, all of my top players do well academically. I've never had my best player be satisfied with being an okay student—until Diana. For someone who is so driven to be the best in basketball, she is perfectly content to be an okay student. She says, "I'm happy with this." She has no A's, no F's, and that is fine with her.

It never really is fine with me. All the things I avoided growing up, I want my players to face. I think it makes them stronger. I think it makes them better. I tell them, for instance, that when I was in high school, I never studied. When people say, "I never opened a book in school but I got straight A's," they are lying. At some point they opened their books, or they wouldn't have gotten straight A's.

Well, I never got straight A's. I didn't open my books. I settled for going to class every day and locking into whatever the teacher was talking about, committing it to memory, then giving it back to them on a test.

I have a great memory. The best. I remember everything. Back in the day, I could tell you about a game that happened six years ago. I could recite the score, who had the ball, where they were standing, and what the person on the other bench was doing. I knew names and faces and dates and times and who all the characters were. I could do the same with my schoolwork. But when it came time to study, and become that A student, I fell short because I was undisciplined. I didn't care, until after the fact, when I saw my grades. Then I was mad. I was mad because I knew I could do better.

I've spent far too much time in that "I wish I would have" mode. Some of it I can fix. Some of it, the chance is gone, and you don't get it back. That's what I am trying to tell Diana about her grades. But Diana isn't really buying it. She says, "I want to be a basketball player. That's what I do." People who play college basketball say that is only one part of their life. They say, "This doesn't define me." But Dee is different. She *wants* to be defined by her play. Her feeling is, "This is who I am. This is who I want to be."

People say Diana Taurasi is one in a million. I don't know. I thought Rebecca was. I thought Nykesha was. I thought Sveta was. Dee seemed different from them, but she wasn't. She seemed different because of her whole demeanor, but when you strip away the façade, she's the same.

What I'm going to miss about her is there's never been anybody that combined all the things you value in a player the way she did. She is a great player, a great practice player, able to engage in everybody and everything all the time.

It's funny. I didn't cry at Senior Night for Diana Taurasi. I knew I would miss her, of course, but Dee is a hard person to get to know deep inside. I was really torn up when Kerry Bascom graduated, when Meghan graduated, when Rebecca graduated, when Jamelle graduated, when Nykesha and Sue and Asjha Jones and Swin Cash and Tamika Williams graduated, when Sveta graduated, because each one of those guys allowed you to get inside them.

Dee never quite lets you do that. Now, I got as deep into her as you can, I think, but I'm not sure even I was able to break it down completely. Her defenses are just so strong.

⊕

Kathy and I take a road trip into New York City in the summer of 2004. We haven't seen Dee in a while. She is training with the Olympic team, and they are playing a team of WNBA All-Stars at Radio City Music Hall. Kathy, Jamelle, Tonya, and I go to see the game. It's a really fun night. Diana and Sue Bird and Swin Cash are playing for the Olympic team. Kesha is playing for the WNBA. Rebecca, who is pregnant with her first child, is doing the broadcasting. A lot of our former and current players are there: Asjha Jones, Maria Conlon, Morgan Valley, Jessica Moore, Ashley Battle. It is a great night for Connecticut.

We wait for Diana after the game, and it's a long wait. She's got to deal with the media, and the WNBA people, and the fans. The hardest part of my relationship with Diana is we rarely have time to talk. It is obvious with all the people around at Radio City that we aren't going to have any time alone. We're standing by the stage after the game, and she comes up to me and grabs me and puts her arms around me. Everyone is standing around, so we start hugging each other, and I start goofing around and kissing her neck, and all our players are yelling, "Get a room!" But while we're kidding around like that, I'm whispering to her, "You miss it, don't you?" She's telling me back, "You have no idea how much I miss it," and I say, "I knew you would."

It is one of those rare times when she tells me what she is really feeling, instead of what she is supposed to be feeling. That's the thing with Dee. She wants you to always think, "Everything is fine." You ask her, "How are things going?" and she says, "Fine." You ask, "How are your teammates in Phoenix?" and she says, "Fine." Meanwhile, they're not fine. They don't understand what she's done for them, because they're too busy being jealous over all the attention she gets, and the endorsements she gets.

That's one thing Dee never had to deal with when she was at Connecticut. We were a team, and everybody pulled for everybody else. We had our good days and our bad days, but at the end of the day we were together, working toward the same thing. When basketball becomes a job, that changes. I'm just happy Diana Taurasi hasn't changed along with it. It must have been great for her to see Morgan and Maria and Jessica and Ashley that night, because they know what she did for them, and they'll never forget it. They wouldn't have missed seeing her for the world.

She wouldn't have missed seeing them either.

On top of being the best player ever to come out of Connecticut, Dee also leaves as one of the most popular to ever play here.

But that's when she leaves. When she comes, she's dealing with a group of upperclassmen who want to wring her neck.

Dee's freshman year ends badly. It should end with a national championship but Shea and Sveta get hurt, and the rest of our players can't recover. We lose to Notre Dame 90–75 in the national semifinals in St. Louis. Kelly Schumacher plays her heart out. She has 12 points and 17 rebounds. She is a senior, and this is her last chance to win another championship. Dee tries to step up and fill the void left by Shea and Sveta, but she shoots 1 for 15 in that game. She is 0 for 11 in three-pointers, and she fouls out with a minute and a half left in the game. As she comes off the floor, she is fighting back tears. I grab her and I shout at her, "Stop crying! This is not your fault! We don't even get here without you!"

Naturally, the media is having a field day with Dee's numbers. The theme is predictable: the kid didn't step up.

It is the last time anyone can say that about Diana Taurasi.

NINE

Diana Taurasi has a miserable summer after her freshman season. I couldn't be happier about that. I know she is coming back with something to prove. I hope her teammates feel the same way.

Our 2001–02 team doesn't have the most depth that we've ever had, but it probably has the greatest combination of factors going for it in order to win the national championship. We have the best guards, the most talent, the most experience, and we have the necessary hunger and drive from the year before. All the elements are in place.

We play, for the most part, with only seven. Our starters are Sue Bird, Asjha Jones, Swin Cash, and Tamika Williams, who are all seniors, and Dee. Our bench is really just Jessica Moore and Ashley Battle. We use Maria Conlon a tad, but it isn't her time yet.

You would think our lack of depth would be an issue, but it isn't because the seniors are so seasoned that they don't get into foul trouble, and they don't do dumb stuff. Jessica proves to be a terrific backup at almost every position. She gives us a ton of versatility that year. We can take Tamika out, put Jessica in, move Swin to small forward. We can take Asjha out, move Tamika inside. We can take Swin out and put Maria in and play Dee at small forward. We can put Ashley Battle in. We can go small, go big, play fast, or play half-court.

At the end of the 2000–01 season, I am unbelievably disappointed in St. Louis because I really feel an opportunity slipped through our fingers. We were the best team. There's no question we were the best team. So it hit home that season that the best team doesn't always win the championship.

The way I am going to approach the 2001–02 season is, "Okay, now we'll see what these guys are made of. They've only got one year left." Diana is a sophomore, which obviously means we are going to be a whole lot better, because she's had one more year of experience.

I've got four seniors who can no longer defer to Shea or Sveta, because they are both gone. Now it's all on their shoulders, and not only that, they've failed. All four of them failed. I didn't point the finger at one of them after St. Louis. I didn't say to one kid, "If you had help up your end, we would have won." It was all four of them.

They know the deal, and they come back with a vengeance. You can see it in training camp. They respond to every single challenge we pose to them in practice. We have this drill where we execute a little three-man weave. At the end of the weave, all the three-point shooters shoot threes, and all the other guys shoot pull-up jumpers. If you make a three, it's worth three. If you shoot a regular jumper, it's worth two. If you miss, your two teammates rebound it and put it back in, and that's worth one.

The goal is to get 35 points in a two-minute segment. But

here's the kicker. Anytime you miss a putback, you go back to zero. If one guy rebounds the ball, and isn't paying full attention, and hits the bottom of the rim, then your team starts over.

I can honestly say they hardly ever have to start over that season. From the very first day, you can see that this group is going to leave nothing to chance. Every day they walk into the gym with the same look on their face. Every day is, "No screwing around today."

The fact that we don't have a lot of players in the rotation probably helps us. There isn't this sense that we have to get everyone involved, or to bring certain guys along, or mull over, "How are these guys going to fit into their roles?" We don't spend a lot of time worrying about whether guys will rise to the challenge. They already know exactly what is expected of them. It is boom, boom, boom and on to the next thing. We know what we have to do. Everybody knows.

The thing that makes our seniors unique that season is they've won one and lost one. They speak very eloquently about both. They are able to say, "I know what it feels like when you win a national championship, and it's the greatest feeling in the world. But I know what it's like to lose one, too, and it stinks. So now I've got a choice. Which feeling do I want to experience again come next April?"

They are a group with no ego, these seniors. The reason I know that about them is they never would have come together if they were looking to be the one and only. If you are Swin Cash, why would you want to share with Asjha Jones? If you are Asjha Jones, why would you want to share with Tamika Williams? The fact that they all came here with no ego made it easier for them to accept Diana, who has enough of an ego for all of them put together. She is a pain in the ass at times, but they are okay with her, because she is going to help them get where they want to go.

Dee takes things a little more seriously as a sophomore. She applies herself more on the defensive end. She accepts criticism a little better. She's maturing, that's all. You know each year her skills are going to continue to improve, because she works on her game so much. Her freshman season, I get on her all the time about not going to the free throw line. We have 35 games in her freshman season, and she goes to the line a grand total of 41 times. I'm saying to her, "You are a 90 percent free throw shooter. How can you only get to the line 41 times?" She does what she always does—she shrugs—but the next season, she comes back and makes a concerted effort to get to the line more. In 2001–02, Diana goes to the line 87 times. By her junior season, she's living at the line. She shoots 146 free throws.

The 2002 championship team has their moments, like all of them. But the beauty of it is, they completely own the venture. They don't have to share it with guys who had been there before. This is their time, and if they want to take it to another level, it's up to them and them alone.

It would be an understatement to say they rise to the challenge. They go out and prove they are worthy of every single press clipping ever written about them. We beat teams by an average of 35 points that season. Nobody really gets close, except for Virginia Tech, which is the only team we don't beat by double figures. We play them in early February at their place, and we're a little off. There is a point in time in that game when I'm thinking, "I can't say a loss here would be bad." It's hard going undefeated. I'm thinking to myself, "Maybe these guys are trying too hard to go undefeated instead of just playing, and maybe a loss here would end all that nonsense."

Of course, as I'm thinking that, they start to pull it out anyway. We're down by four or five late in the game, and Sue Bird makes a huge shot in the lane off a pick-and-roll that only Sue Bird can make. Then Tamika Williams steals two inbounds passes and that's all she wrote. We win 59–50, and nobody gets closer than 12 the rest of the season.

Tamika Williams was—and still is today—maybe the most popular player among the coaches of anybody that came here. I just think her personality is so terrific. Her father was a Vietnam vet and he came back and was a DJ, among other things, and he is absolutely the most outgoing guy. He is funny, and embracing, and Tamika takes after him. She's a lot of fun, and very nurturing, always bringing people together.

If you talk to Tamika and you're not laughing, you don't have a sense of humor. Tamika and Meghan Pattyson, to me, epitomize the spirit of UConn basketball.

One thing about Tamika was I thought she was never able to get to the level she could have reached because she was too willing to play a secondary role. She was more apt to say, "Go ahead, Swin. Go ahead, Sue. You guys do it and I'll hang back here and check out the scene."

She'd have these unbelievable games and you'd say, "C'mon Tamika, have those every night," and she'd say, "Nah, not really. I'll just be here to enjoy the camaraderie and the whole team thing." But then we're down at Virginia Tech, and there's a chance we'll lose, so she says, "Well, all right, then. I'll just steal this pass so we can win the game."

Our rock—our true leader that year—is Sue Bird. She is very quiet, somewhat reserved. I've often said Sue Bird is the Derek Jeter of women's basketball. She doesn't say a lot, she doesn't demand a lot of attention, and she's not looking for headlines. But when it's the end of the game, Sue Bird wants the ball in her hands, and she's very quietly saying, "I'm going to make the play when it has to be made. I'm going to do the right thing, because I always do. And afterwards, I don't want a parade for it. I don't want to crack open any champagne because I make a shot. I just want you to understand this is what I do. I live for big moments."

Sue's personality doesn't lend itself to conflict, or battles with me. Sue is, above everything else, a pleaser. The other guys are annoying. They *love* being annoying. They love the give-and-take. I love being around that. I love them trying to get me, and me trying to get them. I love playing those games. They are fun to me. They are a challenge.

Sue is never going to open herself up for that. She is not going to allow you to find the little cracks in her armor. She's not going to look too hard for your cracks either. Having said that, in her senior season, there are some instances late in the year, when she can feel the end coming, that for the first time her emotions bubble to the surface.

We are scrimmaging in preparation for the NCAA tournament. Sue rarely gets into it with anybody. She's generally right. If you are talking about a scene in a movie with her, you better re-create it exactly right, because she knows it. If you start quoting the lyrics to a song, you better sing it right, because she knows all the words. Whatever is going on, she's got it right.

In this particular case, we are scrimmaging with our practice players, who are male students from campus. I start using them in 1994. I'm sure other programs do it, too. It's the year we are 35–0 and we're pretty good, and Pam and

Jennifer and Rebecca are hanging out with a bunch of guys who play intramurals at the school and played high school basketball on some pretty competitive boys' teams. I say to them one day, "Why don't you show up at practice?" When they get there, I say, "Let's pick up our girls full-court." Well, Pam and Jen think they're pretty good until they start trying to get the ball up the floor against these guys. They are about to have a heart attack after five minutes, because they can't get the ball over half-court. It's a real shocker to them. I'm thinking to myself, "This might not be good. I might destroy their confidence." But, typical me, I'm going to needle them about it. I say the next day, "You know what? My mistake. Those guys are too good and they are messing with your heads, so the hell with it. Let's go back to playing with the girls."

Jen is pissed. She says, "Yeah, we'll see." So the guys start coming on a semi-regular basis. It gets pretty intense. So one day I see Howie Dickenman, the men's assistant, in the hall and I tell him, "By the way, I've seen some of your practice guys, and they suck. We've got a couple of guys who are really good." That son of a bitch. Doesn't he walk through the gym one day and start watching our guys and the next thing you know, I've lost Greg Yeoman, one of our best. He's got a uniform on and he's sitting on the end of the bench for the men's team.

Now, Howie is one of my best friends. He is the godfather of my son, Michael. He's a terrific guy—but I'm still ticked at him for stealing Greg Yeoman.

It's been a great thing for us to play against men. There's not much in it for the guys. We make them lose sometimes. We don't let them block shots. They get out of hand occasionally and I have to yell at them. But I love having them because they have a high level of respect for our players and we respect them. They become a big part of our team and we miss them when they leave.

On this particular day in practice, one of our practice guys, Tom Tedesco, makes a shot. I don't think Sue tries very hard to contest it, and I get on her about it. I go up to her and I say, "All I was asking for was one stop. One stop. That's all we needed in this situation. I can understand if one of the freshmen or someone who doesn't know any better lets that happen, but you know what? You didn't even try to contest it."

Sue looks at me and says, "Oh, I didn't, huh?" Now, for her to question me, or to say anything at all, was absolutely stunning. It is just so uncharacteristic of her. So now I'm mad. I snap at her. I say, "Oh, so you think you contested that shot? You're saying I made this up? What, do you think I came to practice and said, 'I think I'll piss off Sue Bird today'?"

Everyone is real quiet, because this kind of exchange between us is so unusual. But I'm not done. I say, "I know what I saw. I'm not making this up. You were not there to contest that shot." Now I go over to Tom. Everyone knows how much I like Tom. He's friendly with my kids. He's been to my house for supper. Sue knows exactly what I'm going to do.

I look at Tom and I say, "So, Tom, was Sue there or not?" Now Tom, the poor kid, is screwed. Here's Sue, who he has known for four years, who is probably his good friend at this point, and here's Coach Auriemma, who is probably going to help him get a job when he graduates. How is the poor kid going to answer this question? He looks like he just wants to die. But I'm not letting him off the hook.

Tom hems and haws and gives me kind of a half answer. He says something like, "Well, she kind of contested it."

Now Sue is really ticked off. She's ticked at Tom for not backing her up. She's ticked at me for getting on her for not contesting the shot. When Tom answers, she says to me, "What do you expect him to say?"

At this point, I'm really pissed off because she's talking back to me, which she has never ever done, and she's getting really upset, because she really believes she was there and Tom was just lucky to hit the shot.

Looking back on it now, if you put a gun to my head, I'd have to say it was a fifty-fifty ball. Someone who wanted to be nice to Sue Bird would have said, "Okay, that was a lucky shot by Tom." Someone who wanted to zing her would say, "Where were you?" I chose that route, and it escalated from there, and Sue kind of lost her composure.

The rest of the team is completely shell-shocked because nothing like this ever happens to Sue Bird. She is in trouble. The shirt goes up to her face. She's embarrassed, and she's crying, and she doesn't want anyone to see her, and she doesn't want to deal with anybody at this point.

Here's the problem: Sue Bird isn't Sue Bird anymore. Now she's just like every other kid. She's no longer the un-flappable goddess who has the game in the palm of her hand. I probably should have put a stop to it, but instead I let her wallow in it for the rest of practice.

When I leave the gym that day I'm ecstatic. Sue Bird has finally showed another side of herself. People don't ever see Sue like that. Everybody has that side, but now they can see, guess what? Even Sue Bird gets affected.

Sue Bird, in my mind, is the standard by which you judge point guards. So they see her struggle and they say, "Man, Sue just broke, so if I ever break it doesn't make me a bad player." I think it's good for people who are viewed as perfect when they get some cracks. It makes them human.

I don't worry about Sue. She's too strong for that. Another kid that doesn't have her inner confidence, or have the same relationship with me, might have left me walking out thinking, "Man, I'm going to have this kid over to dinner, and bring out the couch and say, 'Tell me all your problems growing up.'" But not Sue.

Sue, more than anything, is someone you can count on, someone who will be there at the end. She always takes care of everything.

The next day, we get together in a circle and she tells the team, "I just want to apologize for what happened. I'll make sure it never happens again." I tell her, "Sue, you don't have to apologize. Everyone already knows. What you did yesterday was so out of character for you, we understand you're sorry it happened." Then I tell her, "I think it was a lucky shot. I don't think Tom could make that shot again in a million years, but the bottom line is, you've got to get your butt over there, just in case." I know in her mind, she walks away still thinking—still knowing—that she was there. She walks away saying, "I know I was there, but if you don't think I was there, I'm sorry for the way I reacted." Typical Sue.

Sue Bird will not fight you on much. She's going to tell you very calmly, "I'm sorry you feel that way, but I'm right. I'm right because I'm Sue Bird and I'm always right."

You know what? It's nice to be Sue Bird.

It's also nice to be her teammates. She gets them the ball just where they need it. She gets them the ball before they even realize they are her best option.

My team is so dutiful and so disciplined during Sue's senior year that it's hard for me to get on any of them. You can't get on Sue. You can't do it with Asjha either. She is just so sensitive. I remember her crying once because she played poorly, and she didn't want to disappoint anyone. Her freshman season, we lose to Louisiana Tech. Asjha isn't getting much accomplished, and I take her out of the game, and she's sitting there all weepy. I turn to Chris Dailey and I say, "How am I supposed to put someone in the game who is crying?" She just wants so desperately to do well, and when she doesn't, she feels so bad that she cries. I don't know what to do with Asjha half the time. What should I do? Start screaming and yelling at her to stop crying? That's not going to do anybody any good.

I'm convinced Asjha has unlimited offensive ability. But the cool thing is she also becomes our best defender. She is one of the most reliable players I've ever had. She never misses a practice. She never misses a game in four years. You can count on her. The only time I get really upset with her is when she passes up open shots and defers to other players. She takes the team thing to an extreme. But by late in her senior year, she isn't passing those shots up anymore, and it makes us really, really good.

In our second-round NCAA tournament game against Iowa, Asjha has 14 points and nine boards in 25 minutes. We win that game 86–48, which means we are advancing to the East Regional semifinals in Milwaukee. It also means we've played our final game of the year at Gampel Pavilion. As we run off the floor, our fans start applauding. They keep on clapping until our seniors come back out of the locker room for one final bow. They want to congratulate what is shaping up to be the best women's college basketball team of all time.

I'm doing a television interview on the court when they

start chanting for the players. They aren't going to stop until Swin, Asjha, Tamika, and Sue come out. When they do, everyone goes crazy. It gives me goose bumps. Our fans are the greatest when it comes to that. Our players are wearing matching T-shirts, and they start dancing and jumping around and high-fiving everybody. It's a great scene.

Our guys do the same thing a few years earlier, in 2000, when we beat Hampton in the first round. Hampton's pep band is the best in the country, so our guys come out and start jamming with the pep band. I can still see Swin out there, showing off her moves.

Swin Cash has a lot to do with why we win it all. She is so smooth out there. I love to sit back and watch her. For all the style she has off the court, she exhibits just as much of it on the court. If she were a guy, she'd be Walt Frazier. He was my favorite player growing up. He had this aura about him, with the nickname "Clyde," and the hats and the suits and all the other things that added to his style.

Swin is the same way. The way she moves, both on and off the court, just exhibits "cool." There's just something about her. Nobody dresses better than Swin. She is always stylin'. She has a tremendous influence on Jessica Moore with her fashion sense.

I went to dinner recently with Swin and she had on a butterscotch leather jacket with matching butterscotch boots and a matching purse. She looks like a million bucks and you say to yourself, "Man, this is so Swin. There is just so much more to her than playing the game." And yet, when it comes time to play the game, she plays it harder and with as much passion and intensity as anyone.

The first time I see Swin, she is a kid, real skinny, with arms and legs flying all over the place. She is running up the floor going a hundred miles an hour, and every time a shot goes up, she's trying to block it. She's trying to block one over here, then runs over and tries to block that one over there, then tries to get this one on the weak side. She blocks it, then rebounds it and dribbles the length of the floor and scores. She is like a whirlwind. She plays that way the entire game. I keep saying, "How can anyone keep up that pace?" But she does. Every night. Then she comes to Connecticut and does the same thing for us.

I have to get on Swin a little bit down the stretch of her senior year, though. She plays very poorly in Milwaukee, which is where the East Regional semifinals are held. She plays lousy against Penn State, who we beat 82–64, and against Old Dominion, the team we knock off to get to the Final Four. Swin Cash, the leading scorer in the Big East that year, has 10 points and two rebounds against Penn State. Against Old Dominion, she has seven points and two rebounds. In two games, two very critical games, she has a grand total of four rebounds.

To be honest, she doesn't play that well in the semifinal win over Tennessee either. Luckily, it doesn't matter. We beat them handily, 79–56, because Asjha has a double double (18 points, 10 rebounds), and so does Diana. Sue Bird is Sue Bird. But Swin Cash is not Swin Cash. She has 12 points and four rebounds against Tennessee, and four of those points come in the last minute, during garbage time.

Normally at that point, with the game well in hand, I empty my bench. Not this time. I call a timeout with about three minutes left, and I let Swin have it. I tell her, "You suck. You were horrible against Penn State and Old Dominion, and you were horrible again tonight against Tennessee. You have nothing to do with this win."

Swin's eyes are filling up a little bit, because she knows I'm right, and she doesn't know how to get out of this funk she is in. But I'm not showing her any mercy. I tell her, "We are not leaving this building until you get your head out of your butt and turn this thing around. You are going to stay in this game with Stacey Marron (our walk-on) and all the other guys who don't play much until I'm convinced you've got your head on straight."

Normally Swin would be sitting there on the bench with all the other starters whooping it up and enjoying the win. I make her stay out there for the rest of the game. She is mad at me, and madder at herself. She's also embarrassed, because everyone in the building knows why she is still out there. Well, doesn't the son of a gun come down and bury a couple of jumpers.

After that game, I'm on the court doing a television interview when Pat Summitt shows up at our locker room. She asks CD for permission to address our team. She comes into our locker room and tells our guys she admires the way they play the game. She tells them they played like champions.

I'm not around when it happens, so I'm not really sure what context to put it in. People ask me what I think about it, and I don't know what to say. I always wonder when something like that happens. What is the motivation for doing it? Is it for publicity? To gain some kind of an edge? I have no idea. I just thought it was a little odd.

My players don't have much of a reaction to it. Pat comes in, tells them they played well, and leaves. They all just shrug and say, "Okay. Cool." They aren't thinking about ulterior motives. They say, "Oh, that was nice," and then they move on.

Swin is still smarting from how she is playing. The great

thing about Swin is she has so much pride in herself, and so much pride in how she is viewed. She is humiliated at the end of that Tennessee game, but she isn't going to allow herself to feel sorry for herself.

I want Swin to play well. I'm not going to enjoy the win unless I know we are coming back to play Oklahoma in the championship game with all our bullets in our gun. I am worried about Oklahoma. They are a very well-coached team. They have Stacey Dales, and LaNeishea Caufield, and Rosalind Ross. Sherri Coale, their coach, is a friend of mine, and I know she will have them ready.

I have to find a way to get Swin ready. The day before the final game, we have an Easter dinner with the team. At the end of the dinner, I tap my glass with a spoon, and I say to them, "Normally, I don't like to bring religion into our team. That's personal, even though I went to Catholic school, coached at a Catholic school, and I believe in my faith with all my heart.

"It's just that I think this particular moment calls for an analogy, so I'm going to make a prediction about what will happen in tomorrow's championship game."

They are all looking at me like I am nuts. Chris and Jamelle and Tonya are glaring at me like, "Don't say anything stupid." I say, "You all know the story of Easter. Jesus was in a cave for three days, and then he came out of the cave and rose from the dead. It's a big part of Catholic religion. Well, do you know what's going to happen tomorrow night? Asjha Jones is going to go over and she's going to remove this giant boulder. As soon as she does that, Swin Cash is going to rise from the dead, and lead us to the national championship.

"I really believe this. Just like Jesus, this is going to be a great resurrection."

By this point, Chris has her head in her hands. Half the kids are laughing their brains out. Asjha is looking at me like I have gone completely mad. Swin is laughing, but she is a deeply religious person, and I'm sure she gets my meaning. Why do I do things like that? In some ways, it gets my team loose. It gets them to stop thinking about how big the game is we are going to play the following day. It gives Swin a chance to laugh off how poorly she has been playing, but also, hopefully, makes her feel like, "I'm going to do exactly what Coach Auriemma predicted."

Some of the parents are at our dinner that night. I'm sure some of them walk away scratching their heads. There's no question I baffle a lot of them with the things I do and the tactics I use to motivate their daughters. But most of them are pretty good about letting me coach my team. Of course, I have some interference from parents. Every coach does. Maybe there is more than I know, because oftentimes I think the worst things are said behind my back, not to my face.

I never mind taking phone calls from the parents. Nykesha Sales's mother called me all the time. She'd call to say, "What's wrong with Kesha?" I'd say, "I don't know, I think she's being a lazy bum." She'd say to me, "Well, then, Coach, just kick her in the butt." And I'd say, "All right, I'll do that, but stop making her those pork chops every time she comes home, because she can't help but eat them, and it messes up her conditioning."

The parents who cause me the worst problems are the ones who call to complain about their daughter's playing time. Obviously everyone thinks his or her child should play.

But they aren't in practice every day watching what I'm watching. The bad part about that is that if they think their darling should play more, the kid is hearing that every time she calls home, and that makes for big problems.

You can't have two coaches. I'm your coach. That's it. You don't go home, or go to your dorm room, and pick up the phone and call home and get coached by someone else. If you want more than one coach, you need to go somewhere else.

The night before our championship game in San Antonio, I have my annual party. A lot of the Connecticut politicians are there. I realize that night how lucky I am we have that kind of support. Every time we go to Washington, D.C., we're in this little gym in Georgetown, and all of a sudden I look up and there's Chris Dodd, our senator, walking in to watch us play.

The support on campus is also unbelievable. We get it from our president, Philip Austin, who comes to all our Final Fours. I've been fortunate enough to spend time with him and have dinner with him, and it's like hanging out with a guy I grew up with. To be able to feel that way about your president is just fantastic.

Of course, the two most pivotal people in the growth of our program are the former athletic director, Lew Perkins, and our current athletic director, Jeff Hathaway. When Jeff is the associate AD at Connecticut, he is the one who runs my program on a daily basis. Even though Lew is there, Jeff is the one I go to for everything. Who can say what would have happened if Jeff wasn't the way he was, willing to get things done for us? At one point he leaves to be the athletic director at Colorado State, but now he's back with us as our AD. I'm thankful each and every day for that.

Obviously the fact that Lew, his predecessor, said, "All right, we're going to make women's basketball big-time" is a huge factor for us. Now, did he say that, or did we make it big-time and he had to ride with it? Who cares? It happened, and he supported us. He was never one of those ADs who said, "It's only women's basketball. If it works, it works." What Lew said was, "We're going to make it work."

Kathy and I talk about that the night before the final game. We recognize how fortunate we are to have our university behind us. And I tell my wife how fortunate I am to have her with me every step of the way, too.

You have to be with the right kind of person to be in this business. My job is unusual. The hours are ridiculous and unpredictable, and I spend more time with other people's kids than with my own. Your family life can really suffer if you're not careful. Kathy and I don't feel sorry for ourselves. Anyone who is successful, whether in owning their own business or working as an executive, is faced with long hours and a lot of travel. We all do the best we can.

It helps if you are with someone who really understands what that commitment is. That's where Kathy comes in.

I'm so lucky to be with her. I'm not sure there are many people who are as fortunate as I am to have someone who completely buys into the lifestyle and the sacrifices and the ups and downs that go with it. Not only that, she's in a position where she ends up being a mom and a friend and a confidante to the players, to the point where she still gets birthday cards and anniversary cards from them. I think she's memorable to them because she has always been able to look at things from a mom's standpoint. She looks at a situation and can say to me, "If that were my daughter, here's what I'd be thinking." She's always coming at me from the players' point of view.

Kathy has this ability to provide balance to almost any situation. If I'm unbelievably angry about something, she's the one who is incredibly calm and diffuses things. When I'm nonchalant about something, she's the one who brings some seriousness to it and reminds me, "Hey, you need to address this. This is important."

She's very good at putting things in the proper perspective. She does that better than anyone in my life—probably because she's been around me for so long. This whole wild ride didn't just happen to me. It happened to both of us. Kathy was in it with me from the beginning. We both started at the bottom and worked our way up together.

That's why I trust her judgment. That's why I listen when she tells me, "Hey, we need to have Diana over for dinner," or "Give me Kesha's phone number. I want to talk to her," or, "Hey, let me give Jessica's mother a call." Now is she doing that because she's married to the head basketball coach, or is she doing it because she genuinely cares for those kids and the parents in our program? That's an easy one. It's because she cares. She has a huge heart and a huge amount of compassion.

I'm not going to get into my personal feelings too much. She knows what we've been through the past thirty-two years. Those things are between her and me.

She knows how much I love her. I probably haven't expressed to her enough times how much she means to me. Sometimes you take it for granted. I never want to take that for granted, and I certainly don't. So that's what I tell her that night in San Antonio.

I wake up the morning of the championship game with a good feeling. I know Sherri will have her team prepared, and she has some really quick guards that could give us trouble, but I just feel our guys can withstand all of that. Oklahoma tries to take away our three-pointers. We are 0 for 9 in threes in that game, because they extend their defense. But when they do that, we just say, "the hell with it" and throw it inside. We finish that game with a 44–25 edge off the glass. Our first 10 points in that game come on offensive rebounds. We are just annihilating them on the boards.

The thing that almost costs us is we have 21 turnovers. They do a good job of pressuring us and causing some of them, but a lot of them happen because Dee starts throwing the ball around. We are trying to blow them out. We get up around 15, and we get impatient and want the game to be over and Diana makes three or four mistakes in a row. She is bordering on being out of control out there. I call a timeout late in the game, and I get in her face. I tell Dee, "The hell with you. You just don't listen. You have your own way of doing things, and you don't care what we do, so the hell with you." Then I look at my other four starters and say, "Screw her. We'll win without her."

Of course, I don't take her out. I'm not crazy.

We go back out there, and by the time we have the next TV timeout, they've cut our lead to six. There's about three minutes or so left in the game. It's only a few minutes earlier that I've chewed Dee out. I've just told her in the last timeout, "These four guys have worked too hard and you are ruining this for them. You are so selfish." I'm accusing her of everything I can think of, whether it's true or not. The whole time I'm doing that, she's just sitting there looking at me as if to say, "Yeah, yeah, yeah."

Well, now this game is starting to get away from us, and the kids are looking at me, and it's our ball, right in front of our bench. My seniors look concerned. They don't say anything, but their eyes are saying, "What are we going to do?" I grab my clipboard and I tell them, "Okay, here's the play. We're going to inbound the ball to Dee, and we're going to run 'special.'"

Special is a play where everyone spots up and we get a guy in the low post. In this case, it's Dee. According to the play, Dee should back her man down, and if they double her, she should kick it out and we knock in a shot. If she's one-on-one, she takes her guy to the basket.

So Dee gets the ball, backs down Oklahoma guard Dionnah Jackson, scores—and gets fouled. It's five fouls on Stacey Dales, one of Oklahoma's best players and their leading scorer in the game, and it's a three-point play by Dee, and it's all over. We win 82–70, and Diana Taurasi, even though she shoots 5 of 16 from the floor, makes the biggest shot of the game.

In a matter of three minutes, we go from telling Dee, "We can't stand you, we hate your guts, you're the worst thing that ever happened to this program," to "Now, listen, Dee. We're going to give you the ball, and you better make sure you win the game." All the seniors are going, "Yeah, Dee, do you understand?" Dee doesn't say much, but you know she's thinking, "I understand. That's why when you were ragging on me I'm saying, 'Yeah, yeah, yeah,' because all I really want to know is, 'When am I getting the ball?'"

It is a terrific send-off for our seniors. We hold a championship parade in downtown Hartford and more than 150,000 people show up. Everyone has declared the 2002 Connecticut champs the best women's team ever. Later that spring,

Sue Bird is the number one pick in the WNBA draft, Swin Cash is the number two pick, Asjha is the number four pick, and Tamika is the number six pick.

That leaves only one starter: Diana. She is an amazing player, and we all know it. She helps send off the seniors with another championship, while at the same time taking a small piece of ownership of her own first title.

I am certain it will not be her last. For Dee, the fun has just begun.

TEN

Our success presents me with opportunities I never dreamed would be available. I have offers for endorsements. I am asked to throw out the first pitch at Fenway Park. I am doing commentary for ESPN. I am commissioned to do instructional videos and motivational speeches.

People all around me want to market my coaching philosophy. They all want to know how I've developed my coaching style. I guess you steal the stuff you like from other great coaches and put your own stamp on it.

I worked with Jim Foster for two years as a high school coach. He's tuned in to the women. He knows how to work the crowd. He's very noncontroversial. He's the professor. He studies the landscape. I also worked for Phil Martelli for two years as a high school coach, then with Debbie Ryan for four years as her assistant at Virginia. I have to say I take something from all of them—but not enough.

Jim Foster and I hook up when I am in college. He has just come back from Vietnam, and I am going to a stupid junior college instead of a four-year college. The junior college itself isn't stupid. My reasons for being there are. My friends are there, it is cheap, and I know I can play basketball there. Pretty good decision, huh?

Anyhow, Jim is about seven or eight years older, and we form an intramural basketball team to play against some prisoners nearby. Jim is the player-coach. I remember him telling me over and over, "Stop driving the lane. Do you understand these guys are in jail for murder?" Jim teaches me a lot of things. I'm only twenty-one when I hook up with him. We're coaching a girls' high school team. He's the varsity coach, and I'm coaching freshman and JV. It is a crazy dead-end job, but one day Jim gets a call from St. Joe's. He gets offered the head women's job. I'm thinking, "What the hell kind of world do we live in where a guy who has been coaching three years of high school gets a college job?" Well, it turns out he's part-time. I go with him, so I guess I'm less than part-time. But the level of competition is good. We play everybody. We play Queens, Montclair State, Cheney State, all those schools that are really good back then. We play Villanova. We play South Carolina, when Magic Johnson's sister is there.

Being with Jim is great socially. His wife, Donna, Kathy, and I spent a lot of time together. Some of my favorite memories are putting together toys for Jim's son on Christmas Eve. We do everything together. I really like coaching with him.

It is really hard in 1979 when Phil offers me a job as the assistant at my old high school, Bishop Kenrick, in Norristown, but I take it. Phil lets me coach the junior varsity and do some scouting. Phil and I are not alike. He is incredibly detail-oriented and time-management oriented. Debbie Ryan is the same way, and I learned from both of them how to plan things.

I am not a very good assistant coach. I suppose outwardly I am, but inwardly I'm not. I don't second-guess the head coach, but I am challenging and questioning them constantly. At first, I just say the stuff to myself. Eventually, I find myself saying it out loud.

When I say things to Phil, he ignores me. So I stop talking. My feeling is, "Screw you." After I stop talking to him, he looks over at me and says, "What's your problem?" I say, "What's the point of me talking if you're not going to listen?" He says, "It's my job to listen. It's your job to talk. So keep talking, and I'll pick out what I want to pick out." That's how Phil Martelli gives me license to offer my ideas. When you are an assistant, you have all the answers. You are always right, because you never have to take the blame when you are wrong.

The years I am with Phil, I think, "This is my niche. I'm going to be a high school coach someday, and if I get lucky, maybe some college will give me a shot." Meanwhile, Phil is becoming one of my best friends. I think he is a tremendous coach. Out of nowhere one day, Phil comes up to me and says, "Listen, I just got a call from Debbie Ryan. She just offered me the assistant's job at Virginia, but I'm not going to take it. I told her to talk to you." I say, "Me? A women's job? Where the hell is the University of Virginia?" I have never been out of Philadelphia.

I don't know if Phil is trying to get rid of me or not. I fly down to Virginia, talk to everyone, and they offer me the job. Now all of a sudden, I'm coaching women's basketball. Part of me is ticked. Part of me still thinks, "I could be the high school coach where I played as a kid, or maybe I could be Phil Martelli and help mold a young college star like Jameer Nelson."

Anyhow, Kathy and I pack up the few things we have and go to Virginia with the attitude of, "If we don't like, it, we'll just come home." We end up staying four years. After those four years, Debbie looks at me one day and says, "You've got to go." She is right. I have to go. I can't contain myself. I am like a racehorse straining at the starting gate. I have too many ideas, and when you are an assistant you are supposed to act like an assistant, but I treat everything like it is my program.

Debbie has enough confidence in me to give me a lot of responsibility, and I don't want to let her down. I feel as though I need to treat the program as my own so it will be as important to me as it is to her. I know with my own assistants, if they don't take some ownership in our team, then we're not any good. I get that concept from my time in Virginia.

While I am the assistant, I am the good cop. I am the one who puts my arm around them and says, "Aw, she doesn't really mean it." I am the guy they come to when they have a problem. I am the one who gently tells them, "C'mon now, suck it up." I'm sure my current players would be amused to learn I was the nice guy once.

Debbie never had a full-time assistant before, and here comes this pain-in-the-ass guy who wants everything. I want Virginia to go from being good to winning the national championship, and I want to skip every step. I am in a big hurry.

I consider Debbie Ryan a great friend. I'm grateful for all she did for me. I'm bad about keeping in touch. I get so caught up in what I'm doing that I'm always disappointed in myself when I don't take the time to stay connected with everybody. If I could do one thing better, that would be it.

I've never forgotten any of the people who have helped me become a better coach. Some of them don't even know me very well. I've picked up things along the way by admiring their teams. I am just so in awe of people like Hubie Brown and Jack Ramsay, because they succeeded in ways that inspired not just players, but other coaches. Of course, I can't be like any of them.

One of my favorite guys is Terry Holland, who was the men's coach at Virginia for many years. I picked up a lot of drills from him. I also learned a lot from watching Jimmy Lynam.

Jimmy used to run a camp in the Poconos, and one of the best days of my life is when I get to work there. I'm the women's assistant at Virginia, and I drive up there to this camp, and the cabin they give me has holes in it, and it's raining, so I end up sleeping in my car because it's the only dry spot I can find—or afford. They pay me $130 to work at the camp. It costs me at least that much in expenses to get there. Still, I wouldn't have missed it. I remember working this three-on-three station, and Jimmy is watching me, and he comes over and he says, "I really like what you are doing." Here is this guy who, at the time, is the head coach of the L.A. Clippers in the NBA, and he likes what I'm doing? I feel like I've died and gone to heaven.

Even though I've taken pieces from a lot of different programs, if I could model my team after anyone's, it would be North Carolina, because they do everything right, and their coach, Dean Smith, was so good. Maybe they didn't win more because they had too many good players. Maybe they had too much of a team concept. All I know is, in terms of sharing the ball those Carolina teams were the best.

When it comes to coaching, I also draw from my Philly roots a lot, which means, play your ass off, press everything, don't give an inch, be tough, don't ever back down. If I could be a Philadelphia-type coach with Carolina players, I'd have it made.

And that's what I've tried to create at Connecticut—the female version of Carolina. What I love about their system is you can have Michael Jordan on a team with a relatively unknown player, and they will both have an equal opportunity in that particular style of game. That's what I've always wanted: to have a player like Maria Conlon, who nobody wanted coming out of high school, starting alongside the best to ever play the game, Diana Taurasi. Cool. Our system allows for that. That kind of teamwork enables you to get to the Final Four because you're unselfish. Now, once you get to the Final Four, you need someone to put the team on their back, and if you have that someone, you win.

I want to tell Dean Smith how much I admired his teams, but it's not like I am hanging out with him on a regular basis. But then, a few years ago, I went to the annual Nike trip for the coaches. It's in Carmel, California, and Nike shows you all the newest stuff and you get to comment on what you like and what you don't like. The best part of the trip is the camaraderie of the coaches. I'm sitting at the table having something to eat with Syracuse men's coach Jim Boeheim and his wife, and there's Dean Smith, walking with a plate toward us. He plops down, and I'm thinking, "Man oh man. This is Dean Smith."

I start telling him how when I was at Virginia, our office was right next door to the men's soccer office. Bruce Arena was the soccer coach, and the two of us became good friends. His office was on the other side of the wall of the visiting men's locker room. Bruce and I used to sit in his office and listen to the pregame, halftime, and postgame speeches of the opposing team. We'd listen in on Jim Valvano, Lefty

Driesell, Bobby Cremins, and Mike Krzyzewski, and, of course, Dean Smith. We'd laugh and laugh, then report to Terry Holland the next day about what was said.

Dean Smith is chuckling as I tell the story. Then he asks about our Connecticut team. He is very gracious. The talk turns to golf, and then the meal is over, and we go our separate ways. Later that night, Bobby Cremins, the former Georgia Tech coach, comes up to me and says, "We need a fourth for tomorrow. Dean wants to know if you're available to play."

It's going to be Cremins and me against Dean Smith and Roy Williams, the two Carolina guys. The next morning, Roy Williams is sick, so he doesn't show. I ask where we're playing, and they say, "Cypress Point." Now, nobody gets on Cypress Point. It's one of the most exclusive golf courses around, but the guy who runs the place is an alumnus of Carolina so of course we're in.

We get there, and I realize Cremins and I have shorts on. I thought about it before we left, because when you play a lot of these exclusive courses, they like you to wear long pants, but it's summer, and I figure Bobby is wearing shorts, so we're okay. Dean, of course, is wearing long pants. As we approach the course, the pro says, "Good morning, Coach, how are you doing? I hate to do this to you, but your guests can't play in shorts."

Cremins is fuming. Right away he knows from all the years of competing against Dean Smith what's going on. "You knew!" he's shouting. "You knew we couldn't wear shorts, and you didn't tell us! You wanted this to happen!" We all can't stop laughing.

We go into the pro shop, and of course they don't sell pants. They sell everything else except pants. We have no choice but to put on some olive green caddy pants they have lying around. They are rain pants. We look like Bill Murray in *Caddyshack*. So we play 18 holes in these ridiculous pants.

Now, all Bobby Cremins wants to do is crush Dean Smith. Dean Smith is the most competitive guy I've ever seen on a golf course. He's over seventy years old, but don't think that matters. We're playing this crazy game where you add up points, and it's a dollar a point depending on the shot you hit. At the end of nine holes, Dean is down something like $15. I'm playing pretty well. So is Bobby. Well, now we're on the back nine, and Dean goes to work. He wins holes number 10, 11, 12, and 13. He just kicks our ass. You'd think this older man might get tired, but it is just the opposite. He comes to life. He wipes us out.

All the Carolina guys are like that. I'm an assistant coach for the women's Olympic team in 2000, and I get to meet Larry Brown. Larry played at Carolina and is a Dean Smith disciple. He's telling me how much he loves the way Sue Bird plays. Brown says he likes watching our team. He asks me, "What's your favorite play?" So I grab a napkin and I say, "Coach, here's what we love to do." I diagram a play for him, and I say, "I got this out of Dean Smith's book. It's stuff you used to do." He said, "Yep, we've been doing that at Carolina for a hundred years. Still works, doesn't it?"

That's the part I love most about the Carolina program—the bond they all have. It's really, really strong. I always hoped my players would feel the same way about playing at Connecticut. I'm not like Dean Smith. I'm not saying that. Our personalities couldn't be any more different. But I believe with all my heart that the way he coaches and teaches basketball is the way it should be played. I want people to feel about my program the way they feel about his. I want my players to feel like once you are in this family, you are always in this family, and it is a very special club.

Having said that, Dean Smith is not the only basketball coach who has influenced me. The guy I used to follow all over the country is Bob Knight. Now, I know Bob Knight is crazy. But I've seen him speak every year since I was twenty-one years old. He hasn't done much of it in the past four or five years. But when I am younger, every time he has a clinic, I go to see it. I love the stuff his teams do. Am I at all like him? No, not at all, but I appreciate how disciplined his Indiana teams are.

Once, after we have a little success at Connecticut, they ask me to speak at this clinic. I'm a nervous wreck, because I know Bob Knight is there, too, and I'm afraid he might be listening. I'm more nervous that day than when I met President Bush and President Clinton at the White House. I keep thinking, "What if he doesn't like what I'm saying?"

When I am just starting out, and making about $16,000 a year, I scrape up some money and fly up to Hartford on the old People Express airline to hear Bob Knight. I stay in a hotel with my buddy Tom Perrin. We have a Holiday Inn room, with two beds. We are there two nights. The second night, Tom says, "Do you mind if a couple guys crash with us tonight?" I say, "But we've only got two beds." He says, "Don't worry. They're a couple of basketball junkies. They'll sleep on the floor." We go out that night for a few beers with the guys, and they're really nice. They're brothers. Their names are Jeff and Stan Van Gundy. I laugh my ass off every time I think about it now. They are both millionaires now. Jeff coached the New York Knicks for years when Patrick Ewing was there, and now he coaches the Houston

Rockets. Stan is the head coach of the Miami Heat, and he's got Shaquille O'Neal and Dwyane Wade.

As much as I enjoy great players, if you ask me whether I'd rather meet Shaq or Hubie Brown, I'll take Hubie. Getting to know some of the truly great coaches in this game has been one of the most rewarding parts of my job.

I've always been a big Hubie Brown fan since his days coaching the Knicks. I used to see him places, at games or at clinics, but I never said anything to him. I'm not really good at walking up to someone and saying, "Hi, how are you doing?" because there's a part of me that thinks, "They are so much better than me at this." I fight with this perception that they are on a different level from me.

On the same Nike trip a few years back, they make us do all these team-building games. They put you on teams with other coaches. One of the games is you have to catch these water balloons without having them break. I'm on a team with (current Golden State Warriors coach) Mike Montgomery and Stanford women's coach Tara VanDerveer and Kentucky men's coach Tubby Smith, and we're supposed to work together and interact with one another and figure out how to catch these balloons. I don't really want any part of it. They shoot the balloon something like forty yards out of this contraption, and we're supposed to catch it with this tarp. I'm the last guy holding on to the tarp, so naturally when the balloon hits, I'm the one who gets soaked. I'm feeling pretty self-conscious, and I'm looking for a way out of these games, so I grab a couple of burgers and a beer, and I see Hubie Brown standing there, so I get up my courage and I go over and talk to him.

Hubie used to do something that we use now called 1–4 high. I think the guys in the NBA have renamed it the

"Hawk series," because Hubie used it while he was coaching the Atlanta Hawks. We adapt it a little bit so that you have one point guard, and your other four players are lined up, two at the foul line extended, one way out on the wing, and the other on the opposite wing. It's almost like an offensive line in football with three receivers. It involves a series where the point guard passes the ball to the wing, then runs what we call a UCLA cut. All of our movements have names. The names come from the person or place that used it and had the most success with it. If someone uses it, but isn't any good at it, they don't get any credit for it.

Anyhow, the point guard passes to the wing then rubs off the post, and that's called a UCLA cut. It's a famous cut. If Southwest Missouri had done it, or West Chester State had done it and finished 12–12, they would not call it the West Chester cut. But because UCLA won ten national championships with it, it's called the UCLA cut, and it's part of Hubie Brown's "Hawk series." Hubie starts many of his series from there, and, after the point guard rubs off the post, Hubie has devised about seventy-five different things that can happen.

I love that Hawk series. It rewards patience, good cuts, and movement without the ball. I'm the kind of guy that if I see something, I try to project how it would work for our team. Our press offense is Hubie Brown–inspired. Our half-court offense against traps is Hubie Brown–inspired. A lot of our 1–3–1 stuff is Hubie Brown–inspired.

People forget Hubie started as a high school and college coach. He needed simple, basic, fundamental plays that even players with minimal talent could run. That's why I like his ideas so much. People have watched our team run the Hawk series, and they write or call me and say, "Can we have your offensive stuff? Do you have it on paper?" Well, the answer is I really don't. First of all, if I wrote it down, it wouldn't make sense to them, because I've tailored it to fit our program and to evolve with our basketball team. Second, just because it works for us, it might not work for other people. And third, you can't really be sure until you actually get out on the court and try it and tweak it and refine it.

If you look at Connecticut's teams over the years, you'll see some Hubie Brown stuff, as well as some of the great stuff Bobby Cremins ran at Georgia Tech when he had great guards like Mark Price. I pick up a lot of it while I am coaching at Virginia. I use quite a bit of the stuff Rick Pitino ran when he coached at Kentucky. I've used the old Holy Cross shuffle.

The Holy Cross shuffle has been around forever. Some of it, I'm sure, has been attributed to current Connecticut men's assistant George Blaney, who was a really successful coach at Holy Cross for years. But George will tell you a lot of it was already in place when he got there.

The shuffle cut was made famous in the fifties. There are lots of different ways to use it. I used to run it with our high school teams. You set up some sort of 1–2–2 formation. One guy dribbles down, the other guy screens, and you make a pass. Then the next guy sets a screen, and the other guy sets a screen on the weak side, and then it's a backdoor cut. It's a continuity offense where you keep going one side to the other. In the pre–shot clock days, you could run it forever.

Villanova coach Harry Parretta runs a lot of the Holy Cross shuffle. His teams are very, very good at it. He calls it the spread offense, but it's the same old-time basketball they used down in Worcester, Massachusetts. Bill Gibbons, who used to be George's assistant at Holy Cross but is now the head women's coach there, runs the shuffle as well as any-body. He's a great coach. His teams overachieve almost every single year.

Again, the key is movement. I love movement. I've never been into setting up four guys low and have this guy go one-on-one and score. I don't want to just run pick-and-roll for-ever. I'm not too interested in dumping it into the post and overpowering someone either. I'm into all five players mov-ing.

The other offense I enjoy watching is Sherri Coale's of-fense in Oklahoma. She's one of the best offensive coaches in the women's game. Again, she coached in high school, and had to figure out how to get less talented players open shots, instead of just giving them the ball. She runs a really nice motion offense. She's a real student of the game who imple-ments some real good old-fashioned fundamental basketball.

If you watch Boston College, you'll see that Cathy Inglese has gotten very creative on the offensive end. Her staff is very innovative when it comes to getting their players shots. Everything involves screening. They do a really, really good job of that.

You wish the women's game displayed more offensive in-novation. I think a lot of it has to do with the fact that the older coaches just don't have the background. Someone like Cathy Inglese, who played the game and has been influ-enced by coaches she admires, has been smart enough to look around and try some new things. Many of the other coaches just don't want to go outside the box.

Sometimes you see things on other teams and it fits your personnel perfectly. I had an interest in the triangle offense made famous by the Chicago Bulls. We began running a ver-sion of it during the 1994–95 season.

I don't know former Bulls coach Phil Jackson at all, but I read a story in a magazine that Jackson's wife at the time is a graduate of Connecticut, so when I see that, I send him some information on our team. That is the year after we are 35–0. I tell him, "Your wife might enjoy this." He writes back, "She's a big fan. We've enjoyed your success." I see an opening there, so I write back and ask if it would be possible to come watch a practice.

He says fine. So I take my son, Michael, who is turning nine, as a birthday present. He is too young to appreciate what we see. Not me. It is terrific.

Chicago assistant coach Tex Winter, the architect of the triangle offense, is very gracious in sharing information. He sits down with me and watches film and points out certain things. Just sitting there, watching practice, I am able to pick up quite a bit. We have already been running the triangle offense, but now I go back and incorporate a few of the new things I see.

Not everyone should run the triangle offense. If you don't have the right personnel, it won't work. There are a lot of teams trying to run it without the right people, and the result is a bunch of kids running around in circles.

Let's say you have Shaq. Then you would run the triangle offense quite differently than if your center was Bill Wennington. Phil Jackson ran it with both players—with Wennington in Chicago and Shaq in L.A. If you have Michael Jordan and Scottie Pippen, you are going to run it a lot differently than if you have John Paxson and B. J. Armstrong. If you take Kobe Bryant away from the triangle offense with the Lakers, when they ran it in 2003–04, then the whole thing would run through Shaq. If you took Shaq out of the triangle offense, it would all run through Kobe. If you took both guys out of the triangle offense, you'd finish sixth.

Consider our 1995 championship team. The triangle accented our strengths. Everything was going through Rebecca Lobo and Kara Wolters, but Jen Rizzotti and Nykesha Sales made it work. Once we got the ball into either Rebecca or Kara, they had to be double-teamed at all times. We had enough talented players slashing through the lane or spotting up and shooting to compensate for those double teams.

When I go back after my visit with Phil Jackson and Tex Winter, it's the start of the 1997–98 season, and Rebecca and Jen are gone. Kara is still there, and I know how to get her involved, but now how do I make Nykesha into a more effective player? She is our Jordan. From what I learn that afternoon in Chicago, we are able to make the triangle offense work like a charm—again. Our record that season is 34–3. We may have won it all if our Jordan—Kesha—didn't tear her Achilles'.

One of the little things I pick up that day is how the guards bring the ball over half-court. You don't pay that much attention to it, but as their guards cross half-court, they cross at the exact same time. If anything, the guard without the ball might be a step or two behind. If you aren't careful, you can allow teams to push your offense so far out that you have eliminated the thing that makes the offense so special, which is penetration. It's so important to get the ball over quickly and assume your position in the offense.

The other thing I find really interesting is that if you are being pressured, and you inbound the ball, the person who throws the ball runs right up the middle. The guy who catches the ball does something different. Instead of turning around and dribbling up the floor, he or she looks for a player cutting. If that player is open, you give him or her the ball. If not, you go to the open side of the floor. Think about it. If you inbound the ball to the left side, then everyone is moving that way, so if you cut against the grain, you are going to be open. What that does is help eliminate the possibility of defenses trapping and pressuring, because now you've got to cover the whole side of the floor instead of running everything on one side.

The main thing that makes the triangle offense work is unselfishness. The whole thing hinges on making the next pass, or making the next cut, even when you know you're not going to get the ball. That's the biggest thing.

If I pass the ball to you and I know I'm going to get it back, then I'm going to cut like a son of a bitch and score. Well, that's great. But the trick is to cut that same way even when I know I'm not going to get the ball. So many times, you see players say to themselves, "Screw it," and just go through the motions. Now not only am I not going to get the ball, because I've made a half-ass cut, but now I haven't opened up an area for anyone else either. You have to make a cut real enough so the defense reacts to you. Then when they do, you cut behind them and off you go.

The thing that really impresses me about the Chicago Bulls is the way Jordan and Scottie Pippen act in practice. They are first in line for every drill. They play hard, and if their teammates don't they are all over them. I've been to a number of different NBA camps, and it seems to me that plenty of stars spend the whole practice trying to get out of doing drills. Jordan and Pippen set the tone.

One thing I've noticed about the top programs in sports, like the Carolina basketball teams, is that they are uniform across the board. I want us to be that way. Our shirts are tucked in at all times. There are no names on the back of our uniforms. We wear socks that are all the same length. I don't really like people to express themselves individually, other than on the court. If we are going to be on the same team, then everyone has to adhere to the same thing.

Today everything is about self-promotion. We didn't start out at Connecticut saying, "Let's be different." We started out saying, "This is what we're going to do to establish who we are." From there it evolved into, "You know what? We're different from everyone else." Then comes a point where we look at it and say, "Should we change it?" I don't think we need to. Our approach is simple, direct, and all about excellence. It reminds me of Penn State football, which I always had a great respect for, or the New York Yankees, who still don't have names on the back of their jerseys.

As we go along, we develop our own signature touches. Before every game, we get together in the center of our locker room, join hands, and yell, "Together!" When we have a home game, our fans stand and clap in unison until we score a basket.

We also have our own practice traditions. A few years ago, Tonya and Jamelle started something called the Breakfast Club. Kids coming in from high school think they are in shape, because they don't know any better. We evaluate them and say, "This kid needs to do extra." The idea is, "How can we get them into shape and good and pissed off at the same time?" So we make them work out in the morning really early, like at 6 a.m. The kids nickname it the Breakfast Club. It can entail anything: running the stadium steps, or swimming in the pool, if they really hate that, or something on the track, like a five-mile run. Whatever bugs the kids most is what Jamelle and Tonya make them do. The idea is to get them to hate the Breakfast Club so much that they will stay in shape and never be required to be part of the "club" again.

One of the things that really bothers me is this idea that you can't weigh in athletes on a regular basis. That's a bunch of crap. People have this mistaken notion that kids will develop an eating disorder if you keep on weighing them. Well, you know what? If a kid doesn't understand when they come to college on a basketball scholarship that there's a certain optimum weight you should be playing at, then they shouldn't come at all. The whole idea that men can be weighed in, but not women, drives me nuts.

They weigh football players. They weigh wrestlers. Are you telling me they can't develop eating disorders? They weigh in basketball players on the men's side. But because they are women, we have to say, "Oh, they're special, they're sensitive, we've got to handle them with kid gloves because they might develop an eating disorder."

Don't misunderstand me. I understand the seriousness of eating disorders. We dealt with it on a daily basis with Shea Ralph. But her disorder had absolutely nothing to do with being weighed in each day. She had problems with eating long before that. We're not trying to hurt these kids by weighing them. We're trying to help them. And it's not even about weight anyway. It's about conditioning.

I want our kids to be the best-conditioned players on the floor, and most of the time, they have been. But for some of them it hasn't been easy. Take Nykesha. She's one of our best all-time players, but when she comes here, and we have her go through our conditioning tests, she runs a 7-minute, 30-second mile. I knew it was coming. She wants to be in great shape, but she has no idea how. I remember her telling me one day, "Coach, I try to get in shape, but then I go home and my mom has been waiting for me. She's been cooking all day, and I get in the house, and she's got those pork chops on the table, and I've just got to eat them."

You learn how to treat each player differently in these situations. Some kids need a lot of prodding. Others are naturals. Svetlana Abrosimova is one of the most well-conditioned athletes I have ever seen. The first day she's with us, she says in her wonderful Russian accent, "So, Coach, what are we doing?" I tell her, "Well, we're running a timed mile. The guards have to finish in 6 minutes, 30 seconds, and the big guys have to be in by 7 minutes." At the time, the record is 6 minutes, which is a pretty quick mile. Pam Webber, who used to run all the time, has the record. Guys like Missy Rose and Jen Rizzotti also kill the test.

So Sveta shows up to run the mile. Missy is there, so they start running together. They've gone around the track three and a half times. It's four times for a mile. They've got about 220 yards left. Sveta says, "How many times more do we go around?" Missy says, "No more. This is the last lap." Sveta says, "Oh, I see," and boom! She takes off. She flies ahead of them and finishes with a 5:40 time. She doesn't even break a sweat. That's the difference between the Russian work ethic and the American work ethic. What they do is day and night compared to us.

Sveta is an incredible competitor and an incredible athlete. In four years at Connecticut, I don't remember her ever being out of breath. She always has her hands up. She is always calling out, "I'm open, I'm open." I told her once, "Put your hands down. You look like someone is holding you up with a pistol in your back." Truth is, Sveta is always ready. She is never too tired to shoot.

I ride her all the time because nothing bothers her, and nothing I send her way wears her down. I do it because, first of all, I love her, and she knows it. Secondly, I know anything I do to her is nothing compared to what her coaches in Europe make her do. In her mind, I am easy on her, even though from an American standard, I am very tough.

I hear that complaint all the time from other coaches. I'm too tough on my players. Really? Ask them if I'm too tough. Ask them if the results are not what they've hoped for. I am tough on them because I want to get the best out of them.

Besides, no matter what I do, somebody won't like it. I'm not going to win any popularity contests in the women's game anytime soon.

There are plenty of people out there who say I'm a self-promoter, but they'd have a hard time proving that. If you look back on what I've done in the twenty years I've been at Connecticut, any of the notoriety I've received is because of my team's success, and the individual players I've produced. It almost has nothing to do with me. There are coaches out there who have done a far better job of promoting themselves.

Part of the problem, I think, is because I receive offers to do some TV work. I never set out to be on television. But because I'm very accessible to the media, and I don't take myself too seriously and I don't take them too seriously, and because I say some things I feel like saying that are definitely different from the "coach-speak" that most other people give you, the TV people look at me and say, "Oh, that's somebody we might want." So when the WNBA starts up, and they are looking for someone to talk about the players, they look to someone like me, who isn't afraid to say things, and who knows the personnel, because half of my players are in the league anyway.

After it's all said and done, the reason anyone knows anything about me is because of the teams we've had and the tremendous success we've enjoyed, and the individuals we've had who have developed into stars, even within the conformity of our program. One of the things I'm most proud of is if you ask someone about Connecticut basketball, they'll start talking about Diana Taurasi or Nykesha Sales or Sue Bird or Swin Cash or Rebecca Lobo. Or they'll say, "That's the school that had that undefeated team back in '95," or "They're the program that got women's basketball off and running." No one is saying, "Connecticut. Oh yeah, that Geno Auriemma is the best." It's not about me. It's about our players.

I shouldn't let my critics get to me. But I do, partly because I feel guilty about all this success, when so many people I grew up with, so many people that I know have worked really hard, don't have that much to show for it. I wonder why no matter how much we accomplish at Connecticut I'm feeling this constant need to prove myself over and over, just like I did when I was twelve years old.

If you think you're ugly and someone tells you every single day that you are beautiful, it doesn't make you beautiful. I want to be liked. I want to be respected. But I'm convinced in some instances that that won't ever happen for me.

I have tried to show the women's game respect. Many, many times, we have played teams that are overmatched, and I have been very mindful about not running up the score. Sometimes people recognize that, and sometimes they don't.

We had a game back in 1998 when we pounded Providence College, 126–48. Their coach at the time was Jim Jabir. He made a statement after the game insinuating we ran up the score, and kicked his team while they were in the "fetal position." I take exception to that. The truth is his guys stopped playing. My guys never did. Some of my starters played 16, 17, and 18 minutes in that game. That's all. What are we supposed do? There's a shot clock. We can't stall. And even if we do, coaches are insulted when you do that. So should I tell my kids, "Play bad and miss on purpose?" It's been a problem for us for years.

Some coaches have recognized the difficult position we are in. In December of 2000, we played Illinois and we beat them 97–55. As bad as the score is, it could have been much, much worse. The coach for Illinois, Teresa Grentz, comes out after the game and says, "Let me say one thing. Geno is a real gentleman. Thank you. Thank you."

The reason she goes out of her way to do that, I discover later, is because Illinois lost earlier in the season to Tennessee 111–62, and Teresa had been really upset. She felt Tennessee had run the score up.

I appreciate Teresa's comments, because she understands what we were trying to do, or not trying to do. At the time, Illinois is really struggling. Teresa has done a lot for the game. I respect her a great deal. She was Chris Dailey's coach at Rutgers, and she's from Philly, but I would have pulled back for anyone, because it's the right thing to do. I don't know why she felt Pat Summitt and her team rubbed it in. I wasn't there. I didn't see the game. My guess is Teresa didn't like Tennessee going out of its way to set up a couple of dunks for Michelle Snow. When you are up by a bunch and you try to orchestrate stuff, that's when you can get yourself into trouble.

Any coach will tell you this is an impossible job to manage. None of us are perfect. None of us have all the answers. We are what we are, and each of us, no matter how successful we are, has our flaws. One thing that bothers me is when coaches want to tell you how hard they work. I'm always leery of someone who tells me how hard they work. If they have to tell you, that should be a sign. Hard workers just work hard and let their results speak for themselves.

There are a lot of coaches out there who work hard non-stop trying to build the kind of program we have. You feel for them for the time and effort that goes into it, because, for whatever reason—not necessarily because you've worked harder—you've been fortunate enough to have this great success. If I add up the number of hours I work and the number of hours someone else that has never been to the Final Four has worked, what if the hours are exactly the same? What if the sweat, the staying out late chasing this game or that game, this recruit or that recruit, and the not being home for three weeks at a time, and being on the phone and watching film till all hours of the night adds up to be the same?

You can't turn around and say, "Well, I win more because that person doesn't put the time in." It's not that simple.

Nothing about this job is simple. You do what you feel is right and hope it works. You hope your kids can run your offense. You hope they can stay healthy. You educate yourself the best you can, and hope it's enough.

Even though you're never really sure it is.

ELEVEN

We are defending national champions and no one is expecting us to do it again in 2002–2003 because Sue, Swin, Asjha, and Tamika are gone, and only Diana is left.

Here's the thing. Everyone has forgotten one person: Maria Conlon.

Maria doesn't play at all her first two years here. She isn't recruited very heavily. Nobody in the top fifty schools recruits Maria. That should tell you something. When you come from a small school in Connecticut, and none of the elite programs are after you, what that says is, "I'm probably not at this level, but if I go to UConn and work hard, who knows what will happen?"

I recruit Maria because I see something. I can't put my finger on it. I go to watch her play and I say to myself, "Damn, why does this kid's team win all the time?" They go undefeated twice. I watch her and say, "Man, I can't coach her." That's because she shows no expression. Zero—nothing good, nothing bad. That bugs the hell out of me. I like my kids to show emotion. I like "Damn!" when something goes wrong, and I like enthusiasm when something goes right. I don't like players feeling sorry for themselves when things go wrong. I also don't want them doing six cartwheels when they do something good.

Maria is already driving me crazy before I even have her. Even when I bring her in to talk with her, there's nothing. No emotion. It's really getting to me.

I say to her one day, "Do you want to come here or not?" She says, "Yeah. I've always wanted to come to Connecticut." She isn't kidding. You go to her house and she's got a little half-court in her backyard. She practices back there, or plays H-O-R-S-E with her dad, and there's a big UConn flag hanging there, and the court is painted UConn blue. So, really. Where do you think she's going to school?

Little girls growing up in Connecticut have become like little boys growing up in Indiana. That's what happens when you have success. I was joking with Kathy about the Red Sox finally winning the World Series. I'm waiting for the first baby to be born named after the Sox. Pedro Sullivan. Can't you see it? It's going to happen, if it hasn't already.

Maria comes to Connecticut, and she's not playing at all in the beginning. Her body language is not conveying very positive things about her. And she's always maligned.

She is definitely one of my hardest projects. She constantly needs to hear from me, "Hey, you're really good." But for two years I refuse to tell her that.

She mopes around if I don't compliment her. She is always telling people, "Coach doesn't like me." I finally tell her, "Hey, Maria, when you start working hard and committing yourself to what we need you to do, then I will tell you I value your contribution. But until you do, you will get nothing from me."

Her first two years with us she does zero. She figures, "They've got Sue Bird and Dee, and I've got no chance, because everyone sees me as this slow, overweight kid from Connecticut, and what am I doing with all these All-Americas?" She convinces herself so thoroughly that everyone views her that way and guess what? She starts believing it herself.

Now, all of sudden, Sue and Swin and all of those guys are gone, and she says to herself, "Hmmm. You know what I'm going to do? I'm going to lose fifteen pounds, and I'm going to get in shape, and I'm going to come back looking so good that Coach will say, 'Wow, man, you've turned it around completely.'"

Sure enough, Maria Conlon comes back for her junior year looking really good. It is the start of 2002–03 season and Maria is playing great for us.

Tonya and Jamelle and Chris are giving her all sorts of positive feedback, but not me. I won't say it. I won't say, "Hey, you're doing great." So what happens? Maria starts moping again. My coaches come to me and say, "You need to talk with Maria. She really needs you to tell her she's good, because she's struggling." I snap back, "I don't give a damn. Let her struggle." I say that because she's pouting. I hate it when my players pout. Well, common sense will tell you that no wonder she's pouting, it's because she's struggling, and she's struggling because she's pouting. Those two things go together.

You would think I could act like the adult in all of this and go up to the kid and bring her in my office and sit her down and say, "Listen, Maria. Relax. Everything is going to be fine. You're my starting point guard, and you are going to play 35 minutes a night, and don't listen to anyone who says you are slow, or you can't do it." Instead, I have to be an idiot. I have to be stubborn and, in this case, stupid and let the whole thing drag on.

Finally, when I can't take it anymore, and I start feeling guilty for dismissing this kid with my usual theory of "Let her figure it out herself," I call her in. This is after my coaches badger me every day, telling me, "You're an idiot. Maria is being a baby, but you're worse. You're the grown-up. Act like it."

I'm getting it from CD, and Jamelle, and Tonya. I'm getting it at home from Kathy. Even my kids are on me.

So I call Maria into my office and I say, "Okay, Maria, what's the matter?" She says, "What am I doing wrong? Because I feel no matter what I do, it's wrong." I say, "Well, now you're feeling sorry for yourself. Is that what you want to be, Maria, a martyr?" Maria is mad now. She says, "What, you don't think I'm working hard enough?" Now the two of us are screaming at each other and you can just see the rage coming out of her. It is obvious she needs to get all of it off her chest.

Finally, after she's done, I say, "Are you happy now?" and she says, "Yeah, but I still don't feel like you believe in me." I say to her, "Maria, how many minutes are you playing?" She says, "I don't know, thirty-something." I say, "If I didn't believe in you, do you honestly believe you would be playing that much?" But that isn't the point. She needs to hear from me that I believe in her.

From then on, Maria Conlon is fine. We have no problems the rest of the season. I could have saved my staff and myself a lot of trouble if I had just talked to Maria earlier. But I can't, because I am too busy being a jerk.

If someone asked me, "What's the one thing you need to

improve upon as a coach?" the answer would be easy. I would say, "I need to recognize that my stubbornness gets me in big trouble."

On the other hand, there was a reason I did what I did and said what I said. Every single guard that I've ever had that had tremendous limitations, I've felt like it was my obligation to make them so strong and so tough that none of those weaknesses would ever appear out on the court. You look at Maria and she was too slow, not athletic enough, not quick enough, and not tough enough. What's going to get Maria in trouble? What could get her into trouble is the same thing that got her in trouble during her freshman and sophomore years—not working hard enough, and backing down once in a while, and not wanting the ball under pressure.

Now she's a junior. What is going to keep us from winning another championship? A team that looks at us and says, "We can attack that kid." Can she be quicker? Faster? No. So what can she do better? Be mentally stronger than she was last year. Bring it to a whole other level. How do you that? You have to constantly challenge her.

Maria and I had a difference of opinion. She wanted me to realize she was working as hard as she could and I should understand. I was coming at her with the idea that she was *not* working as hard as she could and was *not* taking it to the next level, and no, I do not understand.

By the time we were done that day, she wanted to jump over the desk and choke me. I was thinking, "Good. Now we're getting someplace."

Had that incident not happened, I don't think Maria and I would be as close as we are today. We are as close as we have ever been. She helped coached the team during the 2004–05 season as a student assistant and she was a big, big help to us.

When you look back, you have to say Maria is one of our best success stories. So few people believed she could do it at this level, and she proved them all wrong. I'm really glad she was able to do that.

Her situation reminds me of when we have Rita Williams. Rita comes into our program as this out-of-control junior college kid from Norwalk, Connecticut. She is 180 degrees different from Jen Rizzotti, who she is supposed to replace when Jen graduates.

The first year Rita is here, Jen is a senior. The two of them have some memorable battles. Rita is pretty quick. I bet if you ask Jen Rizzotti how many times she's been stripped in her life, most of them were by Rita Williams in practice. But when it comes to work ethic, if you look at Jen, on a scale of 1 to 10 she's at a 15. At this juncture of Rita's career, on a scale of 1 to 10, she's a negative 4. So there isn't a whole lot of love lost between the guys who have just won a national championship the previous year and these new kids coming in who haven't won anything.

Now, off the court, Rita is a real sweetheart. But on the court, she has issues. Our players don't treat Rita very well in the beginning. Jen and Jamelle are seniors, and they are constantly on her. They are telling her every day, "C'mon. Work harder! Put some effort into that cut. Put some muscle on that pass!" My players are pretty good at policing themselves.

So it's 1996 and we're in Chicago. We're practicing before our game with Vanderbilt, which, if we win, will send us to the Final Four. We're at a high school doing some drills, and Rita is in la-la land, and Jen and Jamelle just tell her, flat out, "Get off the court." I don't say a word. I don't have to say a word. Rita leaves the court. We beat Vanderbilt, and she doesn't play.

Rita is ostracized for a long period of time. I know it isn't easy. She realizes she has two choices: quit, or get with the program, because her teammates are right and she is wrong.

So now we come back the following season, and Jen and Jamelle are gone, and Rita is going to be our starting point guard? Are you serious? We're going to go from Jen Rizzotti, who led us to a championship, to this wild thing who doesn't work hard enough?

That's where Tonya comes in. She takes Rita under her wing that spring and the next fall. Tonya is the perfect person for the job. She is someone who has always been able to connect with our players in her own quiet way.

Tonya was an unbelievable player for Virginia. She's one of the best players in ACC history. Everyone just assumes she went to UConn. She probably should have gone here. She is one of those kids who has appeared on everyone's radar from the time she was in the sixth grade. She grew up in Boston and played in a city program for Alfreda Harris, who has done a tremendous amount for the kids in Boston and Roxbury. I could have recruited her, but I figure she is too good for Connecticut at that point. Had I known at the time she is such a homebody, maybe we would have had a shot.

We play Virginia in the Final Four in 1991, and Tonya is giving us fits. There is a loose ball in front of our bench and she is chasing after it, and she grabs the ball and falls out of bounds right near our bench. I grab her and pick her up and pretend to carry her off the court to get rid of her. She makes all the key free throws down the stretch to beat us. So when it is time for us to find an assistant coach, I call Debbie Ryan and ask about Tonya.

I bring her down, and she won't say boo. For a while, I am wondering how helpful she is going to be with the players and recruits, because she is so quiet. I couldn't have been more wrong. Tonya is so invaluable to us because her relationship with our kids is just incredible, and her ability to get through to the kids during individual workouts is really impressive.

Tonya is the one who gets to Rita. She is the one who makes her understand what she has to do to become successful here.

I'm rooting for Rita, because she has this lovable personality off the court that exudes all this warmth. She's the kind of kid you just want to put your arms around and love to death. So I see her during the course of the summer and I ask around. I ask how she's playing and how she's doing in summer school. I want to know if she's going to class. I want to know if she is committed to this. Sometimes, the reports I'm getting are, "Well, she's doing okay." So one day I go over to her and I say, "Rita, you know, I'm really encouraged. I'm really looking forward to this coming season. As a matter of fact, I think you've got a real chance to be a great backup guard for us."

The look on her face is priceless. She's knocked flat on her back. I say to her, "No, really, man. Based on what I see right now, you have the backup point guard job all locked up."

Now fall rolls around, and practice starts, and they are killing Rita in the papers. They are saying it's never going to work with Rita running the team. But they are comparing her to Jen, and that's not fair. I tell the writers, "Look, Jen did it this way. Now we're going to do it Rita's way."

Well, how did Rita's way work out? We are 30–0 heading into the NCAA tournament. We lose to Tennessee because Shea Ralph gets hurt. So much for Rita Williams not being good enough.

In the end, you can say the same thing about Maria Conlon.

Of course, it doesn't hurt that Maria is playing alongside Diana Taurasi. She has the most incredible season I've ever seen in 2002–03. Whenever the situation calls for it, Dee does something absolutely amazing. Then, a few days later, she does it again.

We play Tennessee at home on January 4 that season, and it's vintage Dee. First of all, she sinks a half-court bomb, which is just luck. But the jumper she nails to tie the game and send it into overtime is ridiculous. Then, in the overtime, she's making plays in the lane, she's making unbelievable passes, just taking the game over. It is one of those games for the ages. It is a game that shows everyone all the things Diana Taurasi can do.

In the middle of this amazing season that Dee is having, we are also about to set a new record for consecutive wins in the women's game. It's not something we spend a lot of time talking about. I can't tell you when the first game of the streak was. I don't even know there is a streak until we are 15 games away from breaking it. It doesn't mean that much to me. It's not like they give you any trophies for it. I guess if we had been able to win 88 in a row that would have excited me. Then we would have been talking about the UCLA men's record. We would have been talking about the longest streak in *all* of college basketball.

The thing about breaking the record is that right in the middle of it Chris Dailey's dad is dying. That makes it a very trying time for all of us. He is a big part of our program. He is our extra scout. The fact that he and Chris are so close makes it difficult. If you ask the kids, I bet that's what they remember more than the streak itself. I don't detect any anxiety about setting the record.

On January 18, we beat Georgetown 72–49 for our 55th consecutive victory, which surpasses the 54 straight that the Louisiana Tech women's team won in 1981–82. Chris isn't with us. Her father has passed away, and she's with her family. I have a migraine that day. I don't even know where it comes from. I've only had two of them in my life. Maybe I just don't want to deal with the streak. I don't really know.

The fact that we are playing Georgetown, and their coach, Pat Knapp, is one of my really good friends, doesn't help matters. We go on this run and they can't score, and I always feel bad when that happens. They are playing like crap, and they just want to get it over with, and then we play like crap, and we just want to get it over with, and I can't stand to watch it.

I don't even care which team wins. I just want to go home. I am in so much pain I can't lift my head. I get to the locker room after we win and I can't look at any lights. I'm in agony. The team doctor comes in and tells me I need to go to the hospital. Jamelle and Tonya have to handle everything. I can't even address the team after the game.

They do some CAT scans, and they are negative, and they tell me I have a migraine. They give me some medicine and I go home and go to bed. It is scary. Maybe the tension of the whole thing catches up to me. Maybe the loss of CD's dad has something to do with it. I have never been so out of it.

It's good training for Jamelle, to be thrown into a situation like that. She addresses the media after the game. She is the head coach for that brief amount of time. It gives her a taste of what it's like.

The streak ends on March 11. We lose 52–48 to Villanova in the Big East championship. We lose to my good friend Harry Parretta. I don't really grasp at that time how remarkable it is to win 70 games in a row. With all the parity in the game today, both in the men's and women's programs, my guess is it probably won't happen again.

While the streak is nice, I suppose, I'm far more impressed with the way our team is coming together. The beauty of this particular season is that there are different people stepping up at different times. Dee is the constant. She is the sun. Everybody else takes turns being the planet she shines on. Dee is doing everything, but then here's Jessica Moore being the perfect inside-outside player who will rebound, score, and play defense. Now Jessica is going into a little funk but here comes Ann Strother, who is ready to play right out of high school, and hits big shot after big shot. Just when Ann starts to hit the wall, there's Maria knocking down shots and making smart plays. Just when, "Damn, Coach is mad at Maria because she's not running things well, and Dee is struggling with injuries and foul trouble," ooh, there's Barbara Turner stepping up and getting 26 points against Notre Dame. Man, Jessica Moore is having problems now, and we're taking a beating inside, and we're in the Final Four, and what the hell are we doing? Hey, Willnett Crockett. Where did you come from? Those 10 rebounds really help.

That's the best way I can describe it. Everybody takes turns contributing a little bit. Just when we start to count on one of the young players, because they have never been in that situation before, they start to disappear a little bit, which is normal. But once they start to disappear, someone else appears out of nowhere. It is perfect.

It is also incredibly nerve-racking.

Our path to the championship is nothing like the previous season. Every game, it seems to me, hangs in the balance. We play Texas Christian University in the second round, and we are down 35–33 at halftime.

The worst thing you can do as a team is to watch a team play a day or two before you play them in the NCAA tournament, because two things can happen. One is they play awful and you think they stink, but they're probably not that bad, otherwise, how did they get there? Or two, they play great, and you go away thinking they are a lot better than they really are. Either way, nothing good comes out of it. In the case of TCU, we watch them play Michigan State, and it's as bad a game as I've seen. So the perception of my players is, "They're not that good."

Well, guess what? They are good. They aren't afraid of us. They take it right to us. It's the kind of game where we need all of Dee's 35 points. It's the kind of game where superstars establish why they are superstars. Without them, you don't get to the Final Four, and you don't win a national championship.

When you win three championships in a row, as we end up doing, you are talking about winning 18 games. You've got to win six straight in each postseason. That's 18 in a row in the NCAA tournament. Something is bound to go wrong in one of those games and you lose—unless you have the one person who can make the difference.

We have that one person. We have Diana Taurasi, and they don't.

Dee goes off in the second half of that TCU game. We rip

off an 18–2 run and she scores 10 of the points. She is also involved in some way in the other eight. We win.

It doesn't get any easier from there. We're killing Purdue in the next game, but we go scoreless in the final eight and a half minutes of the game, and they go on a 20–4 run. We win 73–64 because we are so far ahead early.

Now we're in the Final Four, and we play Texas. We have no business winning that game. They play better than us. They are more talented than us. We win because we're Connecticut and we expect to win. We have been in that situation before, and they haven't. They outplay us for 37 minutes, but in the final three minutes, when it's time to win the game, they can't do it. It's not their fault. They just can't.

We can't stop them. Stacy Stephens is killing us inside. We finally put Willnett in and she plays great. Just great. She is the X factor in our season. Without Will, we don't get a championship. Even so, we are struggling down the stretch because they are so athletic and so talented. So I call a time-out and do something I never—ever—do. I say, "We're playing zone the rest of the way." It stops Texas in their tracks. All the stuff they've been doing, all of a sudden it goes out the window.

We hang on to win, 71–69. Maria hits two big free throws. She has only one turnover, I think. Then, in the championship game, she has no turnovers. In 77 minutes of the Final Four, she only coughs it up once.

I am thrilled for her. It's a credit to her mental toughness. I could say no one expected Maria to be really good at UConn except for me. I recruited her, so I'm smarter than everyone else, and take that, you dopes who criticized her. But the bottom line is I didn't expect her to be that good either. When I recruited her, do you think I said, "Hey, this kid is going to be solid as a rock for us in two championship games"? No way. I didn't. What I said was, "This kid has a chance to play a nice little role for us."

I coach her like I coach everyone else. I get pissed at her, and I criticize her for every little thing I don't like. Some kids take that and say, "Screw it, I'm not doing this." But the ones who get to be good players say, "Oh yeah? We'll see." That's what Maria does. She makes herself into a great player.

By the time we got to the Final Four, there was nothing Tennessee or Minnesota or anybody could have done to rattle her because, guess what? After putting up with my bullshit, asking her to go out and handle the ball against those guys? It was a piece of cake.

We play Tennessee—again—for the national championship. As we're preparing for the game, I'm trying to figure out how to get my team ready. Some people have these thoughts come to them that make them say, "I think I'll do this. Wouldn't that be a nice thing to do?" Every once in a while I get one of those thoughts, but most of my thoughts are, "How can I rub someone the wrong way, just for the fun of it?" I guess I'm just an ass. I like to irk people.

So it's a couple of hours before the game, and I'm wandering around with one of our writers, Randy Smith, from the *Manchester Journal*. I like to walk around with him to kill time. I remember Randy saying before the game how talented Tennessee is and how improbable it is that we are in the championship game, because we lost all those seniors from last year. And then he says, "Well, the perception is you are Connecticut, so you'll win regardless." I say, "Wait a minute. Just because we're from Connecticut means we're going to win, no matter who we put out there?"

And then it dawns on me. I walk into the locker room when my players aren't there and write down the names of last year's starters: Sue, Asjha, Swin, Tamika, and Dee. I do it for two reasons. One, to bug the hell out of them, and two, to let them know they are not in this by themselves.

I call them in and I say to Jessica Moore, "Jess, this is not you playing against Tennessee. This is you doing everything Asjha taught you to do. She's going to be right there with you, the entire 40 minutes." Then I say to Barbara Turner, "Barbara, this is not just you playing against Tennessee. This is Swin and everything she stands for. It's you and Swin." I do the same with Maria. It's Maria and Sue. I want them to feel there is another person inside them besides themselves.

We beat Tennessee 73–68. Dee scores 28. She's a perfect 8 for 8 from the line. Maria has 11 points, six assists, and no turnovers. Ann Strother is huge. She hits three three-pointers and finishes with 17 points. She hits a couple of clutch free throws in the final minute and Ashley Battle comes up with a big steal, and we're celebrating again.

One of the best parts about being champion is you get invited to the White House to meet the president. That, believe me, is a memory to last a lifetime.

The first time we go is with our undefeated team in 1995. It is a very, very big deal. I walk around my house before we leave saying, "I'm going to the White House. I'm going to meet President Clinton."

Back then we go with the champion of the men's teams, which in our case is UCLA. There's a great deal of planning that goes into picking the date and organizing the visit.

We charter a plane to go down to Washington, D.C. and

there's a lot of excitement. Everyone wants to go, so we have all sorts of people on the plane—players, coaches, boosters, university officials, state officials, and fans. The plane we have has just been used by the Rolling Stones, so our kids are saying, "Hey, we're like rock stars."

Everybody has his or her own perception of what this experience is going to be like. Everyone is saying, "This is what I'm going to do when I meet the president." A lot of the older guys on the plane, most of them boosters, have their own viewpoints. The part I find interesting is a lot of them do not care for President Clinton or his politics. So they go down there saying, "I'm not going down there to meet him. I'm going down because I'm a Connecticut fan."

When we arrive, we go through a security check. We stand outside the gate and get checked off by the guards who have a list of names of expected guests, and we show an ID card and boom! We're in. We take a little tour of the White House. There is a room set aside, and President Clinton is supposed to come out and speak. The two teams are at podiums on either side, and he's expected to walk through this door to a lectern with the presidential seal on it and say a few words.

There is a big delay. It's a very, very long delay. It turns out a U.S. jet has been shot down over Bosnia, and the president has to deal with it.

When he finally comes out, he speaks to our group as if he'd been preparing to meet these two basketball teams for the past month. I guess that's what makes you president. He makes us feel like nothing else is going on in the world. He makes us feel like we are the most important people in the building. He gets everything right. He knows all about our team.

————

The captains from UCLA and our captains, Rebecca Lobo and Pam Webber, give President Clinton a jersey. The president invites both UCLA coach Jim Harrick and me to say a few words. He is standing behind me as I am talking, and I make a couple of jokes, and I hear him laughing, and it's this eerie feeling, knowing the president is standing behind you.

Then President Clinton does something that I guess is typical of him. He ushers us into another room off to the side, and every member of the team has their picture taken with him. So, when you get home, you have a team shot as well as a personal shot. I have one of President Clinton, my daughter Jenna, and myself.

Meanwhile, all those people who were on the plane saying, "He's not my kind of guy" are shaking hands with this man and talking to him, and their jaws are hanging down. That's not just the power of the presidency—it's also the charisma of Bill Clinton.

Nearly five years later, we win again and we're in the locker room celebrating, and they bring in a conference speakerphone and say, "President Clinton is going to call to congratulate you, can you hang around for a couple of minutes?" We say, "Sure!" Well, five minutes go by, then ten, then twenty minutes. A woman comes on and says, "The president will be right with you." Now another ten or twenty minutes go by, and we're at the point where we have to do the postgame press conferences, and the kids have to do their random drug testing and all that. Finally we make a decision. We tell the woman at the president's office, "Sorry, but we've go to go." We never get a chance to talk to him.

We don't end up going to the White House that year. Michigan State is the men's champion and our two schools can't agree on a date that will work for both programs. It is such a shame it didn't work out. It would have been a great opportunity for those kids.

Anyhow, a couple of weeks go by, and I'm home with my son, Michael, watching a baseball game on television and all of a sudden the phone rings. I hear Michael say, "Yes, right, okay then, hold on." He says to me, "Someone is on the line saying they are Secret Service. I think it's a prank." I take the phone and someone says, "Coach Auriemma, can you give us your social security number?" I tell it to him. He says, "Can you hold a second, please? It's President Clinton calling from Air Force One." Sure enough, President Clinton is on the phone. We talk for about five minutes. He says, "Sorry we didn't connect after you won." He talks about our team, and tells me how much he loves Sue Bird. We don't talk about anything else except basketball. It's obvious the president follows the game very closely.

When I hang up, my son says, "Who was that?" I tell him, "It was President Clinton." He says, "No, c'mon, who was it?" I say, "It was the president of the United States, calling our house."

By the time we win again in 2002, George W. Bush is in office. It's the spring after September 11, and security is very tight. In spite of that, President Bush still wants to meet with us, but he's also going to meet with the men's and women's hockey champions, too, so there will be four teams.

The experience with President Bush couldn't have been any more different than the one with President Clinton. People aren't kidding when they say these two men are total opposites. Bush has them set up four podiums outside of the White House in the Rose Garden. We've got all our dignitaries with us—people like U.S. Senators Joe Lieberman and Chris Dodd. We are briefed by a group of government officials who tell us, "The president will meet with you at one o'clock, and he'll be done at one-thirty."

When we meet with President Clinton, it was like, "The president will be here shortly," and when you ask how long we'll have, they say, "Until he feels like leaving."

At precisely 1:01 p.m., here comes George W. Bush. He walks right up to the podium and begins speaking. Sue Bird and Swin Cash are up there. The president addresses the two hockey teams, the men's basketball team, which is Maryland that year, then us. When he gets to us, he screws up my name. He says something like "Areema" instead of Auriemma. He starts laughing at himself and says, "Well, whatever the hell that guy's name is, he really can coach." It is a good save. He shakes hands with everyone and gets his picture taken with the group. We are last. He comes up to me and says, "Sorry I screwed up your name." I say, "Don't worry about it." He says, "Oh, no. I'm not." Obviously he has much bigger things to worry about. He walks out the door at exactly 1:29 p.m. He's done.

One year later, in 2003, we are back at the White House again as champions. It's the same setup. We're on the same schedule, and just like last time, President Bush is on time right down to the minute. He walks in the room and he says, "Where's Geno? How are you doing?" I'm thinking to myself, "Very smart. He's not even going to try and pronounce it this time." I say to him, "Well, Mr. President, we're back." And he says, "And I'm still here." He waits a minute and then he says, "I think you told me you'd be back." I smile at him and I say, "I did, didn't I?"

So now it is 2004, and we've won three championships in a row, and we're doing three in a row with George W. There's a lot of stuff going on in the world. There's trouble in

Afghanistan, and trouble in Iraq, and he is under a tremendous amount of pressure. You can see it in his face. He's smiling, but he's wearing the look of a man with a lot on his mind. I say, "Just hang in there, man," and he says, "Thanks, Geno. Thanks." There's kind of this awkward silence, and then I tell him, "You know, an old coach told me this once. He said, 'The dogs will bark, but the caravan rolls on.'" The president shakes my hand and says, "You are absolutely right."

I go back and tell Hubie Brown I was quoting him to the president. Hubie is the first one I heard that saying from. It means, in essence, that no matter what you do, someone is going to say you are not doing it right, or you could do it better. You can't listen to all that crap. You've got to just keep moving on. I've learned that the hard way.

Fans are not shy about writing to me and telling me what they don't like about my coaching style. Most of the time, the letters are about me shouting at the players. People don't like that. I also hear a lot about the bad language I use. I know it's a problem, and all I can say is, I'm working on it. I know my language isn't good sometimes.

I'm constantly challenging myself to do better when I'm addressing my team, because it's not fair to use that language. I would not want anybody to speak to my kids like that. Even though it's not directed at anybody, I know that's no excuse. I'm trying to be more cognizant of it.

But sometimes even the very best players in the country can drive you crazy.

TWELVE

If Dee was the sun for our 2003 championship season, then all you can say about the next year is some cloud cover rolls in.

I start out convinced it's going to be a great season. I expect all the kids to take another big step up in their development. I think—we all think—with Dee in her senior season, her light is going to shine even brighter and bigger than ever.

We are wrong. Dee just isn't able to do what she did the year before. The other guys aren't able to raise their level. All of them get a little better, but they don't sustain it.

Dee is Don Quixote in her senior year. We just prop her up and let everyone think she is alive and well and as great as ever. If they had only known how banged up she was. That's why she doesn't dominate, because she doesn't have the energy or the physical ability to pull it off. Her body betrays her, so she's forced to save her energy for when we really need it.

The difference between the 2003 championship season and the 2004 championship season is that when Dee struggles, now we struggle, too. And, uncharacteristically, we tank a couple of times.

There is no greater example of that than when we play Duke on CBS. It's January 3, and we're 8–0, and we're two of the top teams in the country, and I still can't believe what happens.

Duke is supposed to be really, really good. But we go out there and destroy them. We are embarrassing them on national television. We're making them look like a junior high school team. But then, with five minutes to go, they turn the tables. They rip off a 30–11 run and *we* look like a grade school team. Now they are embarrassing us on national television.

When I watch the film afterwards, I'm sick. We turn the ball over too much. We give them too many second-chance points. We blow a 35–18 halftime lead, and a 59–42 lead with 17 minutes left, and a 12-point lead with five minutes to go. Dee hits a jumper to put us ahead, 67–65, with about five seconds to play, but then Jessica Foley hits a three at the buzzer for Duke.

It's over. We have humiliated ourselves in front of the entire country.

That loss snaps a streak of 69 straight home wins for us. We are tied with Tennessee for the NCAA record going into that Duke game, but we can't hang on.

It is the perfect game to illustrate our team. We can blow anyone out in the country, and we can look like the worst team in the country.

It's a lesson to me as a coach that your players are only as good as you think they are. The last five minutes of that game, I don't think my players are any good, so they live down to my expectations. I don't say anything particularly bad to them in the huddle, because I am so flabbergasted that we are blowing this lead.

We have a 12-point lead with five minutes to go and we don't win the game? Are you kidding me? What my team needs at that point is me to tell them, "Listen, guys, do you know how many times we've been in this situation? Lots of times. Teams try to come back on us and our response is boom, boom, boom! We knock them out. So don't worry." That's what I should be saying. Instead, I am so frustrated with them that I keep harping on the fact that I can't believe we've gotten ourselves into this mess.

Obviously that isn't too helpful in turning things around. So they go back out there and throw the ball away again, and I've got to call another timeout. Then, all of sudden, we're in the middle of this desperate situation, and none of us are sure how it happened.

The problem we run into is Dee is the only one I trust to inbound the ball cleanly. The other problem is Dee is the only person I want to receive the inbounds pass. We finally settle on having Barbara Turner inbound the ball, and she throws it away. We turn to Jessica Moore, and have her inbound the ball, and she throws it to Dee. Now all Dee has to do is dribble it up the court. But for reasons known only to her, she turns around and tries to throw a home run pass. Here's our first-team All-America player, the best player in the country, and she throws the ball away. I say to her, "Dee, what on earth possessed you to do that?" She answers me, "I dunno."

I dunno? I can't believe this. She walks off the court with this look on her face as if to say, "Hey, man, what about you? What the hell are you doing?" I've already blown three time-outs, and our best player has this total blank look on her face.

We're screwed.

It's like the tennis matches I used to play in college. You win the first set 6–2. It's a three-set match. You're up 4–2 in the second set, but you lose your concentration and your opponent comes back and wins the second set 6–4, and now all of a sudden you're like, "What the hell?" Now the big advantage you had is gone. Now it's tied. Now you are in a third set, and all you can harp on is how you let that overwhelming win in the first set deteriorate into this. Poof! You're fried. You've blown a circuit, and you're done.

We learn a lot that day—all of us. It is a real reminder to me how far we need to go. During the season, I tell my players every five minutes, "Figure it out." I want them to figure it out on their own, because when it comes time for the NCAA tournament, they've got to make split-second decisions that will make or break our season. I can see they have a lot of work to do before they will be able to make those decisions on their own.

I can't get past that Duke game. All we have to do is inbound the ball, get it across half-court, and we win going away. Well, we can't do it. Why? Because we get sloppy. Well, isn't it the coach's job to make sure that doesn't happen? I guess it is. I get sloppy sometimes. What we do that day is unacceptable, and it's a reflection on both my players and me. The game is supposed to be played a certain way and we don't do it. We should play the game perfectly. You hear that and you figure, "Geez, this must be coming from a guy who is incredibly disciplined, who has all his ducks in a row, who is a stickler for every detail." Well, bullshit. This is from a person who wishes he could be that way. This is from a person who is trying to make his players see the value of being that way.

I'm forever in that "I wish I could have" mode and it drives me crazy. Like right now. I wish I could lose ten pounds. Every night at the end of the day, I think about what I could have done to help me reach that goal, and I haven't done it. The same thing happens when I'm coaching. I go back and look at the film and say, "Damn, I wish we would have done that differently."

That's why I'm constantly striving for perfection. When we are up 25 points and Barbara Turner gets the ball and without looking where she's going charges into a player and gets called for an offensive foul, I'm livid. You know why? If she does that in a two-point game, it's going to cost us. "Well," you say, "it isn't a two-point game. It's a 25-point game." The young kids have a hard time with it, too. When I start screaming at them, they look at me, and think, "Why is he killing me? We're up by 30." They don't understand I'm coaching the Final Four two years from now. I'm preparing them to stay mentally tough at all times, regardless of the circumstances.

Sometimes I wish I was more organized, but I'm not by the book. I will never be. I can't put those ducks in a row, day after day. That's not my personality. That is Chris Dailey's personality. I'm not a follower of any kind of order. There's classical music, and there's jazz music. Classical has a constant rhythm to it. Jazz starts out a certain way, then goes off on a whole other tangent. Then it comes back. Then it goes away. Then it comes back again. That's me. Now, if it keeps going away and never comes back, that's crappy jazz. But if there's a common thread, you wind up saying, "Yeah, that's pretty cool."

No one is telling me I'm pretty cool after that loss to Duke. It's a frustrating day for everybody. It's apparent to me my team is playing for March and April. I talk to Phil Martelli about it. He asks me if they're playing hard. I tell him they are. They always do. But the team has gotten to a point where they lose their concentration and say, "I just don't want to work that hard. I'll play hard, but I don't want to work that hard."

That worries me. It gnaws at me. It's hard to coach the same guys two years in a row. There are no seniors from the championship team in 2003, so now we've got essentially the same roster returning.

It's like when somebody puts a salad in front of you. For five straight days, you eat the same salad. On the first day, it tastes great. By the fifth day, you never want to see it again. On the sixth day, they give you a salad, but they throw in a couple of different ingredients and you say, "Man, this tastes really good." So what we have in 2003–04 is the same salad with no new ingredients.

It makes for a trying season—one of the most trying of my career. The wear and tear of it is difficult. As much as the team wants to be good, they are having trouble sustaining that for the entire year. What do they have to prove? The year before they had a ton to prove. Diana wanted to prove, "We're not just a bunch of slugs living off a great senior class." That motivated her as much as anything.

Here's the other thing that puts me over the edge in 2003–04. Dee is a senior, a leader, the best player in the country, so her teammates, whenever they get into trouble, say, "Aaaw, screw it. Let Diana do it." I'm already being really hard on Dee, because I want her to play even better than she did in her junior season. I realize eventually she was so good the previous year there might not be any way for her to improve on that.

Still, I want her to try. I'm ordering her to try. It's too hard. She can't. She's struggling with a ton of injuries. Her back is bothering her all the time, and she's got problems with her ankles, and she's wearing down. Our trainer, Rosemary Ragle, is her best friend that season. She spends more time with Dee than anyone else. I see Dee's confidence eroding a little bit, and I never—ever—expected to see that.

We can't get Dee to sit out. She needs to rest her body because she's so banged up, but she's one of those kids who lives to practice. She craves it. She tells me, "Coach, seriously, I'd rather miss a game than miss practice." I tell her, "Dee, please. No one will think less of you if you sit out once in a while. We need you to do that." But, like everything else over the past four years, she's fighting me every step of the way.

In the meantime, the other guys are absolutely no help. I'm thinking these players are ready to show their upside, but early on, Ann Strother isn't that much better, and Barbara Turner isn't that much better, and Jessica Moore is too inconsistent. We lose Nicole Wolff right away with a knee injury. It breaks your heart. She misses most of the previous year, too, with a stress fracture.

Two times Nicole has to sit there and watch us win a national championship. It's hard to keep her part of it when she's not playing. It's hard to keep her in the nest. I tell her she has to keep herself in the nest. One of the best things about going to college is being thrown into a new environment and figuring out how you fit. If you are a smart kid, like Nicole is, you say to yourself, "Where do I stand? How do I function in this situation? How do I stay connected to the program so it doesn't look like the train has left the station and I'm not on it?"

Nicole is a kind of shy, introverted kid who puts a lot of pressure on herself. She gets perfect grades the first semester, and then gets a 3.5 grade point average the second semester and is ready to jump off the Bissell Bridge, whereas we've got a couple of kids who would kill to have their GPA from both semesters add up to 3.5. Nicole is a quiet person who doesn't naturally interact with a whole lot of people. But now, because of her situation, she is forced to go out of her way to be part of things. It's not an easy thing to do, but Nicole does it.

The other thing you have to remember about Nicole is she's tough as nails. She has grown up with basketball. Her father is the men's coach at Boston University, so she knows how it works. I really want Nicole to succeed. She works so hard, and she's one of the nicest kids you'll ever meet. If she can stay healthy, she will be a Rhodes Scholar candidate.

She comes in her freshman year and wins a starting job, but then she misses some shots and loses her confidence a little bit. She is so hard on herself. You can see it on her face. She's thinking, "I'm letting the team down." Well, then she gets hurt and she has to sit on the bench and watch. One game, I say to her, "It sucks, doesn't it, watching us play like this." Her eyes fill up a little bit and I say, "Bet you'd do anything to go 0 for 7 from the floor, huh?" She says, "Yeah, that doesn't seem so bad anymore." So you hope the silver lining from the injuries is she doesn't care so much anymore when she misses shots.

Nicole is out for the 2003–04 season, and Ashley Battle has all sorts of bumps and bruises, and Maria is pouting, and we're getting nothing from the freshmen, but somehow we are winning. My coaches keep telling me, "It will sort itself out." Then why do I feel like the roof is about to cave in?

It all comes tumbling down ten days after the Duke game. We go to Notre Dame and we get spanked, 66–51. Dee falters a little in this game. She's 4 of 15 from the floor, and she scores 11 points. Jacqueline Batteast has a big game for Notre Dame.

We are quiet leaving the court. The players go into the locker room and we keep going to the coach's room. In between those two rooms are the showers and the bathroom.

The coaches are sitting there feeling lousy. None of us are saying much. All of a sudden we hear this noise coming from the shower area. Even though the door is closed, we can hear this banging. We can hear a voice crying. Jamelle says, "Who is that?" We keep listening. I say, "Oh crap. It's Dee."

I walk over, open the door, and there she is. There's our team leader, our rock, sitting on a bench, swaying back and forth and banging her elbows against the wall. She's crying, and she's talking to herself, and it's all coming out. The first thing I think of when I see Diana like that is, "This is what it must be like to work in a heroin rehab center." I say that because she is shaking and she's suffering, and she has no idea how to get out of this. She is in withdrawal, like some kind of drug addict.

I have never seen Dee like this. And all at once, my heart really goes out to her. I grab her, and I hug her, and I tell her it's not her fault, and we're going to fix it, but she isn't listening. She doesn't believe me. It hits you then what this poor kid has been through. Unless you've been in her shoes, in a situation where you get all the credit for what happens— and you've never been quite comfortable with that—and then you also get all the blame when things go wrong, you can't possibly understand. But when she's sitting there, you remember she's just a kid, and that no kid should have to deal with this kind of pressure.

My wife and I were talking about something like this during the World Series. Kathy says to me, "How come when a pitcher throws a pitch and the guy hits a home run, it's the pitcher's fault? Why can't it be that the batter did a good job hitting the ball?" I say, "It's the pitcher's fault because he threw the pitch. He gets paid for getting the hitter out. The hitter gets rewarded for his job. Everyone says, 'Yo, that was a helluva hit.' Meanwhile, they say to the pitcher, 'Yo, that was a lousy pitch.' Even if the pitcher throws a great pitch and the guy manages to hit it out, he's still not off the hook. It's his job to get the guy out, no matter what."

Now, the difference is that pitcher is an adult making $15 million a year. In Dee's case, we're talking about a twenty-year-old kid. When we lose the Duke game, everyone says, "Man, what's wrong with Dee?" Now all of a sudden we go to practice and Dee is thinking, "Everything I did last year clicked, and everything I did was right. I pushed all the right buttons. And now everything I try doesn't work. I am still me. Can't they realize I'm hurt? Can't they realize I'm carrying these guys all the time? I carried them all last year. Someone has to help me."

Of course, because she's Diana Taurasi, she says none of that. She just keeps it all bottled up inside. She never says anything like that, but her actions after the Notre Dame game say it all.

Dee will tell you she played badly against Notre Dame. She was bad—but not awful. She was just bad enough so we didn't win. Now she is sitting there crying and banging her fists against the wall, and she looks like someone who just wants all this crap out of her system. She looks like someone who has run out of answers.

The other kids are stunned and a little scared. They are in the locker room, and they can't see her in the shower area. They can only hear her. I'm trying to console Dee for what seems like a long time, and I think Ashley Battle and Jessica Moore might have come over eventually, but they're not sure if they should be there. It's too late, anyway. They had their chance, and they didn't help her.

You'd like to think it's an opportunity for these other players to say, "Don't worry, Dee. You can count on us." After that, they do try. It happens for about eight or nine games. They take a little more responsibility, which is good. But it's still all going to come down to Dee.

A couple of days after the Notre Dame loss, I call my team together. I tell them, "You have to understand the load Diana is carrying. Nobody bitches at Dee more than I do. Nobody demands more from her than I do. And you know what? She never complains. She doesn't complain about her ankle problems, about her back problems, about getting triple-teamed, about getting fouled, about the fact you guys are a bunch of slugs and she has to lug you around again.

"She put you on her back last year and won you a national championship. You have a national championship because of her. You will never be able to repay her for what she did for you guys. And right now she is crying out to you guys for help. All she wants from you right now is to see what she is going through and be there and bail her out a little bit."

At this point, Dee has her head down, and you can see the tears coming out of her eyes, because these are all the things she has wanted to say, but never would.

The other players take it to heart. They really do. They

try their best. But it's like me grabbing my son, giving him the keys to my car, and telling him, "Go to New York and pick up my friend at the Four Seasons." He just got his permit. How the hell is he going to do that? You can't ask Ann and Barbara to do stuff they aren't prepared to do yet. Imagine me going to Maria and saying, "Yo, Maria, I'm not going to play Dee for a couple of weeks. So you just do everything she does, okay?" Forget about it. That's not going to happen. It's wrong to expect it to happen.

Maria is a senior that year, too, but she has only one year of experience. The first two years, Maria is what I call a 20–20–20 guy. That means she gets in either when we're up 20, down 20, or with 20 seconds left. You don't develop a lot of game experience when you are a 20–20–20 guy.

I usually have rules about subbing in kids at the end of the game. It's three minutes or nothing, unless it's a national championship, or unless I need to take one of the players who has done really well out for an ovation. In that case, if Dee needs to come out, and there's only 40 seconds left, then that's how it goes. Under normal circumstances, though, I don't like sticking someone in for 20 seconds. I hated that as a player. It's humiliating, and most times, it's unnecessary.

My intent is not to embarrass kids. But sometimes it happens, because they are so stubborn or so spoiled, and the only way I can get through to them is to do something that will grab their attention.

After being a head coach for twenty years, I'm starting to realize kids have changed. They are more coddled. They have it so much easier than my first Connecticut team. It dawned on me a few weeks ago when I got stuck behind a school bus. When I was a kid, I always took the bus to school.

Not the school bus—the city bus. I'd walk with my mother three blocks to the bus stop. We'd get on together, take it twelve blocks to the main bus terminal, then I'd change buses and go in one direction to school, and she'd continue on the bus another six blocks or so to work. I was usually the only kid on the bus. But that's the way it goes. It was the only way I could get to school.

I think kids today have lost something. The bus I got stuck behind stopped at every street corner. At one stop, six kids got on. The next stop, which was thirty or forty yards away, tops, another group of kids got on. I'm thinking to myself, "Why can't they just walk to that other bus stop?" That's what missing. We do everything for our kids today. Life has become too easy. That's one reason coaching, to me, is not just about basketball. It's about teaching kids how to get along in life.

Everyone is so spoiled today. And guess what? I was spoiled in my day, too. I always had enough food, I always had just enough clothes to wear, and I had my one baseball glove that was going to have to last me a whole bunch of years.

I'm sure my father was looking at me and saying, "I can't believe this kid doesn't work." I was twelve. By the time he was twelve, he had been working for a while. I'm sure my dad's father was looking at him when he was eight and saying, "I can't believe this kid doesn't work." You hope every kid is forced to do something he or she doesn't want to do, so they learn. I had to do things I didn't want to do, too, but I look back and I'm glad. It has made me tougher. It has made me better.

If I really want to tease my mother, I start talking to her about when we were growing up. I'll say to her, "Mom, tell me again about the stuff I got for Christmas when we lived in Italy." She looks at me and says, "Christmas? You didn't get nothing for Christmas." I don't think I got a Christmas gift until I was about ten. The only reason I got one was because we were living in America, and everybody gets Christmas gifts, so you've got to get them, too. My mother, God bless her, never got Christmas gifts as a child. When you are tying pieces of cardboard together as shoes, you aren't handing out gifts.

Now, I could tell my team stories about growing up in Italy and how I didn't have much, but I know better. I know better than to sound like an old man who says, "When I was your age . . ."

Some of this stuff they have to figure out on their own.

The NCAA tournament is getting close, and I don't like where Dee's head is. She's being a baby. She's acting like a twenty-one-year-old that has been dragging a bunch of slugs around for two years. It's gotten to her, and she can't do it anymore. She needs my help and support, and in typical fashion, I'm not giving it to her.

She's pouting and getting ticked off at me because I'm all over her ass. I say to her, "Who do you want me to get on? You want me to get on the other guys? If I thought they could handle it, don't you think I'd do it?"

I know her well enough to know when something is up. When she wanders into my office, if she sits on the couch to the left of my desk, she just wants to hang out and tell me how great she is without actually saying it. But when she sits in the chair in front of my desk, I know something is wrong.

Of course, it takes a while for her to tell me. First we have to go through the "I'm Diana Taurasi, nothing bothers me, I'm cool, I've got ice in my veins" routine.

So one day she comes in and slumps into the chair in front of my desk and I say, "So Dee, what's wrong?" She says, "Huh? Oh, nothing." I say, "Oh, nothing, huh? Hey, I don't know much, but it seems to me that you are tired of being Diana Taurasi. It seems to me being Diana Taurasi is one big pain in the ass right now, and you wish you weren't her."

Well, that does it. She loses it. She breaks down crying in my office. That's when I tell her, "This is going to end badly for you if you're not careful. You can't hide from what you are. You are Diana Taurasi, and everyone thinks you are invincible, and you have to be on stage all the time. It sucks to have to do everything right everywhere you go, doesn't it?"

She says, "Yes, it does. I'm sick of it." I tell her, "I know, but that's too bad. This is how it is. Stop pouting, because no one is going to leave you alone. I'm not going to leave you alone. I'm on you because you are the only one who can handle it. If I leave you alone and you do it your way, you're going to be disappointed."

A couple of weeks later, we lose to Boston College in the semifinals of the Big East tournament. That is it. She's had enough. I can tell by Diana's face she will not let us lose again. We play Auburn in the second round of the NCAAs and we hold them scoreless for more than 16 minutes of the second half. It's my fiftieth birthday, and Ann Strother and Maria Conlon give me a gift: four three-pointers each.

We play UC Santa Barbara in the next game. They have a 6-foot-8 center named Lindsay Taylor. Jessica Moore plays great defense on her. We beat them by eight. We knock off Penn State. We hold off Minnesota.

We will be playing for the national championship—again. Our men's team wins the championship, too, and we have a chance to become the first Division I school in history to win both the men's and women's crowns in the same season.

We do it. We do it against Tennessee. One of their top players, Loree Moore, is out with an injury. Dee is Dee. She's the best player on the floor. Jessica Moore explodes for a bunch of big baskets in the second half. Barbara Turner, who gives up three inches to their big men, is immense off the boards. She gives us a terrific performance. Ann Strother hits some big, big shots.

When the game ends and the buzzer sounds, Diana punts the ball into the stands. The expression on her face is one of immense relief.

Her career here is over. She has locked up the storybook ending. I watch her and think how far we have come. I think back to that old gym with the leaky roof and I can't believe it has been transformed into this.

I look into the stands and I see Lester Baum, one of our oldest and most loyal fans. He is married to Devra, who one day introduces me to her sister, Esther Newberg, who becomes my agent for this book. Lester has been a supporter of our team forever. He and Devra endow a number of scholarships for the women's basketball program. They understand the journey. They have been on it with me.

Years ago, when we are in the old gym, we're playing Providence, which is much better than us at the time. There are two hundred fans in the stands, at the most. Lester is sitting in the end zone to my left. We're holding the ball because it's the only chance we have to shorten the game and steal a win. Lester is watching, and he's getting pissed, so he starts screaming to my players, "Shoot the ball!" This goes on until I can't take it anymore. We're in the middle of the game, and

I turn to Lester and shout, "Lester, shut up! We're trying to hold the ball." He says, "Oh, okay, Geno."

Imagine me trying to tell Lester something now in the middle of our game? It's so loud in Gampel Pavilion, I can barely hear my assistants, who are sitting right next to me.

The support our program has enjoyed is unbelievable. So many people have been there for us, like Mrs. Benson, who found out it was my birthday one day about twelve years ago and brought me a cake. Ever since then, she brings cookies and cakes to the office when she finds out one of our staff members is having a birthday.

We have a lot of boosters. I'm sure some of them give big money to our program, but I don't know who they are. I don't want to know. I don't want to have to treat them a certain way.

I've had a number of people who have been extremely supportive to Kathy and me during our time in Connecticut. It's hard for me to establish close friendships, because I'm not the most accommodating guy in the world when it comes to planning things, because in this job, your schedule changes all the time. You hope people understand. Some do, and some don't. Those that do—and they are too many to list here—help you so much. We feel so lucky to have been welcomed into the community of Manchester, and the community of the University of Connecticut.

It's the same for the players. They have one another, but there's a whole other support group out there on campus for them.

Dee is named Most Outstanding Player of the NCAA tournament. She has made sure it ends the way it should end. She puts an exclamation point on her reputation as the best player in the game.

I make up my mind that I'm going to let this one last win wash over me a little longer. I'm going to celebrate with Diana, who has challenged me as much as any player I've ever had. I'm going to enjoy these kids, like Morgan Valley and Ashley Battle and Maria Conlon, who have sacrificed so much to get here. I'm going to revel in their success.

There are no sentimental words exchanged between Dee and me. That's not how we do it. We both know what we mean to each other. I've never felt the need to tell her.

Months after Dee is gone a reporter asks her to describe her relationship with me. She says, "Every single day he hits you and hits you and hits you. And, if you are still standing in March, he'll embrace you."

I wish the embrace could last.

But Dee has to move on, and so do we.

THIRTEEN

It is just seconds after we have beaten Tennessee to win our third consecutive national championship, and the very first person I need to talk to is Pat Summitt. Moments after the buzzer sounds, we meet at center court and speak briefly. Everyone who follows college basketball wants to know what I say to her.

I tell them it is none of their business.

Months later, the curiosity over our private discussion lingers. Friends, acquaintances, even total strangers pull me aside and say, "C'mon, you can tell me. What were you two talking about?"

I'm sure some of them found it amazing that we were talking at all. There's no question that Pat wasn't very happy with me in the spring of 2004. She didn't appreciate some of the comments I had made about her and her program the past couple of years. I have a tendency to be sarcastic when the writers ask me questions. That's my sense of humor. I say things that are supposed to be funny, but not everybody interprets them that way.

I say things I guess people think I shouldn't say.

Like the time I call Tennessee the "Evil Empire." That is in 2003, and it is the week before the Final Four, and we are on course to play Tennessee for the national championship. At this point, our programs have developed a pretty heated rivalry. A Connecticut-Tennessee showdown is what everyone wants to see. We're the defending national champions that season, and we've beaten the Lady Vols twice in the championship game before.

Someone asks me to explain the significance of the two teams possibly playing each other again for bragging rights. So I say, "Well, we're from New England and they're the Evil Empire, and our job is to eliminate them." I figure everyone knows I am making a reference to the great baseball rivalry between the Boston Red Sox and the New York Yankees. The Red Sox president, Larry Lucchino, had generated a lot of publicity by calling the Yankees the "Evil Empire," and I am playing off of that.

Most people get it. The numb nuts that don't understand it make it out to be a *Star Wars* reference, like I was saying I was Harrison Ford, the good guy, and Pat Summitt was Darth Vader. They just didn't get it.

The unfortunate part is Pat didn't get it either.

I suppose I should back up a little and explain how we get to this point. In the beginning, Pat and I have a very cordial relationship, but over time, that relationship really disintegrates. I'll take partial responsibility for that. I have a tendency to shoot from the hip and say whatever comes into my head. Oftentimes, I make comments about Tennessee or their coach that are not appreciated.

It all comes to a head in the fall of 2003, when Harry Parretta, the coach at Villanova, calls me up. Now, Harry and I have been friends forever. He says to me, "Geno, I got a call from Pat Summitt, and she wants me to help her with her offense. She wants some new ideas. Would you be all right with that?"

I say to him, "Why would you have to ask me that? I don't have any feelings about it one way or another. Although, Harry, I will tell you I think it's a little odd."

Here's the best friend I have in the Big East, a guy I've known for thirty years, and suddenly our biggest rival is calling him for help with their offense? It seems a little funny to me, but I'm not going to get too bothered by it.

So I say, "Listen, Harry, I'm going to call Pat right now and tell her after she spends three days with you, she'll be so screwed up she won't know what to do with her team, because nobody ever understands what the hell you are saying."

Harry laughs, and that is the end of it. Later on, people tell me that Pat didn't just call Harry out of the blue, that Harry saw her at a clinic and said, "Call me, I'll help you with your offense." I don't really know which story to believe. I guess it really doesn't matter.

Anyhow, Harry goes down to Tennessee and works with their team, and every time I talk to him, I put a little dig in. I say, "Man, Harry, you must be exhausted coaching your team, and helping the men's team down there at Villanova, plus coaching Tennessee. Where do you find the time?"

So now the NCAA tournament rolls around, and of course they put Villanova in Tennessee's bracket, and all ESPN is talking about is Harry and Pat. The two teams are set to play each other, and the game is in Knoxville, and Pat invites the whole Villanova team and the coaching staff over for a cookout at her house before the game. Now, I'm saying to myself,

"Who the hell does that? And who goes?" I think it is the most bizarre thing I've ever heard.

Pat gives Harry a lucky tie. He shows up the day of their game wearing it. It is crazy. It has just gone too far. I'm trying to hold it in, but I can't. It's just too funny to me.

Anyway, we win our regional game against Purdue, and here come the writers. They want to know what I think of Harry and Pat. Villanova had beaten us earlier that year, so they want to know if I think Harry has given Pat any insights into our team. So I say, "I'm not worried about that. Pat is going to coach her team the way she coaches her team. But what I am really sick of is this Harry and Pat stuff. If I hear one more story about the two of them, I'm going to throw up. They're over each other's house, they're having a cookout, they are in the hot tub together, probably. How far is this going to go?"

The writers are laughing, and I'm laughing as I say it, but obviously it doesn't go over too well. Pat never says anything to me, but I get word she is ticked off.

Harry isn't mad at all, but he does call me up to say, "What are you doing?" I shoot back with, "Yo, how's the hot tub?" He says, "You've got to stop." I say, "No, you've got to stop, because you know, she's married and you're married and you better cut it out, or people will start talking."

Harry is laughing, but he says to me, "Stop perpetuating this. It's getting out of hand." I tell him, "Oh, come on. I'm just having some fun." Harry says, "Well, I've got all these reporters calling me, asking me what I think," and I say, "Good. I have to deal with reporters every day. I'm glad it's your turn."

I get a lot of grief for what I say. I was just having some fun, and, in a roundabout way, my players didn't have to answer questions about the Final Four and Tennessee and all that, because all the stupid stuff between Harry and Pat and myself takes over. Well, then, on top of it, I make my Evil Empire comments, and now the Tennessee people are really out to get me.

I guess it is my fault for assuming that Pat Summitt would understand the reference to the Evil Empire, or that *anyone* would understand it. The truth of it is, Pat gets caught in the crossfire between Harry and me. Where we come from, in Philly, you make fun of the people you like. If you don't like them, you wouldn't even talk about them. You'd say, "Don't ask me about that person. Just ask me about my team."

I wasn't about to let a chance to have some fun at Harry's expense go by. His cozy little relationship with Pat was too good to pass up. What she probably doesn't understand is the person on the other end of it could have been Pat Summitt or Pat Sajak. It wouldn't have mattered. My target was Harry.

In any case, we go out and beat Tennessee for the national championship, and that just adds fuel to the fire.

That summer, I'm at a recruiting camp in Chicago, and I confront Pat. I had sent her a note following our championship game to apologize. I said, "Obviously I was trying to be funny, but it didn't go over so well, so I'm sorry if I caused a distraction." She never answered me.

So I go up to her in Chicago and ask if she got my note, and she says she did. Then she says, "What's this all about? How did it get to this point?" And I say, "Well, it used to be Connecticut versus Tennessee, but somewhere along the way, it became me versus you, and I'm not all that comfortable with that."

I still believe that in her mind, it had also become her versus me, to see who was the best coach, the best recruiter, who had the best strategy, all that crazy stuff that the media loves.

Pat says she didn't see it that way. So I tell her, "You know what? You are perceived as the golden girl of women's basketball, and I've got a chip on my shoulder because I don't like it. That's how I feel. I feel like there are things I'm going to have to overcome that you will never have to overcome."

I tell her, "See Ceal Barry, the Colorado coach, over there? You were just with her for an hour, going over x's and o's. Do you know a few years back that Ceal Barry called me and wanted to come up to Connecticut to go over our triangle offense? I told her we would be glad to help her. She spent three days with us. I went over everything we did with her. I watched film with her, gave her drills, and reviewed strategy. She sent me a note afterwards saying, 'I can't believe you did that, I never knew you before and I'm so grateful.'

"Well, now Ceal Barry walks right by me without looking at me. So where is that coming from? Because we recruited some kids from Colorado? I've got this reputation as an arrogant son of a bitch, a guy who is unapproachable. Oh really? I'll do anything for anybody. Just ask me. Call me. But then don't act like you don't know me because I got some players you wanted."

Pat says, "Well, I don't know anything about that." And she really didn't. I was just trying to prove a point. This is the kind of stuff I'm up against. And because of it, I'm out to kick everyone's butt.

Some of it is just natural. I don't want to come off as "Oh, poor Geno Auriemma, he's a guy coaching women's basketball and woe is me, it's me against the world," but it *is* different being a man coaching the women's game. There are always going to be certain people who don't want you to succeed, just because you are a man.

When I start out, I'm an assistant coach at Virginia, then later a head coach in an obscure Connecticut program. There are some perceived superpowers out there that are looked upon as the giant aircraft carriers, while programs like mine are seen as the SS *Minnow*. Those superpowers decide the future of women's college basketball. They decide who is in and who is out. It is like organized crime, in some ways.

So when you start out, you want nothing more than to beat those superpowers. You respect some of them for what they do, and how they do it. Some of them even become your friends. Some will never be your friend, because you disagree with just about everything they do, and how they do it. That's not to say they can't be successful. It's not a matter of wrong or right. It's a matter of style.

Pat and I are very different. From the beginning, neither one of us is too big on talking to each other, although at one point the two of us share information on our contracts. We also coach an All-America All-Star team together that plays against the U.S. Olympic team in 1995. I really don't understand why we have to be co-coaches. Just pick one of us and get it over with. But they want to keep everybody happy. To tell you the truth, I think it is silly. How are the two of us going to coach one game? But they like the idea of it.

Geno and Pat. Isn't that cute?

I've always respected Pat for what she's done for the women's game. She's had great success, and she's promoted our sport. In fact, the opportunity for us to play Tennessee the very first time came about because we were supposed to play North Carolina on Martin Luther King Day in 1995 on ESPN, and they wouldn't agree to do it. We are a very good team that year. ESPN tries but can't pull the deal together with Carolina. They keep saying no, for whatever reason. ESPN comes back to me and says, "Who can we get?" It has to be Connecticut and somebody, because they owe the Big East a televised game.

They call around to Virginia and some other schools, but they all have reasons why they can't play. So I say, "Call Pat." I knew exactly what would happen. They ask her, and she says, "Absolutely." Pat has always been very good at understanding what it's all about. She knows it would be good for the women's game, even though it means bringing her team to our place. You have to give her credit for that.

She understands Tennessee needs another rival. No matter how many battles they have with Georgia, or LSU, or Stanford, or Old Dominion, or Texas, or Louisiana Tech, 80 percent of the country really doesn't care. Like it or not, the media is East Coast–based. Pat is smart enough to understand we are in the right market geographically. As good as her program is, a large number of people in the South don't care, because they are only concerned with college football and their bowl games.

Down South, a Florida versus Florida State football game is a big event. Florida State versus Miami football is a big event. Every time Kentucky plays basketball, it's a big event. Here in the Northeast, when the Yankees play the Red Sox it's a big event. When the Celtics play the Lakers it's a big event. That's how it works in the Northeast. It is a big-event region. Whatever the sport, if it's big enough, we'll latch on to it.

So now we've got a little something going on, and Tennessee agrees to play us, and the *New York Times* decides to cover it. All of a sudden, it's not just the *Hartford Courant* anymore. All of a sudden, people are going to read about Connecticut and Tennessee everywhere. When the *New York Times* starts covering something, the whole world is aware of it.

So here comes Tennessee to Storrs, and by the time they get there, it's a very big deal. We are ranked No. 2 in the country and they are ranked No. 1. That's the game where Jen Rizzotti hits a big three-pointer at the end to win it for us. That's the game that puts us permanently on the national map, for beating the seemingly untouchable Tennessee Vols.

Jamelle Elliott will tell you that what she remembers most about that game is she guards Nikki McCray. Nikki is Tennessee's best athlete, and Jamelle is probably our worst athlete, but she is out there guarding her. I do it because I feel Jamelle can front her and be strong enough not to let Nikki go backdoor. Jamelle is smart. Smart as hell. I've coached a lot of bright players, but Jamelle is the smartest and the toughest. You want to put her on the court at critical parts of the game.

Pat is very gracious after the loss. She pays tribute to Connecticut and everything is fine. That is in January of 1995. We don't get too excited because we have a feeling we'll see them again in the NCAA tournament. We meet them in Minneapolis for the national championship. We are undefeated, and have just beaten Stanford by 27 points in the semifinals. After our game is over, the reporters ask Stanford coach Tara VanDerveer who will win the final, Tennessee or Connecticut. She says, "Connecticut has no chance." Now, we've just beaten her ass 87–60, and you might think that might have made an impression on her. But nobody is going to bet against Pat, the golden girl—at least not publicly.

It's like women trying to break into the old boys' network.

I am a man trying to break into the old girls' network. The best way to do that, I figure, is to beat everybody. Including Tennessee.

And that's what we do. We beat Tennessee for our first national championship.

We've got another date with Tennessee the following January, in 1996. We go to Knoxville to play in their gym. They've won 69 straight at home. We go in there and beat them, 59–53. There isn't nearly as much animosity as there is now, but suddenly we're 3–0 against Tennessee, and no one has ever done that, so the rivalry is starting to get hot.

We know we're going to see them again in the Final Four. That spring, we play them in the national semifinals. I don't understand why the NCAA didn't set it up so we would play them in the finals, because we are definitely the best two teams in the country, but that's how they did it.

Tennessee beats us in overtime, in what I think is one of the greatest college women's games ever played. It's one of those games in which everyone steps up. Nykesha hits an unbelievable three to send it into overtime. Our guys play well. Their guys play well. As well as Jen played the previous year in the championship game, and completely dominated, Tennessee's Michelle Marciniak completely dominates this game.

Kara Wolters fouls out, and we don't have enough players to keep up with them. Our guys are exhausted. I have this conversation with Jamelle near the end of the game. I say to her, "J, they keep running the same play, a high pick-and-roll. You've got to get around that screen and help." She says to me, "Coach, I know, but I can't get there." I remember feeling really bad for her. She really couldn't get there.

I address the media after the game and congratulate Tennessee. I tell them, "It was their turn. Last year, Jen Rizzotti was in her locker room celebrating a national championship. This year, she's in there crying, and Michelle Marciniak is experiencing what she had."

I never like losing, but I feel okay about what happened that night. Our team played well. It is just that Tennessee played better. It was their turn.

We go into the 1996–97 season with a good feeling. Tennessee has added Chamique Holdsclaw, and she's a monster, but we've still got some players of our own who know how to get it done: Shea Ralph and Kesha and Kara Wolters. They come to the Hartford Civic Center to play us in January of that season. We blow them out. We just kill them, 72–57. It is really stunning, but while this is happening, Ann Meyers, the ESPN commentator, who is watching us destroy Tennessee, is talking about Pat Summitt running for governor, about Pat's orange blazers, about Pat this and Pat that. All of this while we're in the middle of a 15–2 run.

I'm watching this all later, when I'm reviewing the tape, and I can't believe it. I'm thinking, "There's nobody out there looking out for us. To my face, Ann Meyers and the rest of them all say, 'You're doing a great job, congratulations,' but when it comes right down to it, there's nobody out there jumping up and down for women's basketball. There's no Dick Vitale going crazy for all the women who are playing this game, and that's too bad."

We are ranked No. 1 in the country heading into the tournament that spring. The 1997 Final Four is in Iowa City, and we're 33–0, and it's just incredible how good we are. I'm sure we're going to win the whole thing. Our backcourt is Kesha and Rita Williams, and nobody has a better one. We have Kara, who is a senior, and Carla Berube, and we've brought in Shea Ralph, who you know is going to be special, and Amy Duran, who is a good player, and we're damn good.

Tennessee loses 10 games that year. I don't know how they lose so many, but they do. Before the season starts, HBO approaches us about doing a documentary on our team and following us for a season. We say we don't think we are interested, so they follow Tennessee around, and end up with a helluva story.

I still think our 1996–97 team is one of the flat-out best teams we've ever had. But in our first-round NCAA tournament game against Lehigh, just three minutes into the game, Shea Ralph gets hurt. She goes down, tears her anterior cruciate ligament in her knee, and we're in trouble. Doug Collins, the former NBA coach of the Chicago Bulls, Detroit Pistons, and Washington Wizards, is watching from the stands. His daughter Kelly plays for Lehigh, and that's why he's there. He comes down afterwards and says to me, "I've heard that sound before. She's torn her ACL."

He knew because he had done it himself. He is really nice, and we kind of developed a friendship after that.

We beat Lehigh, and we manage to knock off Iowa and Illinois without Shea to get to the Midwest Regional championship, where Tennessee is waiting for us. They beat us 91–81, and it is devastating, because we are so good, but our kids just don't know how to deal with Shea being hurt. They are writing "Shea" on their sneakers, the whole thing. You would have thought the kid died. We should have had a memorial for her.

Look, everyone felt bad. I felt bad. The kids felt bad, Shea felt bad, our fans felt bad, but we still had a championship to win, and we forgot about that. Not only did we lose Shea, we lost a game we should have won.

We turn the ball over 17 times in that game. We shoot 48.1 percent from the free throw line. Kesha has big numbers (26 points and 14 rebounds), and we don't quit, even being down 12 at halftime, but Holdsclaw is too good.

Tennessee has won its second straight national championship. We play them the following year, during the 1997–98 season, and Holdsclaw is a year older, and they add Tamika Catchings and Semeka Randall, and we're just not as good as them. There's nothing we can do about it. They just have too many good players. After they beat us during the regular season, 84–69, Randall makes a comment that Connecticut is scared. That bothers me for a minute, but then I think, "Well, maybe that's just kids talking." I can tell you my players didn't like it—at all. There is no doubt the rivalry is starting to get pretty intense.

We finish that season 30–3, and we lose to North Carolina State in the tournament. Tennessee wins its third consecutive national championship, and they own the women's game.

Now it's our turn for a big recruiting year. We get Tamika Williams and Swin Cash and Sue Bird and Asjha Jones. Tennessee recruits Swin, too, but I think she is watching Tennessee dominate and says to herself, "They've already done it there. They've already got their stars. Maybe I'll go someplace to be the person that helps knock them off."

It takes a while for that to happen. Tennessee is still pretty dominant, and it's not until 1999–2000, when Sue Bird is a sophomore, Shea is back healthy, and we have Sveta, Tamika, and Swin, that we're ready to seriously challenge them again. Sveta is just a scoring machine, but she drives me crazy because she won't play any defense.

So we host Tennessee at our place, and Shea plays a great

second half, and Semeka Randall is unbelievable for them down the stretch. They win 72–71, and it is another great game between two great programs.

But what I remember most about that day is the morning of the game. I piss Svetlana off at shootaround. She is getting on my nerves, which she does a lot, and for whatever reason I pick that day to get really mad at her, and it costs us. I really rip into her at the shootaround, and she's ticked off.

The game goes back and forth, one great shot after another, one great play after another. Randall makes an impossible shot for Tennessee, and we're down one with about 10 seconds left in the game.

We inbound the ball to Sveta, because I know she can get end line to end line in about four seconds. To my amazement, they let us inbound the ball to her. Sveta gets the ball and takes off. She's inside the circle. I've coached this girl for so many hours at that this point that I can tell you that never—not in a million years—would I expect her to pass up the shot.

But she does. She passes the ball. Tamika Williams, who is moving to go up for the offensive rebound, is startled by the pass, and can't handle it.

We lose the game by one point.

I'm convinced to this day that Sveta passed up that shot because she was pissed at me, or feeling insecure from what happened that morning, or had somehow lost her confidence. I say to her after the game, "Why did you pass the ball?" She says to me, in her Russian lilt, "Eh, she was open." I say, "Bullshit. There have been people wide open your whole career and you never passed them the ball when you were open, especially in that situation."

What can you say? You've got to live with it. I was okay

with how it ended. We put the ball in our best player's hands, and the kid decided to pass. If she shoots and it goes in, we win. If she shoots and it doesn't go in, we lose.

It's like giving your quarterback the ball on fourth and 10 on the 20-yard line, and you need a touchdown to win. Whatever he's going to do, you've got to be okay with it, because you've given him the ball.

The best thing about Sveta is it is forgotten the next day. I have to give her a hard time. She knows that. It is part of this ongoing Russian-American war we are having.

A lot of people say it is the best thing that we lose to Tennessee that January, because we aren't undefeated anymore, and some of the pressure is off our team. I guess that might be true. We win all the rest of our games, and we meet Tennessee again for the 2000 national championship.

That's the Final Four that is in Philadelphia, the one where we have a big bash the night before and get home around 3 a.m., and have a fantastic time—all before we've won anything.

The next day at shootaround, I'm feeling pretty good about our team. Jay Bilas, who used to play for Duke, is working for ESPN, and he doesn't know that much about women's basketball at that point. But he knows the game. He's watching practice, and he asks me, "What do you think?" I say to him, "Hey, you played, so you'll know what I'm talking about.

"We're going to spread the floor and force them into defending a lot of different cuts we're going to make. That's how we'll combat their size and quickness. If they can't stop it, we'll blow them out. If they do stop it, it will be a helluva game."

We get out there, and never in my wildest dreams do I expect it to go the way it did. It's a 30-point game. It is just astonishing how well we execute, and how well we play defensively. We couldn't have drawn it up any better. Shea Ralph is terrific. She only misses one shot all day. Asjha Jones has eight rebounds. Kelly Schumacher, our center, blocks nine shots. Sveta is Sveta—brilliant. And Sue Bird, our point guard, is close to perfect. She doesn't commit a single turnover during either game of the Final Four. We win going away, 71–52.

It is the perfect weekend. To look across and see my high school coach, Buddy Gardler, cheering us on, to see my family, and the guys I grew up with clapping for us, it is just a blast.

Now 2000–01 comes along, and we're playing Tennessee twice. It's not so pleasant anymore, for either team. There's just too much at stake. When we go to Knoxville, we're the enemy. When they come to Storrs, it's the same thing. It is a full-blown rivalry, and the bad feelings are starting to develop.

I'm not sure exactly when things turned really sour, but it might have something to do with their assistant coach, Al Brown, who was there from 1995 to 2002.

Anytime we were playing in a tournament, he'd come to our practices and write down everything we were doing. There wasn't anything illegal about that back then. It was allowed. Our practices were open, although that has since changed. He'd bring a notebook and start charting our plays and our drills. I thought it was just bush league. I'd turn to CD and get all pissed off, because we'd never do that to someone.

So one day we're running through our stuff, and he's sitting there with his big yellow legal pad, and I call the team together in a huddle. I say to them, "See that guy over there? He's writing down everything we do. So here's what we're going to do. We're going to run stuff from three years ago, and we're going to let him fill up his legal pad with it, and then we're never going to use it."

That is exactly what we do. We have some fun with it.

Not everyone appreciates my sarcasm. Not everyone understands my humor. I guess my competitiveness and my jealousy and my paranoia, if that's what you want to call it, get the best of me sometimes. I have this feeling that Pat gets preferential treatment from everybody, that she's untouchable, because she's Pat. Think about it. Can you imagine what they all would have been saying if I sent Jamelle or CD to their practice with a yellow legal pad? But because it's Pat, it's okay.

I understand that's because of what she's done, and I understand she's accomplished so much, more than any other women's coach in the history of the game. But I guess I feel like I'll never be treated like that, no matter what our team accomplishes.

The commonsense thing would be to just forget about it. Why waste time and energy on it? Most of the time I don't, but once in a while I walk around pissed off with a chip on my shoulder, and I carry it into games, and, I guess, it finally starts to spill out with comments like the "Evil Empire."

The thing that hits home most is how everybody is so quick to talk about what great coaches Pat and I are, and what adjustments we make, and this and that, and I'm laughing, thinking, "No one is ever going to say that about a bunch of these other coaches." You know why? Because it's not true, about any of us, including Pat and me. The bottom line is, when you're talking about me or Pat or a handful of others, you are talking about coaches who rarely have to contend with bad players. We always start with a stacked deck. What's so hard about that?

To no one's surprise, Tennessee and Connecticut are headed for another showdown in the Final Four in 2004. Earlier that season, we beat them 81–67. We fully expect to see them in the final, but first they have a bit of a scare. They nip Baylor on a controversial call at the end of the game in the early rounds of the tournament. The score is tied 69–69 and the referees call a foul on Baylor with 0.2 seconds left, which enables Tennessee to win it from the line. The Baylor people argue time had expired and the game should have gone into overtime. It's big news for a couple of days.

We have a pretty easy path to the championship. We beat Penn, Auburn, and Santa Barbara, then beat Penn State by 17 points at the Hartford Civic Center to advance to the Final Four. We beat Minnesota by nine points to set up yet another rematch with Tennessee.

Naturally, Pat and I are everyone's favorite story line. The day before the final, some dopey reporter asks Pat, "Let's say you are driving down the road, and Geno's car is stuck. Do you pull over and help him?" She says, "Well, certainly I would. The question you should ask him is, would he?"

Then they ask her why the two of us don't have much of a relationship. She answers, "This is the relationship he wants. I don't have his cell phone number, we don't talk. This is what he created."

Now it's my turn. They ask me whether I'd pick Pat up if she was broken down on the side of the road, and I say, "That's the dumbest damn question I've ever heard. Whoever posed that question is stupid." I tell them, "If you are a basketball writer, ask me some basketball questions about Connecticut and Tennessee. If you are writing for *People* magazine, you are in the wrong place. I hope Pat was smart enough not to answer that question."

Someone says, "She did answer it. She said she would stop and pick you up." So I say, "She would? Well, I'd rather walk."

So now it's the day of the game, and the national anthem is being played at the 10-minute mark, and Pat and I are both out there. We're walking off the court, and I grab her arm. I say, "Hey Pat, you finally have someone you can hate more than me now." She stops and says, "Who?"

I answer, "Rene Portland. Did you hear what she said today?"

Rene Portland is the women's coach at Penn State. She received some lifetime achievement award the day before the final, and in front of all the coaches from all around the country she stands up and says, "The only reason those two teams are playing for the national championship tomorrow is bad seeding and bad officiating."

She is saying the only reason we got there was because we beat her ass at the Hartford Civic Center, and the only reason Tennessee got there was because they got that call against Baylor. She chooses that opportunity, in front of everyone in our profession, to make those comments.

It is totally disrespectful and I'm ticked off.

Rene Portland is one of those coaches who was there in the beginning of the "modern era" of women's basketball, even before the NCAA took over. Marianne Stanley, Pat Summitt, Jody Conradt, Debbie Ryan, Rene Portland, and a few others worked really, really hard to get the game to the level that it has gotten to today.

Each of them handles that a little differently. The way Rene handles it is, "We're Penn State, and you're not." In other words, we're better than you. Our kids are smarter, and better, because we're Penn State. That kind of attitude always pisses me off. Now, if you're Pat Summitt and you want to act that way, then fine. You've earned it. But Pat doesn't act that way. We don't act that way. People that do? My feeling is, "Kiss my ass."

I remember when we are trying to build our program in the eighties. We wanted to play people who were better than us, because that's the only way you improve. I contact Penn State because they are an East Coast team. They say, "Why would we waste our time playing you guys? What's in it for us?" Their attitude is, "Come here and play us five times, and maybe we'll come to your place." Meanwhile, we call C. Vivian Stringer at Iowa and ask, "Can we come out and play in your tournament?" and she says, "Fine. Come on out." We call Tara VanDerveer at Stanford and ask, "Can we play in your tournament?" and she says, "Sure."

So here's the cool part. We go out to Iowa's tournament in 1989, and guess who we play? Penn State. We beat them in overtime, in a great, great game. It is sweet. I really, really enjoyed it. Now, all these years later, Rene Portland makes these comments at the Final Four, and to me, it shows her true colors. It's all a bunch of sour grapes.

Pat is just as furious as I am about what Rene says. She's in an uproar. I tell her, "Rene Portland needs to be held accountable for this. Someone needs to say something to her." Pat agrees as we walk off the court together.

Now it's just before tip-off and as Pat walks by our bench, I say, "Hey. You know that quote about me saying I'd rather walk? Well, if you had your Mercedes, I'd take a ride."

We beat Tennessee 70–61 for our fifth championship. It is Diana Taurasi's final college game and she isn't going to settle for anything but a win.

When the game is over, Pat comes over to shake my hand, and I tell her, "Don't listen to all this crap you hear and read. Sometimes I just say things for fun. It's not meant to be at your expense. I have tremendous respect for what you've done, and how you do it, and that will always be true." She says, "I really appreciate that."

When I get back to Storrs, I write her another note telling her I thought the 2003–04 season was her best job of coaching. She lost Loree Moore for most of the year, but her team still didn't fold, and it is an incredible achievement on her part. She writes right back. She says, "You've taken the game to another level. Your program has set a new standard that we all now have to try and reach. Enjoy your summer."

Believe me, I did.

Epilogue

I thought I had prepared myself for the 2004–05 basketball season. I knew we were going to struggle at times. I knew that without Diana and Maria we would be asking players to lead who had never led before.

Still, I was excited. It was the first time in a long while that nobody expected us to do anything. Nobody was picking us to win a national championship. Nobody was even picking us to finish in the Top 10. "Good," I remember thinking to myself. "Maybe we'll surprise them all."

Or maybe not.

Here's the truth: you can't prepare yourself for a season like we just had. You just can't prepare yourself for all of the inconsistencies. You can't prepare for looking like a national championship team on Monday, but then looking like an NIT team on Wednesday. If you ask any great coach, they'll tell you that is what drives them crazy more than anything. You play great one night, and you say to yourself, "Wow, we've got something here," then the next night you go out and you can't do anything right. That kind of roller-coaster season, with all the highs and lows, really wears you out. I'm sure it wore the players out, too.

I go to them one day and say, "I think you guys have been playing tricks on me. I think you got together in the locker room and said, 'Hey, we've been playing really well the last two weeks. What do you say we screw everything up on purpose today just to mess Coach up?'" I tell them, "I swear you are having secret meetings to intentionally mess up everything we are doing."

Naturally when I'm saying this, they're looking at me as if I'm out of my mind. But sometimes it actually felt that way to me—that they couldn't have possibly done so many stupid things unless they had a plan. I had forgotten how little the freshmen know when they are given the ball and the responsibility of getting us into our offense. We asked Ketia Swanier and Mel Thomas to do that, and they struggled with it. It's like giving the football to a rookie quarterback and telling him, "Here, run the show." At times, he can, when things are going well, his confidence level is high, and he can see the field clearly. But when things aren't going well and it's all coming down on him, he feels like he is in a washer, being turned upside down and all around, and it's an unbelievable nightmare. When you add the fact that we are trying to play at the highest possible level, that churning feeling is even worse.

Our record this past season was 25–8. Eight losses. That's considered a lot in these parts. We took some beatings. Michigan State demolished us at the Hartford Civic Center by 16 points. It was humiliating. Something like that hadn't happened to us in a long, long time. They just whacked us. And here's the funny thing—it was only a two-point game at halftime. But then we came out in the second half and showed a side of us that we couldn't shake all year. We showed the side that when things aren't going well, it's every woman for herself.

Michigan State had something to do with that. They were a great team. They went all the way to the finals this year. Their guard Lindsey Bowen reminded me of some of our great guards from Connecticut. In that game at the Civic Center, she was fearless. She took—and made—big shots. She played inspired basketball.

I was surprised that some of our more experienced players weren't able to step up a little more during the year. Then again, when you think about it, players like Ashley Battle and Jessica Moore had never been put in a situation where it was up to them to make sure we won the game. They get to their final seasons and all of a sudden, that's where they are. We needed them to do more than perhaps they were capable of doing.

It's hard, unless you have all the ingredients. It's easy to turn the reins over to Diana Taurasi or Sue Bird because they have all the skills you need. They can pass, shoot, and defend. The kids we had this season were pretty specific. They were specialists in some ways. And here we were asking them to do a little bit of everything under tremendous pressure.

I saw a lot of those blank stares last season, just like the ones I used to get from Asjha, Swin, and Tamika. I remember one afternoon when we were trying to run a drill. We had ten players at half court. We were running a five-on-zero drill. I explain the drill to the players, and then say to them, "Okay, here's the option I want you to execute."

So five of them go down there and they run the wrong thing. I stop them and say, "Jessica Moore. What did I just ask you to do?" She looks at me like I'm speaking Chinese. She finally says, "I didn't hear what you said." I look at her and say, "Let me get this straight. You just went down to execute something without knowing what it was?" I turned to my coaches and I said, "We're dead."

You know why we were dead? Because Jessica is one of the smart ones. If one of the smart ones doesn't know what the hell we're doing, what are the dumb ones thinking?

It got better as we went along. I had trouble, at times, motivating them. At one point during the season, I kicked them out of their locker room. I had done the same thing years ago, when Meghan Pattyson was playing. We had only been in Gampel about a year, and I believed the team was lacking commitment and feeling sorry for themselves because Kerry Bascom and Laura Lishness had graduated and we were losing games we shouldn't have lost. I figured they had stopped appreciating what they had, so I took away their locker room.

They were knocked on their heels by it. It was a shock to their system. They were saying, "I can't believe this is happening to us." The reason it worked so well was because they knew what the other side was. They had lived in that cramped old locker room before and they didn't want to go back to it.

The group we have now didn't react the same way. It's like when you tell your kid, "Go to your room." Okay, sure. Why not? They've got a computer in their room. They've got PlayStation in there, so what's the big deal? When I chased last year's team out of the locker room, it bothered them for about a day, but they still had their Blackberrys and their laptops and their headphones. Their attitude was, "Okay, then. We'll just get changed somewhere else."

We had some bizarre things occur last season. We played Tennessee at the Hartford Civic Center and were up five with just a little over a minute to go and couldn't hold on. Even so, we had Ann Strother at the line with practically no time left and three free throws to shoot. If she makes three, we win. If she makes two, we tie. If she makes only one, we lose.

She makes one. We lose.

As if we needed any more drama in our lives, we have a recruit, one of the best players in the country, in Hartford on an unofficial visit that weekend. She is making the rounds with her dad, looking at various schools. There's a huge snowstorm, and on the morning of the game, I tell them we will be shooting around at the Civic Center at 8:30 a.m., and if they'd like to join us, they should meet us in the lobby of the Goodwin Hotel. It gets to be 8:29, and I figure they're not coming, so we leave.

About five minutes into the shootaround, I see the young lady walking into the arena with a policeman. She's crying. My life is flashing before me. I'm thinking, "What happened? Was she mugged? Was her dad hit by a car? Has someone gotten arrested?" Chris runs over there, and I put our players through a few more drills, then I join her.

It turns out the recruit and her dad were trying to get into the shootaround, and they went to the wrong entrance of the Civic Center. It was closed. Her dad slipped on the ice and broke his ankle. He was in an ambulance on the way to St. Francis Hospital. I'm thinking to myself, "Are you kidding me? What should we do? How do we manage this? How do we get her and her dad home?"

The dad needs surgery. They put eight screws in his ankle, as well as a plate. I'm thinking, "Sure, great. We're definitely getting this kid. She's probably on the phone right now telling everyone, 'My father just broke his ankle. UConn is definitely the place for me.'"

She did have a terrific sense of humor, though. I was asking her how her dad was doing, and she said he'd be okay, and then she said, "But you know, if I do come here, we may have to rename this arena after my family. You see, my father is a personal injury attorney; he deals with a lot of worker compensation cases, and I'm guessing we'll own this building before the day is out."

By the time this book comes out, we should know what school she has chosen. She's had Tennessee, Notre Dame, Stanford, and Connecticut at the top of her list. She's from the West Coast, so Stanford has me worried the most. I think it's down to Stanford and Connecticut. Stay tuned.

I know the 2004–05 season was hard on our players who had been there awhile. When we started our NCAA tournament run, the media kept putting up the same graphic on the screen. No one on our team had ever lost an NCAA postseason game. Our team as a whole was undefeated—the older kids because they had won three years in a row, and the new kids because they hadn't played in any tournament games yet.

That was bound to end, but when it did, with a loss to Stanford in the Sweet Sixteen, it hit them hard. Players like Barbara Turner and Jessica Moore and Ashley Battle, who have been around a long time, took it to heart.

Barbara Turner, unfortunately, suffered from a number of injuries that kept her from being the Barbara Turner we've seen in the past. When Barbara is on top of her game, she's as good as any forward we've had. The injuries have clouded her career a little bit. This year she wasn't first, second, or third team All–Big East, and I think that really shook her. I think she's mad. I hope she is. She has only one year left to become the old Barbara Turner who helped us win championships.

The person who suffered most from Dee and Maria's departure was probably Ann Strother. She got a lot of open shots when Dee and Maria were out there with her. Now all of a sudden nobody is knocking down shots, and they don't feel like they have to guard Mel Thomas or Morgan Valley, and they guard Ashley Battle only once in a while, so now everyone is focusing on Ann Strother. So she's not getting the shots she used to get. That means she needs to learn how to move better without the ball. She has to learn to get in the lane more. She has to learn how to play a whole new game. I thought she adapted pretty well, but not as well as we needed her to.

I'm sure people are wondering why she looked so lost in our NCAA tournament game against Stanford. Here's the problem: the day before that game, Ann couldn't move her neck. At all. I really wasn't sure she would be able to play in that game. She took some medication to help her, and she had trouble with it. She was kind of out of it, to tell you the truth. She just wasn't sharp. That's not an indication of the kind of player she is, or will be.

Ann is key this season. So is Willnett Crockett, who will be a senior. She is the most wonderful and maddening player I've ever been around. Here's how it starts with her. We're doing individual instruction in September of her freshman year, but I'm out recruiting so I haven't been around the kids that much. When I get back, Jamelle says to me, "Coach, when practice starts, you need to be really, really prepared." I say, "For what?" She says, "For Will.

You've never experienced anything like it in your life." I say, "In terms of what?" Jamelle says, "Work ethic. It's bad. Worse than anything you can imagine."

Jamelle is right. We struggle every day to get Will to play beyond the "I can't" stage. She'd practice well, then awful. Well, then awful. It is nonstop. Then we play Tennessee in the first really big game of her freshman year and she saves the day. I'm thinking, "Where did this come from?" It's the same thing sophomore year: awful early in the season, then come the Final Four, she's the best player out there. The pattern repeats itself in 2003–04.

So here's my theory on Willnett Crockett. She is like a bear. She hibernates from September 1 to March 1, then wakes up and plays like an All-America.

I have a talk with her and tell her I can't live with that. I tell her, "What scares me, Will, is I have to depend on you next year to do the same things Jessica Moore did this year. And you haven't proven to me you can do it. So if you were me, how would you feel?"

She answers, "I'd feel pretty confident, Coach. Because I have no choice. This is my last year."

"So you mean the other years it was, 'If I do it this year, I do it, but if I don't, I don't?'" She says, "No, not really," but we both know that's right. That's frustrating. Will has one more year to break the pattern. She is one of the nicest, sweetest, most sensitive kids we've ever had here. But she needs to give us the same effort, start to finish.

The one thing I was pleasantly surprised about in 2004–05 was our defense. Our defense was unbelievably good. It generated a lot of our offense, which was a good thing, because we couldn't score all season. One of the problems with our team was that we had to play with the lead. If we had the lead, I could massage it and control the tempo of the game. Some of our biggest wins last season were because we were able to hold the lead. It happened at Notre Dame, and when we beat Texas here in Connecticut, and when we played Rutgers.

We found out some things in the final month of the season. Ketia and Mel got some invaluable experience in March, and, I think, played their best basketball. They both have the skills and the temperament to be good players here at Connecticut. They are only going to get better. Will, as we already discussed, proved that when she feels like it, she can be big, strong, quick, and the best offensive player on the floor. She can also defend anyone.

Charde Houston, at times, looked like one of the top 5 to 10 players in the country. To say she even scratched the surface of her abilities is an overstatement. She has so much potential and ability, but she has no idea how to tap into it. She probably got frustrated with us, because every day we were frustrated with her. All she knows is that when she gets the ball, she's going in that direction, because there's the rim. That's okay—most of the time. But she's an incredible passer, which people don't know about, and she can block shots. She can guard forwards, centers, it doesn't matter. There were fifteen-minute intervals in practice when she was the best player I've ever coached. Then, there were fifteen-minute intervals when I couldn't believe I ever recruited her.

I'm telling you right now: Charde could be the best player we've ever had. It's up to her. She has the physical skills, but I don't know if she has the mental makeup to do it.

Nicole Wolff is a player who needs to find a way to relax. She hamstrung herself last season by playing so uptight.

We had our share of highlights in 2004–05. We came on strong in the final month of the season and beat Rutgers to win the Big East title. That was a helluva win.

Ashley Battle and Jessica Moore were both second-round picks in the WNBA draft. They both want to continue to play basketball and I hope they get the chance.

Diana Taurasi came back and got her degree. When I heard through the grapevine that she thought she'd be too busy to finish up, I really got upset. Diana's parents never went to college. The fact that she did was a tremendous source of pride for them. I tried to explain to her that by not getting her degree, she'd be written off as just another dumb jock. I told her she'd just be perpetuating the idea that great players give lip service about going to school, and that would be wrong. I sent her an e-mail telling her she could never set foot on my court again if she didn't come back and enroll in school. She sent me a two-word answer: yes, sir.

In early April, I got together with Dee, Maria, Jessica, AB, and Morgan Valley. We got our pictures taken with the five of them wearing their caps and gowns. I always said, "You think winning three championships in a row was improbable? I thought five of them graduating was a lot more improbable."

Something else happened last spring. I finally contacted Heidi Law, the player who left Connecticut so troubled and unhappy, the one who had written me that letter detailing all the ways I had let her down. In early March, I got her e-mail address and sent her a quick note. She answered it, then sent me a little card wishing us luck in the tournament.

I'll feel better when I've talked to Heidi face-to-face. By the time this book comes out, I hope I will have seen her.

We have a reunion every summer, and she has never come. This year, I'm going to call and personally invite her.

It has been an interesting journey, this life of coaching. From the time I was thirty to forty years old, I thought of myself as someone who was constantly trying to teach players what I knew about basketball, what I knew about being twenty, and what I knew about growing up and becoming successful.

But from ages forty to fifty, it seems as if I've spent the last ten years finding out from my players what it really means to be successful. I've learned more from them this last decade than they've learned from me. Every day, they force me to look at things in a different way.

I can't say it's all been enjoyable, because there are times you wish everybody understood what you were doing. There are times you wished other people appreciated how much you cared. I've grown tired of living in a fishbowl. I'm tired of being scrutinized over every little thing. I wish I could separate who I am from what I do, but unfortunately, these two things have become synonymous.

Who knows what will happen this season? We have some great freshmen coming in. A lot will depend on how much the current players can grow into their responsibilities.

The NCAA champion in 2005 was neither Connecticut nor Tennessee. It was Baylor. I wasn't surprised. Kim Mulkey-Robertson, besides being one of my favorite people, is as good, if not better, than any of the coaches of her generation. She's tough, she's intense, she's engaging, she's in touch with her players, she knows the game, and she has a passion for everything.

Her team reflected her personality. They had a toughness about them that enabled them to surpass even what their physical abilities made them capable of achieving. I was really, really happy for them when they won.

I remember how it feels.

I plan on feeling that way again really soon.

A Personal Note from the Coauthor

I didn't know what to think of Geno Auriemma at first either.

I know what I saw as soon as I signed on for this project: a passionate, driven coach who spared no one's feelings in the heat of a game—or in the private confines of the practice floor. It didn't matter whether you were Diana Taurasi, Barbara Turner, or walk-on Stacey Marron, if you screwed up you were going to hear about it.

How did these women feel about Geno, who refused to stop badgering them until he squeezed every last ounce of talent out of them? Did they love him? Hate him? Fear him?

The answer is all of the above, at one time or another. But what you can't possibly understand until you spend some time with these players is how much affection they feel for their coach once their experience is complete. I've covered countless basketball teams, both male and female, college and professional, and in almost twenty-five years as a sports journalist I have never—ever—encountered a group of athletes who are as fiercely protective of their coach as this one.

Their loyalty is genuine, and Geno has earned it. You've read, in his own words, how he tried to mold these women into champions. But the part he left out was how generous and kind he was to these players long after the games were over.

He told you that when assistant coach Jamelle Elliott's mother tragically died in a fire, he and his staff rushed back from the Final Four to be there for her. What he failed to tell you was that he paid for all the funeral arrangements, and took great pains to make sure each and every player on his team made it to Washington, D.C., so they could go together, in force, to the service.

"It wasn't the money," Elliott explained. "I knew I could pay that back. But I can never repay the support and the love he provided me and my family during the most difficult time of our lives."

He helped Kerry Bascom cope with the loss of her mother, and associate Chris Dailey with the loss of her dad. He counseled Shea Ralph through an eating disorder, and Swin Cash through both personal and business matters.

Some of Geno's most considerate gestures have been subtle. When Sue Bird returned to her native New York for the first time in a UConn uniform to play St. John's, she was hopeful her mother could host a dinner for the team. But when she got hold of the team's itinerary, it became apparent it would be impossible because they were scheduled to bus to New York the day of the game.

"I was a little disappointed," she said, "but then I put it out of my mind. The next day, I find out Coach had totally rearranged our schedule so we could go to my mom's house and have our pregame meal there. It may sound like a little thing, but it meant a great deal to me."

A Personal Note from the Coauthor

Meghan Pattyson, the player in the book whom Geno lambasted after a poor first semester academically, went on to graduate with honors and accept a job broadcasting women's basketball. The pay was minimal, so she ate dinner nearly every night at the Auriemma house. "If I didn't," Pattyson said, "I wouldn't have had any food."

Pattyson was subsequently offered a television opportunity with Lifetime, but knew doing it properly would entail airfare as well as hotel and rental car costs.

"I wanted the job, but I didn't see how I could make it work financially," she said. "My own parents don't even know this, but I went to Geno and asked to borrow some money. I think I cried when I asked him, because I was so embarrassed. He wrote me a check for $1,000.

"I worked really hard over the next few months to pay off some bills and take care of my rent. Then I wrote him a long letter to thank him and enclosed the money I owed him. I don't know why I bothered. He never cashed the check."

Connecticut's all-time leading scorer, Nykesha Sales, never borrowed any money from Geno Auriemma, yet she insists she will be forever indebted to him for the way he helped her grow as a person. Asked to articulate what he meant to her, she found herself choking back tears.

"He changed my life," Sales said. "He made me see myself in a way I never would have. The basketball was one thing. But what he taught me about being a good person is what I'll remember most. I have tried for five years now to write him a letter to thank him, but I can't seem to put it into words."

Rebecca Lobo, the first national recruit Auriemma ever landed, has remained close to her ex-coach even after he put her through a grueling self-examination that left her initially contemplating a transfer.

Those hard times are not what Lobo remembers about Geno. She recalls instead her junior season, when her mother was battling breast cancer and her immune system was weakened. Auriemma arranged to have an area cordoned off where Mrs. Lobo could be safely sequestered from the fans but still enjoy the game.

Lobo will never forget her struggles during her tenure with the 1996 Olympic team, when she played a limited role and clashed with Coach Tara VanDerveer. The person she called for solace was Geno, who reminded her, "Be who you are. Don't try to be more. Don't let yourself be less."

It has long been Geno's goal to create the "North Carolina" of women's basketball. By that he means a highly decorated program with players who feel a permanent attachment and connection to their school. If you are wondering whether he succeeded, drop in on his annual New Year's Eve party, where the house is teeming with former players. Check out his summer home, the regular gathering spot for UConn basketball alums. Pattyson became so close to Geno and his family that she asked his wife, Kathy, to be her matron of honor. Rita Williams calls him every Father's Day. Sue Bird regularly corresponded with him from Russia last spring. Recent graduate Jessica Moore, who lost her dad when she was young, dissolved into tears on Senior Night when trying to explain what Geno, her "second father," has done for her.

Some rival college teams have dubbed the Connecticut program "the cult." It is meant to be dismissive; it is, in fact, a wonderful compliment to a special collection of athletes who remain connected through the efforts of their coach.

A Personal Note from the Coauthor

But don't make the mistake of thinking this means Geno has gone soft. He'll still berate his players throughout a three-hour practice *then* invite them over for supper that evening.

"He might not talk to you all night at dinner," Diana Taurasi said, "but there you are, in his house, eating with his family. And that's when you know, no matter what, he's on your side."

I spent eight months with Geno Auriemma helping him write this book, and here's what I've figured out about him: there's a method to the love, the hate, and the fear.

Of course it is to make sure the UConn women become the best players they can be.

But the real trick is to make sure they become the best people they can be while they're at it.

—Jackie MacMullan
March 2005

Index

Index

Index

Index

Index

Index

Index

Index

Index

Index

Index